Sixteen, Sixty-One

NATALIE LUCAS

Sixteen, Sixty-One

A memoir

authonomy
by HarperCollins*Publishers*

The Friday Project
An imprint of HarperCollins
77–85 Fulham Palace Road
Hammersmith, London W6 8JB

www.harpercollins.co.uk
www.authonomy.com

First published in 2013 by authonomy

ISBN: 9780007523559

Printed and bound in Great Britain by Clays Ltd, St Ives plc

Typeset in Minion by Palimpsest Book Production Ltd, Falkirk, Stirlingshire

Sixteen, Sixty-One is the powerful true story of an illicit intergenerational affair. Names, locations, and some events have been changed to protect me, my family, those for whom I care deeply and others for whom I really don't.

For Trish, who saved my life

Preface

14th May 2007

~~Dear Matthew~~
~~Dear Mr Wright~~
~~Dear Albert Sumac~~
~~Dear Bastard~~
Dear Ghost,

My therapist keeps asking what I'd say to you if I had the chance. I wonder this myself: what *will* I say if we bump into each other when I return home this summer? I see your grey eyes coolly inspecting my appearance, noticing I've put on weight and look plainer with my hair this length. I imagine you composing an email after the event, though you no longer have my address, so perhaps it'll be a letter. It will tell me I've turned into my mother or that I was cruel to return or that you're shocked by how evil I've become. The worst thing you could write would be that you're proud of me.

None of this will have been provoked. I see myself still moving on the same strip of pavement, heading for a collision, and I see the moment of horrified surprise that will wash your tanned face of its careful persona, a flash of reality, followed by your collecting yourself, straightening your spine and telling me how nice it is to see me, how was studying abroad?

But I cannot see my own face in this. I cannot form a response, hysterical or otherwise. All I can picture are fantasies of keying your car and smearing pig's blood on your door, of scratching the letters P-A-E-D-O on your bonnet and hurling bricks through your French windows. Sometimes I scare myself thinking I actually would post a petrol bomb through your letterbox if I could be sure Annabelle was out. And if I wasn't a wimpy English Literature student with no idea how to make a petrol bomb.

I imagine you now, reading this and laughing. This means you've won, doesn't it? You are still inside me. At sixteen, you filled me with love and that was bad, but now you fill me with hate and this is worse. I hate that you have this power still. Are you flattered? Maybe this is better for you: most people can be loved, there is nothing extraordinary in that. Even the plebs you scorn have their Valentine's cards and wedding bands. But how many people are utterly despised? How many people are in someone else's thoughts every day and in their nightmares every night? You should be proud: you've achieved some kind of immortality, even if you haven't written that book you said you would, filmed your screenplay, or established your name.

I hate you by any name.

Sincerely,

~~Nat~~
~~Harriet~~
~~Lilith~~
Natalie

PART ONE

1

I was fifteen when my second life began.

It was the summer of 2000. Other things that happened that summer included Julie Fellows allowing Tom Pepper to touch her nipples for the first time, Sam Roberts claiming to have gone all the way with Rose Taylor and her denying it, Wayne Price getting permanently excluded for selling his crushed-up medication on the playground, Mrs Forman resigning her post as head of English amid rumours of an affair with the new science teacher, Pete Sampras winning his thirteenth Grand Slam title at Wimbledon, the leaders of North and South Korea meeting for the first time and the *News of the World* campaigning for new legislation giving parents the right to know whether a convicted paedophile lived in their area.

Sheltered from such dramas, my first life had been pretty regular. I grew up in a small town in the countryside. I had a mother, a father and a brother. My parents separated when I was eleven, but my mum, my brother and I only moved across town, a few streets away. After we moved, I fell out with my dad for a few years. He began dating twenty-three-year-olds, going to raves and acting like a teenager. I began revising for my SATs, reading books and swapping notes with boys in class. I had my first kiss when I was eleven – with Harry Heeley on the bus back from swimming practice while Kayla Weatherford timed us with her digital watch and Danny King looked out for Mrs Rice walking up the aisle. Shortly after that I started secondary school, where I held hands with Ben Legg, Robbie Burton, Chris Price, Michael Peterson, Stephen Hunt, Simon Shaw, Steven Critchley, David Robson, Gavin Gregs, Reece Cook and a guy at youth club known as Spike.

My favourite item of clothing was a floor-length denim skirt I could hardly walk in. My dark blonde hair reached my shoulder blades in a thick tangle, curtaining my face when I wanted to hide from the world. I'd recently purchased my first pair of tweezers and a box of Jolen personal bleach but had yet to use either, thus noticeable hairs shadowed both my upper lip and between my brows. I was short, not even five foot one – a situation I had tried to rectify a month ago by convincing my dad to spend £16 on five-inch silver platform sandals. I'd worn them with denim pedal-pushers to go shopping and would never again remove the Bowie-esque disasters from beneath my bed.

I considered a day a good one if I managed to avoid embarrassing myself during the seven excruciating hours spent at my mediocre school in the next town. They were few. Most recently, the blonde, bronzed netball captain had seemed to befriend me in order to confirm rumours that I had a crush on Stuart Oxford and, moments after I confided in her, summoned him to tell me – over the sniggers of all around – that he had a girlfriend (a hockey-playing, make-up wearing, French-kissing, Winona Ryder-look-alike girlfriend), but if she and all the other girls in this and every other school coincidentally fell in a vat of beauty-destroying acid, perhaps he'd take me to the cinema. Later that week, I'd also managed to alienate Rachael, the one friend I still had, while we secretly watched her sister's *Sex and the City* videos by claiming with confidence that spooning was a kinky form of anal sex and I thought it disgusting. She'd asked her sister to clarify and told me at school the next day that I was full of shit and would probably die a virgin.

While on the topic, though I'd had a few boyfriends and even touched Peter Booth's thing after we'd been 'going out' for six months (but only for a second before feeling utterly repulsed, darting out of the tent to find another cherry-flavoured Hooch and telling him I didn't want to be his girlfriend any more), I had never handled a condom, still believed you could get pregnant from oral sex and had a poster of Dean Cain dressed as Superman on my wardrobe door that I'd torn out of *Shout* magazine at the age of twelve.

However, for all my naiveties, I was worldly-wise enough to realise owning up to them was out of the question. I may have known nothing about boys or sex that I hadn't read in the Barbara Taylor Bradford novels my mum left in the loo, but I had never received less than an A*. I studied long words in the dictionary with the same voracity others my age collected Pokemon cards, I watched the news rather than cartoons and I made it a point to have every adult who met me comment, at least to themselves, 'She's so mature for her age.'

Why was I mature? One therapy analysis would conclude it had something to do with being a product of a broken home, my parents splitting up the same year I transferred from primary to secondary school and my devastated mother telling me every nasty thing she could think about my father as we packed our family lives into boxes and moved out of the thirteen-room Georgian detached house that had been a home for the first eleven years of my life. Another would suggest it was down to the amount I read and my stubborn insistence on skipping straight from *The Famous Five* to Anita Shreve, Margaret Atwood, Pat Barker and Paul Auster, bypassing entirely those *Goosebumps* and *Point Horror* years that might shape an average teenager's development. And another theory entirely would say that, as of yet, I wasn't any more mature for my age than every other teenager who wants to be grown: that it was what came next that thrust me into an adult world with a child's mind.

My second life began one Saturday in March when I begrudgingly followed my mum to a tea party at a neighbour's house. We lived on a row of skinny Edwardian semis on the edge of town, the gardens backing on to a small wood beyond which acres of farmland stretched towards the horizon. The party was at the end of the street. Even my brother James decided this outing required sufficiently little effort to warrant attending, so the three of us plodded the few dozen steps along the pavement to be ushered through to the open-plan kitchen of number twenty-seven.

Once inside, the host Annabelle handed us mugs of tea and directed us through clumps of people to help ourselves from the buffet table. I loaded a plate with sausage rolls and fairy cakes and scuttled to a chair in the corner. When I'd swallowed my first mouthful and was reaching for my sugary tea, a voice spoke from my left.

'I hate these things.'

I looked over and saw the mildly familiar face of Annabelle's husband.

'Isn't this your party?' I placed another sausage roll on my tongue and, noting the glass of wine in his hand, wondered if he was drunk.

'Oh yeah, of course you have to put on a show, keep them all happy.'

'What d'you mean?' I asked, only half interested.

'See over there?' He pointed. 'My in-laws. She chairs the WI and he sets the church quiz every Tuesday. If I didn't throw a party, especially for a "big" birthday like this, I'd be hung, drawn and quartered by the gossipy blue-rinse brigade. Barbara'd come knocking on our door asking Annabelle what's wrong, was I ill? Were we having marital problems? Annabelle would try to shut her mother up and Barb'd shriek, "*What will everyone say?*" and we'd end up having a party just to calm her down anyway. Much easier this way.'

I tried to stifle a giggle and almost choked on a large flake of pastry as he put on an old woman's voice and flailed his arms in prim horror.

'I'm sure it's not as bad as all that. How old are you anyway?'

'How old do you think I am?' He looked at me with a smile.

'Oh no, now you'll get offended.'

'I promise I won't.'

'Hmm, okay. Well, you said it's a big one, and I'm pretty sure you're older than my parents, so I guess it must be fifty.'

'HA!' His face cracked into a grin and he spilt a little wine on his beige trousers as he chuckled to himself.

'What?'

'I think you're my new best friend.'

'What, are you older? Fifty-five?'

'Nope.' He grinned.

'Well you can't be sixty, I don't believe you're sixty.' Sixty was the age of grandparents, that pensionable age where spines curved and walking sticks were suddenly required. The man before me was a little wrinkled and his hair was silver, but his skin was brown, his eyes sparkled and his limbs moved with muscular ease. He certainly betrayed no signs of qualifying for free prescriptions on the NHS. I liked him; he was funny; he couldn't be sixty.

But he was nodding.

'Wow.'

'Yep, I was born in the first half of the last century. It scares me because I don't feel that old, but I can remember the coronation of Queen Elizabeth.'

I was silent.

'You don't even know when that was, do you? Oh dear. 1953. I was eleven. But that's enough of old-fuddy-duddy talk anyway; let's speak of youthful things. What rubbish are they teaching you at school these days?'

'I'm revising for my GCSEs,' I replied importantly, dismissing his implication that my studies were anything but monumental.

9

'And next week I have to pick what subjects to do for A-Level. It's pretty stressful.'

'What are you going to take?'

'Well, at the moment, I think it'll be Maths, Further Maths, Business and Geography, but I'm not sure.'

He recoiled. 'Yikes, what would you want to do those for?'

'What's wrong with them?'

'Nothing, they're just all so dull.' He faked a long, loud yawn. 'What do you want to be when you grow up?'

'An actuary . . . or maybe a lawyer.'

'Oh dear. Child, you're going to have a boring life. Have you met the people who go into those professions? They have no gnosis, no emotions, no pulse. They're just money-grubbing machines.'

'That's not true,' I replied defensively, though I'd no idea what 'gnosis' meant. 'Some of the work's really interesting. And I like numbers.'

'But what about the poetry? The passion?'

'What do you mean?'

'Don't you do English and Art? Aren't there any subjects that make you feel excited, spark your creativity?'

'Well, sure. I love English and I gave up Art in Year 9 but I still like sketching and things. They're not exactly practical career options, though.'

'Says who?'

'Um, my mum, my teachers, the careers adviser.'

'What do they know? They're stuck in unfulfilling jobs that sap all creativity. What would the world be like if every artist since Shakespeare had followed the advice of their careers advisers and become lawyers instead?'

I was silent.

'What they don't want to tell you is that none of it's real. Earning money and following the system isn't real living, it's just what you have to do in order to find the space to live. The whole thing is an elaborate unreality designed to make us conform. Have you read *Nineteen Eighty-Four*?'

I shook my head.

'What about Hermann Hesse?'

'No.'

'I tell you what, you say you like English, how about I lend you some books? You can take them away and when you're done, come and have a pot of tea with me and we'll talk about this actuary business.'

I took away *Steppenwolf* and *The Outsider* that day. *Nineteen Eighty-Four*, *Brave New World*, *Mrs Dalloway*, *The Age of Innocence*, *Brighton Rock*, *The Plague*, *The Bell Jar*, *The Pupil* and *Sophie's World* followed.

Each time I returned a book, Matthew would carry it down the stairs and place it delicately on the farmhouse table while he boiled the kettle. After nestling the cosy on the pot, he'd offer me a chair and, sitting opposite me, begin: 'So, what did it make you think?'

'I don't know.' I was shy at first; worried my thoughts wouldn't be deep enough, worried I would have missed the point of the prose, that I wasn't reading as I was meant to, that he might think me stupid.

'Come on, there's no right or wrong answer. I just want to know how the book affected you.'

Gradually, I allowed myself to answer.

'It made me wonder why people have to conform.' (Camus)

'It made me think one single day can offer more beauty and pain than a whole lifetime.' (Woolf)

'It made me question whether a society can condition you to accept anything and, if so, whether there's any such thing as right or wrong.' (Huxley)

'It made me think philosophy is like maths: just logic applied to the world. So, if you think hard enough, there must be an answer, but that religion seems to get in the way.' (Gaarder)

'It made me think I should dislike the character, but I didn't.' (Hesse)

'It made me wish I'd been born in that time.' (Sartre)

And, of course, like every girl my age: 'It reminded me of me.' (Plath)

'Excellent.' Matthew smiled. 'Existentialism asks all those questions and comes to the conclusion that the only thing that's for certain is that we exist; we are here. Nothing else is real. All this crap society puts into our heads: money, work, school, cars, class, status, children, wives – everything we're supposed to care about – it's completely unreal. True reality is what's in our minds. And when you accept that, you realise that conforming to society's rules just makes you a sheep. You might as well die now. Only a few people have the courage to truly accept this and those are the few that stick their heads above the manhole-cover, who make art and seek out love. I call them Uncles. They're usually persecuted for it, but at least they're living.'

'Why "Uncles"?' I asked.

He frowned as if I'd missed the point, but shrugged and replied, 'Because parents are too close, they fuck you up, so it's down to Uncles, relatives with a little distance, to guide you through life. When I was slightly older than you I found a mentor, I called him Uncle. It was a sign of respect back then, but now I know it means more.'

I considered his words after I left. I watched my mum cooking dinner and wondered if she had ever stuck her head above the manhole-cover. I observed James playing on the PlayStation and decided he hadn't yet realised the world was unreal. Visiting my dad at the weekend, I looked at him tinkering in the shed and thought perhaps he'd never read Camus.

I sat on my bed and looked out the window.

That is unreal, I thought. *Only I am real.*

At school, I began to feel I was play-acting in my unreality. It made it easier to deal with the popular girls who told me to pluck my eyebrows, but I found my reality a little lonely. I felt like Matthew was the only person who understood it, so I began visiting him more often. If school and home and youth club and the Post Office were all unreal, Matthew's kitchen and the pack of cards between us were real.

Annabelle often busied herself in her bedroom, but always asked if I wanted to stay for dinner. The three of us gossiped about the neighbours over shepherd's pie and sometimes climbed the stairs to watch *Friends* in their living room. I shared the second sofa with the cat.

One evening, after I'd brushed my teeth and was climbing into bed, my mum knocked on my door.

'Can I come in?'

'Of course.'

'I just wanted to say goodnight.'

She looked uncomfortable.

'Sweetie, I know you're spending a lot of time with Matthew and that you're fond of him. I just want you to be a little careful with him.'

'What on earth do you mean?' She didn't reply and I looked at her in astonishment. 'That's ridiculous!'

'I know, he's a lovely man and I'm sure he wouldn't do anything, but I'm a mother and I have to worry. So just promise me you'll look after yourself.'

I made the promise and muttered angrily to myself as she left about just wanting a father figure because she'd picked such a rotten one in the first place.

When I told Matthew of the conversation the following day, he looked concerned.

'Your mother's a nice woman, but she's steeped in the unreality. She'll never be an Uncle and she'll never understand. You may have to be more careful from now on.'

'What do you mean?'

13

Instead of answering me, he sent me away with a collection of Oscar Wilde plays, one of which, *The Importance of Being Earnest*, was indicated with a bookmark.

On page 259 I found a word had been circled in pencil.

> ALGERNON: . . . What you really are is a Bunburyist. I was
> quite right in saying you were a Bunburyist. You are one of
> the most advanced Bunburyists I know.
>
> JACK: What on earth do you mean?
>
> ALGERNON: You have invented a very useful younger brother
> called Ernest, in order that you may be able to come up to
> town as often as you like. I have invented an invaluable
> permanent invalid called Bunbury, in order that I may be
> able to go down into the country whenever I choose. Bunbury
> is perfectly invaluable. If it wasn't for Bunbury's extraordi-
> nary bad health, for instance, I wouldn't be able to dine with
> you at Willis's tonight, for I have been really engaged to Aunt
> Augusta for more than a week.

'You think I should create my own Mr Bunbury?' I asked the next time I saw Matthew.

'Sure,' he smiled, leading me to his study. 'Bunburying is an essential part of life.'

'I'm not sure I want to lie, though.' I perched instinctively on the navy chaise longue.

'I know you don't, because you're honest and true.' Matthew sighed and sat heavily beside me. 'But sadly you'll have to if you want to live freely. It's the dreadful irony of life that all Uncles really want is to live pure, innocent lives, but society forces them to play its sordid little games.'

'So, do you have a Bunbury?' I turned to face him.

'I have many Bunburys my dear,' he answered with a wink. 'I've even had to assume whole other identities.'

After making me promise not to tell anyone, he unlocked a

drawer in his desk and showed me the credit cards he had in other names.

Albert Sumac.

Leonard Bloom.

Charles Cain.

'I mainly just use the first one. It's been necessary for me to hide certain parts of my life from other parts of my life,' he paused as he relocked the drawer. 'For, um, financial reasons as well as personal ones.'

'You've stolen money?' I hiccupped.

'You're very blunt.' His lips curled into that lazy smile I liked.

'I don't think I'll be shocked.' I sat up straight, feeling suddenly adult. 'I'm just curious.'

Matthew returned to the chaise and spoke quietly to the book-case on his left. 'I took what I needed from my last employer when I left, yes. My son helped me hide it in the Channel Islands, and later I invested it in property in Kew. It was a one-off thing; now I just do a little tinkering of the books with my racing clients and the housing association where one of my flats is. They pay me – well, Albert – to manage the building and I skim a little off the top. It's no worse than the banks do every day.'

'And the personal reasons?' I whispered excitedly.

'Ah.' He turned his wrinkled eyes to me. 'Well, I'm afraid you might be shocked by those.'

'I'm not a child!' I blurted.

'You're right, you're not a child. Okay, well I suppose you'll find out sometime.' He glanced quickly towards the closed door before whispering that he and Annabelle had an 'arrangement'. I listened to his words with wide-eyes, neither daring to ask for details about this 'arrangement' nor questioning for one moment whether this might be the sort of line all adulterous men use to justify their actions.

'You mean you see other women?' My voice hit an embarrass-ingly-high note.

'Shhh!' He sat back with a grin. 'I think you're trying to make

15

me blush today. Yes, I have other women. It's a necessity of being an Uncle . . . and a man.'

I mulled over this for a moment, and then asked, 'How many?'

'Excuse me?' He raised one caterpillar eyebrow.

'Sorry, you don't have to tell me,' I mumbled. 'I'm just curious how many women you've "needed"?'

'In my whole life?' he chuckled. 'Annabelle asked me that once and made me count. I think it was sixty-three.'

'You're lying!' I choked. 'That's ridiculous. It's probably impossible.'

'I wish it was,' he sighed. 'Sadly, there have only been a few I really cared about. For some, I can't even remember their names.'

Over the coming weeks, in between philosophical discussions about art and Uncles and gossipy chats about next-door's decision to cut down the oak tree, Matthew told me about the women in his life.

'I used to have to sneak girls past the witch I lodged with. We tried every trick in the book. As far as she knew, I had seven sisters who would each visit me on a different night of the week. Stupid old bag!'

I knew it was weird being told these stories, but I enjoyed them. I imagined them as scenes from black-and-white movies flickering through my mind and tried to work out what my silver-haired friend must have been like as a young man.

'Sometimes, if I liked a girl, I'd treat her to a hotel room. But in those days they wouldn't let just anyone into hotels, so you had to pretend to have just got married or, if the manager had a heart, you could make up some sob story about her dad being out to get you but you just being a nice lad after all.'

'My friend Thomas had this plan to put a mattress in the back of his van, but I think it got him more slaps than shags.'

'I once kissed three generations of the same family. I was in love with Mrs Shelby when I was six and she gave me a kiss after the school play, then later I dated her daughter Jenny, and when she got too old and grey, I took out her daughter Rose.'

'Jocelyn was an actress. She never had a penny, but her breasts were magnificent.'

'Linda was a secretary and used to steal office supplies for me, so I could work from my flat. I hated going into Fleet Street; drinking was the only thing that made it bearable.'

'Amy was fun; she didn't mind doing it outside or in the car.'

'Julie almost killed me. She came to pick me up from work so we could go to the pictures, but what I didn't know was that she'd found out I was going with her flatmate too. Everything seemed normal and she stayed quiet as I chatted about my day, until she turned onto the motorway and just kept accelerating until we were going 120mph and I was clutching the door handle for dear life.'

'Kate was beautiful, but she peed herself when she had an orgasm. I could never get into that.'

'Elizabeth and I used to eat at the best restaurants, and then run out without paying. It put us on such a high. But she always fancied my friend more than me.'

'Lucy wanted to marry me.'

'Irene did marry me: trapped me into it by getting pregnant. I was still in Norfolk in those days and you couldn't run out on a girl in farm country. It was different in the city. I liked the city.'

'Marie – Annabelle's friend whom I was seeing before her – was utterly neurotic. The stupid cow used to cry after sex and then insist on cooking me bacon and eggs, even in the middle of the night.'

After hearing these tales, when the teapot was cold or empty and Annabelle was making quiet fumbling noises in the hall – indicating she wanted some attention now – I would stumble onto the street and stare bewilderedly at the pavement I had plodded so many times before. I imagined the seven-year-old me, clad in

17

a gingham dress and kicking stones with sensible shoes, and I wondered how she and I were still in the same place, how I could know so much now, yet still have to pretend to be the same little girl living the same little life in the same little town.

One day Matthew played me a Leonard Cohen album and began speaking in a much more serious tone.

'Of course, what I was looking for yet was afraid to find all those years was what I had right at the beginning. When I went to university, my family made a big deal about it because I was the first one of us not to work on the farm. I wanted to go to Oxford, of course, but I failed my Latin, so Exeter it was. I was reading English Literature and rushed to join the department paper, to set up a John Donne society and to establish the best way to sneak books past the librarians. I was so innocent then, hardly thinking about girls.

'Suzanne was in one of my lectures. She was from Paris and wore only black. All the boys were in love with her, but for some reason she came over to speak to me. I bought her a hot chocolate at a café and she took me back to meet her flatmate Marie-Anne.'

I noticed with something approaching panic that a tear had dribbled from Matthew's eyeball.

'We had from November to June together and it was perfect. The three of us lived in harmony: Marie-Anne and I both totally in love with Suzanne and loving each other for our mutual predicament. I would watch Suzanne spread out on the bed on spring afternoons, reading poetry aloud as Marie-Anne ran a razor ever so gently over her pubic bone, then softly kissed the raw skin.

'But that upstart Mickey Robinson decided to publish something in the campus paper about our *ménage à trois* as he called it. It was the biggest scandal of the term and I was hauled into the Dean's office. He was so embarrassed he couldn't even look me in the face when he told me I was being sent down. Suzanne's parents were informed and she was summoned back to France

18

before any of us could say goodbye. But it was Marie-Anne who took it the worst.'

He was crying fully now and, borrowing a gesture learnt from films rather than life, I walked over to his chair and wrapped my skinny arms over his shoulders.

'What happened to Marie-Anne?' I asked softly.

'She hanged herself in our flat. The landlady found her. I wasn't even allowed to go to the funeral.'

But I'm getting ahead of myself. Before I learnt about Suzanne and the others, before I'd committed too fully to my second life, Matthew and I had to organise my Bunbury.

'It's regrettable, but I think it would be safest if we offered your mother a reason for you to come here so often.'

'What sort of reason?'

'Well, perhaps you could work for me. I'll employ you to sort my books and maybe put my horseracing accounts on the computer. How about that?'

I'd never thought about what Matthew 'did'. I knew he'd once been a journalist and was vaguely aware he now made money offering betting tips to a mysterious collection of 'clients', but generally I imagined he spent his days reading poetry and waiting for my visits. In contrast to my workaholic parents, Matthew's life was so theoretical and luxurious that the concept of him sat in front of a computer concentrating on paid employment was almost laughable.

'I really could do with sorting through my books – both the horsing ones, and these,' he said, brushing his hand over an old edition of *To the Lighthouse*. 'I'd like them in order throughout the house. We could do it together and drink cups of tea and discuss the dead poets as we go. As far as your mother's concerned, you'd just be earning a bit of pocket money helping out a scatterbrained old gambler.'

Thus I began 'working' for Matthew. The legitimacy of this

work was never clear; sometimes he would thrust a small amount of money into my hand as a kind of payment 'to show Mummy', but most of the time I just spent my Saturday and Sunday afternoons reclining on his chaise longue reading scraps of verse from the anthologies we were meant to be alphabetising.

Sometimes I felt a pang of guilt when I returned home and my mum asked me how the afternoon had gone, if we'd got much done. But mostly I rationalised that it wasn't a lie as such and, anyway, such measures were only necessary because she and everyone else who thought it odd for a teenager to spend so much time with a sexagenarian were so steeped in the dismal unreality of the world they couldn't see the true beauty of friendship. Besides, Matthew was adept at sensing my angst and, whenever I began to slip too far into the vicinity of guilt and shame, I would find an email waiting in my inbox, pulling me back to the beautiful world of literature and poetry:

From: Matthew Wright <theoutsider@worldopen.co.uk>
To: Natalie Lucas <sexy_chocolate69@sweetmail.com>
Sent: 12 July 2000, 08:27:31
Subject: Your worries

I know you struggle with the lies, but never forget what is real. You feel guilty about your Ma, who herself feels guilty about you and her Ma and all of the world, simply because she's trying too hard. She can't see the beauty.

But you, my angel (my Uncle), can. And that is a gift (for me as well as you).

Edmond Rostand said: 'The dream alone is of interest.' So, my darling, let us dream.
MW

* * *

About halfway through the summer, just after my sixteenth birthday, we began discussing love. We read the Romantics, then moved on to Whitman and finally picked up some collections by Leonard Cohen. I liked the singsong neatness of Blake and the hallmark sentiments of Burns, but Matthew would always reach for *Leaves of Grass* or mumble the lyrics to 'Death of a Ladies' Man'.

We discussed unrequited, inexpressible and forbidden love; we talked about communities running people out of town, countries stoning women for infidelity and religions turning their backs on faithful worshippers. We watched *The Wicker Man* and flicked through the writings of the Marquis de Sade. We reread extracts from *Brave New World* and talked about the concept of everyone 'belonging' to one another. He told me monogamy was just as abstract an idea as polygamy and we discussed his relationship with Annabelle once more. We talked about the line between friendship and love, about why the world has to be so blind to the possibilities of their overlap. Sometime in late August, Matthew told me he loved me and I wrote in my diary that he was not being improper.

A lingering hug became our ritual goodbye. Back in my bedroom I would miss his arms and want the safe feeling of being enveloped by a true friend. We swapped 'I love you's in emails and notes through the letterbox. We knew the others wouldn't understand, but we also knew that it was true and innocent.

My Bunbury evolved so that once I returned to school to begin the sixth form I had permanent employment archiving Matthew's racing tips at the weekends. I never went near his computer, but sometimes he'd tell me about reading the form and calculating probabilities so I could blag my way through knowing about gambling. Through a slow accumulation of half-truths and almost-lies, Matthew and I constructed a wall around our friendship that allowed us to spend intense afternoons discussing Uncles, love and poetry. The neighbours, my parents and his in-laws ceased raising their eyebrows and gradually came to expect us to sit together at parties, to dawdle behind or step out ahead on Sunday afternoon walks and to be found together when we were nowhere else.

My diary during that time was a scruffy composition book I'd covered with an angsty painting on squared graph paper. I'd bought it as I walked through the town one Thursday in Year 11 after Josephine Cuthbert had taunted me about my crush on Adam Hound and my brother had poked me in the arm for the duration of our bus ride.

Arriving home, I'd slammed the front door and ran up to my room at the top of my house. I'd spread my paints and brushes over the floor and began making crude, angry marks. After a while, my mum had knocked tentatively at the door. She asked what was wrong and listened sympathetically for a while as I sobbed and tried to describe the hideous impossibility of school and life and myself.

When I paused to hiccup my breath, she glanced towards the window, sighed, and said, 'Well, I'm sure it will get better. It could be a lot worse – at least you have food on your plate. Dinner will be at seven.'

She left and I grabbed a pen. My first entry looked like this:

21/03/2000
'Maybe it's not the school,' she said. 'It's happened before.' Does she think I don't know that? Does she think that every day I don't wish I could fit in, just lazily walk into school and be greeted by a few proper friends instead of worrying who I'm going to burden myself with next?! I hate it. I hate school. I know I've never really been able to settle down with good friends, not at primary school either, but I just think that if I reinvent myself one more time then maybe someone will like me. And sixth form is different. If I could just switch schools one more time I shouldn't get so much

of the 'keen bean' stuff. It's only a week until the end of term, thank God. Maybe I'll make it.

Why the hell am I writing this crap? I hate diaries. They're pointless and I always write in them for a month or two and then stop. It'll probably be the way of this one. I just don't get the point of writing something no one is ever going to read. But then it scares me to rely on memories. I don't want to forget things, especially not the bad stuff, because that's what reminds you not to live in the past but the present.

I don't think I live in either, though. Half the time I seem to be daydreaming: thinking, scheming, planning. And then when I wake up it all hits me again and I get a great wave of depression at the sorry facts of my life.

You probably want to slap me right now. I would. I mean, there are starving kids in Africa and I'm complaining that I have no friends! Not really comparable, I know. My mum says I'm self-indulgent. She cries a lot of the time too, though. I just have issues, you could call it paranoia (is it 'io'?). I mean, I always find I don't trust people. Why should I? I don't trust myself even. I'm two-faced and I lie, so how can I expect all the other girls not to be bitching behind my back? I can't stand myself. I cringe as I say things and I hate being shy. I hate the way I go red and my eyes fill up with water at the slightest things. I hate biting my nails, I hate how people intimidate me just because they don't hate themselves. I don't hate the way I look all the time, but I'm forever wishing I was someone else.

By the time Matthew got his hands on my diary, there were many pages of similar complaints about my mother, school, nobody understanding me and the black bags under my eyes. But there were a couple of other things that made me hesitate when he gently asked to read my thoughts.

'I want to know you inside out.'

23

'I know you're writing it because you want to be read, so why not let me?'

'It would be the most intimate act imaginable.'

Firstly, of course, I worried because by this time he featured quite extensively. There was probably nothing in there I wouldn't say to his face given we'd developed such an open form of conversation, but still, what would it be like to have him see things like this in ink:

14/08/00

The only Uncle I have is Matthew, who is four times my age. It scares me because I've become quite dependent on him but he's going to leave me. Be it death or moving to Bournemouth like Annabelle's always talking about or me going off to university, he's not always going to be here and that makes me want to weep.

22/08/00

Of course, I wouldn't go there. Yuk. I can't believe my mind just came up with that. He's just my best friend and I'm looking for a father figure. It must be all those French films we're watching.

29/08/00

I can't help it. I was in the chemist's the other day and the woman in front looked ancient. She had a prescription three pages long. I looked over her shoulder and read her date of birth. 1926. She was 74. All I could think was that, when I'm thirty, that'll be Matthew. He'll turn seventy the same year I'm twenty-six.

The second thing that I worried would set my diary apart from any other sixteen-year-old's Matthew happened to read was the confession that had made one of my ex-boyfriends, Todd, exclaim, 'Oh God, you're just confused. Every girl I've ever met says that. Get over it, you're not a lesbian!' I didn't know if I was a lesbian or not, but after the incident with Todd I stopped admitting seriously to friends that I thought I might like girls. I did, however, scrawl lines and lines about my concerns and ventured tentative explorations behind the mask of alcohol.

22/03/00

I figured out why I'm writing a diary. It's because I watched Girl, Interrupted *(my favourite film, along with* American Beauty *and* The Virgin Suicides*) and she writes a diary in that. I guess I thought it might help me figure out some of my feelings. Watching that film again was really scary. It's about a girl with Borderline Personality Disorder and the scary bit is I could relate to everything she said: all about not fitting in, not being listened to, not being able to just accept life and finding it easier to live in a fantasy land. The only thing I didn't really relate to was the whole promiscuous thing – still being a virgin and all. But even that's quite shady because I think that if I had the confidence, I may be promiscuous. I keep thinking about shagging some random girl. I don't even know how it would work but I look at Jenna and Claire and Becky in class and I just want to press my lips onto theirs. Sometimes I worry they can see my thoughts, so I tell them I was thinking about Juan, this fit new Spanish guy in my tutor group. But, truth is, I'm far more interested in the lesbian thing. I heard some girls in the year below got really drunk last Saturday and all took each other's tops off and had an orgy. All the girls in the toilets squealed with horror and said to keep away from them in PE in case they perved on us, but I just wanted to ask who they were and how I could make friends. Am I a freak?*

Matthew had asked me ages ago whether I kept a diary and what security measures I had to prevent my brother and parents from reading it. He'd also asked in a teasing tone what secrets I recorded there and whether I kept secrets from him. For a few weeks I'd been entertaining the idea of letting him see it, of allowing another person to read me. I'd read and reread my own hand, wondering what Matthew might make of it: would he be shocked by my curiosities about my sexuality? Would he laugh at my immaturity? Would he think I was a bad daughter because I wrote angrily about my mother? Would he realise I was a loser with no friends at school and not want to spend time with me any more? Would he be offended by my thoughts about him? Would he still like me?

Eventually these doubts were outweighed by the heavy desire to be known: for a single person in the world to understand all that was in my head and help me work it out. One Sunday, after we'd had tea and chatted about Emily Dickinson, I removed the tatty book from my backpack and, with a trembling hand, offered it to Matthew. I paced miserably home and woke a dozen times in the night wondering if I had an email from him.

The next day, Matthew hung my diary from our doorknob in a plastic Safeway's bag, along with two other items. The first was a new, spiral-bound, orange-flowered notebook; the second, a palm-sized engraved metal shape that Google later informed me was an ankh, the Egyptian symbol for immortality. My immediate concern, though, was the printed page wrapped around the object:

Extract from *The Act of Creation* by Arthur Koestler

The ordinary mortal in our urban civilisation moves virtually all his life on the Trivial Plane.

You are not ordinary, Natalie.

I saw Matthew a few hours later and all seemed normal, but as he poured me a cup of tea he asked nonchalantly, 'Why didn't you tell me you were wondering about such things?'

I looked at him blankly.

'It's perfectly natural. In fact, it's essential for Uncles to be open to love in any possible form. Most people go through their lives too afraid to admit their desires; they lock them up and only let out what their mummies say is okay, then end up in dead-end marriages having sex twice a year and finding their wives have been having an affair with the gardener.'

I giggled at his wild, angry gesticulations.

'Your friends at school are just threatened by your insight. They probably go home and masturbate over you, wishing they had the guts to follow through.'

'I don't know about that,' I smiled. 'But is it okay then? Is it normal?'

'Why on earth would you want to be normal?' he chided. 'But of course it's okay for you, it's what you feel. It's exciting.'

There wasn't a day that innocence turned to deception and friendship to seduction. The declarations of love and the poetry we were reading lent themselves to hypothetical discussions about erotic possibilities, but they began in the abstract.

'If society is so wrong that it forbids a perfectly healthy friendship between an old man and a young girl,' I'd ask, 'how can we be sure that everything else it deems "wrong" isn't just as natural?'

'Exactly,' Matthew would grin. 'The machine is there to perpetuate itself, not to protect us. You must find your own rules.'

'But it's absurd that a society it doesn't affect in the slightest condemns it so forcefully. What difference does it make to Mrs Roberts and my mum and Pat down the road whether you're my best friend and I want to tell you I love you?'

'None.'

'And obviously I don't, but what difference would it make if I wanted that to be romantic love? As long as it made you and me happy and Annabelle was not hurt by it, who else could it possibly affect?'

'No one.'

'And it makes you wonder what else we're being conditioned to disapprove of. Why is euthanasia banned? Why is bigamy

27

illegal? Why can't tribes live as they want? Homosexuals get married? Lesbians adopt? Prostitutes work in the open and couples swing?'

'Because true freedom is too much for most people. Only Uncles realise the true possibilities of love and life. And sadly it means they must spend their lives fighting against society just to stay alive.'

By mid-September, we'd all but given up on sorting books. Instead, we'd carry a tray of tea and Eccles cakes into his study and close the door. We'd sit sideways on the chaise and I'd snuggle into his arm while cradling a cup in two hands. Being cuddled by Matthew was my favourite thing and I conveniently ignored the occasional slip of his hand or sniff of my hair.

Sometimes, if we were having an impassioned debate about literature or the world, our faces would get close, our eyes locked together in intensity. One day, his argument trailed off and I thought I must have won my point, but his face remained close and my eyes couldn't turn away. I felt something tingle in my throat and shoulders. I had a sensation like pressing a bruise and became strangely aware of my sandalled toes. Was it my imagination, or was his face inching closer, were his eyelids drooping closed?

I pulled away and straightened my T-shirt.

Matthew reached for his mug and sat back, smiling.

'You almost let me kiss you then.'

'No I didn't!' I blurted out, then blushed.

Matthew sipped his tea and muttered, 'Two roads diverged in a yellow wood,' before replacing his cup and asking what time I'd be able to come tomorrow.

The scene of the almost-kiss was repeated a few days later on the couch in the living room and again over the table in the kitchen. Each time, I allowed myself to indulge that dizzying feeling for a moment longer; smelling his musky cologne and studying his wrinkled lips; tasting and enjoying the unknown before being plunged into the confusing rapids of shame and regret.

I wrote pages in my diary each night, convinced this elastic band of emotions was true passion and I was the only person ever to have felt it so potently. And every second or third weekend, Matthew read my angst-ridden thoughts and told me my soul was beautiful, my life would be incredible.

On 28th September, Matthew succeeded. I wrote in my diary it was 'Nothing huge, but special all the same.'

That evening, he sent me an email:

From: Matthew Wright <theoutsider@worldopen.co.uk>
To: Natalie Lucas <sexy_chocolate69@sweetmail.com>
Sent: 28 September 2000, 22:37:31
Subject: Thank you

Your mind was beautiful today, your body pure bliss. I
belong to you.
Ancient Person of thy heart

You can probably see where this is going now. It wasn't quite as clear-cut and sordid as it might appear. Naive as I may have seemed thus far, I realised there were certain lines that required more consideration than others before crossing.

While the kissing gradually led to 'sorting books' in a horizontal position in the top room, I was quite insistent that whatever his hands and mouth did to please me, his belt-buckle was not going to budge. And though we sent emails most evenings telling the other of our desire, dreaming of total abandonment from the safety of separate bedrooms and discussing the orgasmic meeting of my 'baby kitten' and his 'throbbing doppelgänger', I was certain of one thing: I didn't want him to be my first.

I was aware mine was an unorthodox adolescence. I realised I could grow to regret it, despite my enlightened knowledge that this was the real world. So, for the sake of damage limitation, I wanted to lose my virginity to someone else. Matthew and I discussed the situation via email only, never referring to it between declarations of love in person.

From: Matthew Wright <theoutsider@worldopen.co.uk>
To: Natalie Lucas <sexy_chocolate69@sweetmail.com>
Sent: 4 October 2000, 09:20:12
Subject: Two roads in a wood

I see you worrying about what the world will think and whether you will be able to take things back, whether you'll regret our friendship in later life or discover you chose the wrong yellow-brick path. I see you struggling to find the answers and I wish I could take your pain away, because this time for me is beautiful and relaxed. As you grow, you will understand the world has its reason and things will happen as they please. Our decisions always seem more significant before we have made them.

So, if in your deliberations you ever worry about me, please don't. I am a happy voyeur of your beautiful mind and the conclusions I know it will eventually reach. I cannot, of course, give you advice, but perhaps if you have your A* mathematician's hat on today, you will appreciate the words of Mr Einstein: 'Pure logical thinking cannot yield us any knowledge of the empirical world; all knowledge of reality starts from experience and ends in it. Propositions arrived at by purely logical means are completely empty of reality.'[1]

---

1   Albert Einstein, *On the Method of Theoretical Physics*, Oxford University Press, 1933.

Follow your heart, my love. I will await.
Your very parfait gentle knight
MW

Every night I'd retreat to my room and attack my diary. Matthew told me the decision was in my hands, but our mutual stumbling block was my virginity. He said he couldn't 'take the lid off' that side of me because the first time would inevitably be disappointing and he didn't want to ruin what we had. I agreed. Everyone said it hurt and I was sure I'd end up hating him. But how could I take the lid off with someone else knowing I was in love with Matthew?

What I needed was a boy my own age who wouldn't mind being used and whom I trusted enough not to tell the rest of the sixth form about my proposition.

Richard was my target. We had been girlfriend and boyfriend for a short while in Year 10 and had remained flirty friends since. Our 'relationship' had ended when Richard had told me, quite seriously, that he had important and dangerous things he had to concentrate on to fulfil his destiny and he couldn't be distracted by the usual trappings of teenage life. The gossip tree soon filtered to me that Richard had confided in his best friend Andy that he had been approached by an old homeless man while on holiday in Greece who had told him he was the Second Messiah and dark powers were approaching that only he could battle. Ever since, Richard had been bidding for Samurai swords on eBay.

To sum it up, in Richard's favour:

- Single
- Too focused to want a girlfriend
- Too self-absorbed to bother caring about my motives for such a deed

31

And, against him:

- Possibly slightly unhinged.

I told Matthew I had decided on a person. I suggested the thing to Richard via MSN Messenger. And Richard agreed. The how and where were a little more complicated, so, though it was only October, we decided on New Year's Eve, knowing somebody would have a party. It was settled. I would pop my cherry as I was meant to: drunk and in someone's parents' bed with an acne-ridden boy I found only mildly attractive, and thus I would be free to explore the world of Uncles with one less worry.

Then came the green candle.

On 4th November, I received the lyrics to a Leonard Cohen song via email. The first line was blown up in bigger font and some words made bold:

I lit a **thin green candle** to make you jealous of me.

Attached was an extract from Matthew's diary:

November 2000

So, old man, what are you going to do?

About what? And who are you calling old? I thought we were only as young as we feel.

Fool. I suppose you're telling me she's the elixir of life?

Natalie? Yes, she might be.

So, what will you do?

I can't hurry her. Her beauty and charm is in her innocence – she needs to find her own way.

But what about you? What about your needs?

My needs are less important than hers.

Less important, perhaps, but no less pressing. Every man has needs; it's foolish to deny them.

Yes, yes, we've been down this path before. I know I must do something.

So?

Well, Suzie keeps pestering me.

The PhD student who snaps at you if you bring her flowers and doesn't care if you don't call? Sounds perfect.

Yes, and she tells me she's spent the past six months in the gym.

But..

But every time I see her she tells me she wants my child.

Yikes.

Indeed. She says I won't have to be involved, but I'm not so sure.

You think she's tricking you?

Not deliberately, but women are irrational, they change their minds, especially when children are involved. I've had enough of that for a lifetime.

So, what's the alternative?

Becky's eager.

The one with the nice bum?

Yes, you perv, the one with the nice bum. But she's not much older than Natalie. Eighteen, and nowhere near as mature.

Could be fun, though.

Yes, perhaps.

But..

But my heart's not in it, I suppose. Even though I know I need something and Natalie's talking about experimenting with some boy from school..

Wait! You're talking about living like a monk while she goes around with spotty teenagers? You're even more of a fool than I thought.

Perhaps. A fool for love?

Pah. It doesn't seem fair at all.

No, but she's a child, I can't expect her to understand. I can't make demands on her.

And what's this email about? Are you lighting a green candle?

No, maybe, no. No, I just want her to know how I feel. Perhaps I won't even send it.

And if you do?

Nothing. Then she'll know I've chosen what I have with her over anything I could have with the others.

How very noble.

Don't be so sarcastic. I mean it. I love her. It's real. For the first time in my measly, ancient life, it's real.

A bubble began to rise in my stomach as I read. Suzie and Becky. Who were they? Why should I care? Matthew said he was not lighting a green candle, but still sent me the lyrics to the song. What could that mean? The basement room where I was reading

34

was lit only by the light of the screen and I imagined myself engulfed by a turquoise flame. I pounded up the stairs to my bedroom and scrabbled beneath my mattress for my diary.

After an hour sprawled on my bed with a biro in my hand and tears in my lashes, I paced back down to the computer, praying my brother hadn't gone to play his stupid *Age of Empires* game and read the email I'd left open on the screen. Happily I passed the living-room door and saw James cross-legged in front of the PlayStation instead.

Back at the keyboard, I hesitated. As much as my fingers tingled to reply 'No, don't! I'm here and, yes, I'll be an Uncle,' my throat longed to scream that this was unfair, that I was being handled and manipulated and an Uncle wouldn't do such a thing.

My fingers won.

From: Natalie Lucas <sexy_chocolate69@sweetmail.com>
To: Matthew Wright <theoutsider@worldopen.co.uk>
Sent: 4 November 2000, 22:42:03
Subject: RE: One of Us Cannot Be Wrong

The flame is burning moss. I have an in-service training day a week on Wednesday – can we find a Bunbury?

Later, in my room, I doodled in my notebook:

> *Am I condemned to be*
> *Number sixty-four?*
> *Will you tell your next girl*
> *This one was a bore?*
>
> *That innocent little kitten*
> *You deflowered so well;*
> *My young naive mind,*
> *To the devil did I sell?*

Will you tell of the chase?
The thrill of the game
That finally won me . . .
To discover I'm too tame?

Not like Suzie,
She was fun.
Not like Becky,
With the 'nice bum'.

Is it worth it?
Will I disappoint?
Will you regret the effort?
Will I score a point?

2

At approximately 3pm on 15th November 2000, in room 107 of The Swan Hotel in Swindon, I lost my virginity. I'd been wearing three-inch heels and an oversized suit-jacket, too much make-up for a teenager and black cotton knickers bought in a pack of five from BHS by my mum. I'd known Matthew had booked a hotel room and I'd lied to my mother about going to the cinema with a friend, but I still padded to the bathroom, self-conscious about my nakedness, and looked in the mirror with surprise. As I peed, I wondered what I had thought usually happened when a sixth-former allowed a sexagenarian to spend £150 on a plush suite that would only be used for an afternoon. Had I thought we would simply continue what we had been doing in his top room? Had I imagined his hands and mouth would always work eagerly to please me without his belt-buckle ever budging? Had I believed we could stay in the no-man's-land of *technically* doing nothing wrong? Had I hoped the past few months contained mere digressions that I could take or leave when the mood struck and walk away with my purity intact?

Perhaps I had. It wasn't as if my bookshelves, teachers or friends could provide a precedent; it wasn't as if there were any rules. But I'd responded to his green candle, hadn't I? I wasn't totally naive:

I'd known what he'd wanted. But I hadn't thought about this while clipping my bra and brushing my teeth this morning. I hadn't said goodbye to my mum thinking that the next time I saw her I'd be, what, a *woman*? I'd thought of my Bunbury: I'd concentrated on not overlabouring my lies but making them seem natural. I'd wondered how easy it was going to be to walk nonchalantly towards the bus stop, then dart off onto North Street and slip unobserved into Matthew's waiting passenger seat. I'd deliberated over whether to hide my heels in my handbag and change into them while crouched in his car, or to risk my mother's disapproving comments about unsuitable footwear for the cinema and just leave the house in them anyway. But I hadn't thought about what it would be like to be in a hotel room with Matthew, about his penis actually sliding inside me, about his body on top of mine, about whether it would hurt or whether I might have forgotten my pill even though I hadn't once since I'd been put on it for period pains in Year 10, about all that advice in sex education classes to use condoms even if you're taking contraceptives because you're not protected from STIs that make your pussy resemble an erupting volcano. With the innocence of a teenager who has spent countless Maths classes giggling with friends and ex-best-friends over code-words for body parts and rumours that the girl at the back puts out for the price of a chocolate bar, I hadn't thought we'd actually *do it*.

I didn't bleed and I didn't cry. I didn't even see his thing. Matthew approached it technically, disappearing into the bathroom and returning in his shirt and underpants, smelling like talcum powder, before undressing me and laying me on the duvet. Next, he rifled through his briefcase and pulled out a bottle of Johnson's Baby Oil, placed it neatly on the bedside table. Then, climbing delicately onto the bed, he fixed his eyes on mine.

'Do you love me?' His demanding tone surprised me and I nodded meekly, letting only a nervous breath escape my lips.

'Yes, I can see the love-light in your eyes.'

And in a few minutes it was over. Matthew offered me a box of tissues to clean the stickiness from between my thighs and pulled his trousers back on.

After I returned from the bathroom, we lay on top of the duvet for a while, me naked, him clothed. I wanted to appear mature, but my head was reeling with excitement and disappointment: *Was that it? Is that what everyone whispers about in school? Am I different now? Will they be able to tell? Will my mother know? Will I remember this as special?* Matthew withdrew his arm from around my stomach and walked to the dressing table to fetch his cigars. I pulled my knees up to my chest and hugged myself.

'What are you doing?' He turned back in amusement and horror.

'Nothing. Just thinking.'

'That's what women do to get pregnant you know – lie back like that. You're not trying to trap me, are you?'

'What? No!' I blushed and sat up straight, embarrassed that I'd let my ignorance show.

'I was just thinking about Meursault,' I said, defaulting to literature as a safe topic where we might speak as equals and forget the mundane realities of his grey hair and my smooth skin.

'Hmm?'

'He's the hero of existentialism, the man who refused to play the game, let alone abide by the rules, and he highlights all that's wrong with the world – all that makes this an impossible place for poets and Uncles to live in – but do you think he ever experienced love? Isn't half the point of the novel that he doesn't feel any passions, doesn't understand the motivations of those around him or why laws must dictate x and y? He's basically just an ordinary man: neither an Uncle nor a sheep. He sticks his head above the parapet, but not for any of the reasons that writers and lovers and you and I do.'

'True. But he's just a character. The point is that Camus was feeling all those things and rebelling through his creation.' Matthew sat back against the headboard, a slight smile curling his lips.

'But Camus didn't actually challenge the law and expectations;

he didn't kill anyone and face punishment but not even experience it as punishment. For most of his life, he played society's games and persona'd like the rest of us.'

'So, you wanted him to martyr himself for a world that wouldn't care?'

'No, but it's just, who should we celebrate? Camus or Meursault? Camus's creation of Meursault almost serves to highlight how thoroughly trapped he himself was by the bullshit of the world.'

'Hence why we have to Bunbury,' he winked at me, exhaling a cloud of smoky air.

'But, I want to know if any Uncles ever find the ideal, ever manage to live fully. That has to be the ideal, right? Otherwise what's the point? Why would we continue? We should all wander into rivers with stones in our pockets or stick our heads in ovens. Because a little bit of poetry is not enough. This escape, being here, being with you is my reality and the rest is just gross, you know that? It makes me cry at night. And if I thought it was going to always be like this, I don't know what I'd do. Sometimes I think I'd rather die on a happy note – that's when I'd consider suicide, after the most ecstatic moment of my life, because the thought of falling after being so high would be totally unbearable.'

Matthew smiled at me and I knew I'd redeemed myself. We were no longer in a plush hotel room with a Bible in the drawer and a disapproving receptionist downstairs; we didn't have to leave in a couple of hours and drive back home to face parents and wives, neighbours and peers; instead we were sitting on a cloud with Virginia Woolf and Edgar Allan Poe, sipping tea with Simone de Beauvoir and Marcel Proust. And on this cloud, Matthew's leathery lips tasted like March daffodils as they pressed to my own. My skin buzzed as he folded me back into his arms, whispering into my neck about Helen of Troy.

We left Swindon around five, me sneaking past reception to the car while Matthew dawdled to tell the concierge he'd received a phone call requesting his immediate return, so alas would not be staying and would not require breakfast in the morning. He drove in silence and as we neared home I ducked my head between my knees in case the passing headlights of a neighbour or relative's vehicle happened to illuminate our incongruous faces. He dropped me off at the other end of town and I changed back into my Nikes to plod home, past the Post Office, grocer's and butcher's, preparing my lies and not-quite-lies in my head.

'Yes, Mum, Claire and I had a great time.' *Claire most probably enjoyed her day off too and I didn't say we had a great time together, so we'll call this true.*

'We went to this cool little café and had cream teas.' *True. It was called the Scribbling Horse and the woman gave us extra cream.*

'*The Road to Eldorado* is okay, it's a bit childish, though.' *You don't have to see the film to know this and, as my mother refuses to watch animations, it seems unlikely I'll be quizzed about plot and character development. Therefore, true, plus extra points for successful Bunbury.*

'Hastings was really crowded.' *Also most likely true . . . I just wasn't there.*

'No, I didn't buy anything, but we did look in some book shops.' *True. Matthew bought a* Collected Letters of Virginia Woolf *and I fingered a first edition Oscar Wilde, but shopping wasn't our main priority.*

'The bus was a little late.' *Okay, this one's a lie, but unavoidable. Five truths and one lie – not bad.*

A few hours later, my mum, my brother and I banged our gate and walked the 300 yards to number fourteen. Lydia answered and led us into the sitting room. Annabelle was already sprawled on the floor with her work-friend Lucy, inspecting hand-made jewellery. Lydia's sister, Hannah, was fussing over a teapot by the bay window, and their frail but sharp-eyed mother, Valerie, was characteristically bent double beside a bookshelf, hunting for a specific volume of her 1948 edition of *The Encyclopaedia Britannica*.

These were my mother's friends: people who had been kind to me since I was in single digits; honorary aunts and uncles who cared for my brother and me like children of a collective. Occasionally I felt a pang of guilty tenderness towards this extended family, but mostly over the past few months I'd begun to see them through Matthew's cruel cynicism, noting their individual quirks and scorning their refusal to stick their heads above the parapet.

'I'm so glad you could come on short notice,' Hannah gushed in over-the-top hostess mode. 'Lucy's showing us her gems. Isn't she good? I'm thinking of taking a course.'

My mum had said we'd been invited to look at jewellery; a kind of Tupperware party with beads I supposed. I'd fancied a cup of tea and James had been bribed with biscuits. I shuffled into the room after my brother and noticed Matthew on the end of the couch, a book in his lap. He made eye contact and I turned away, willing my cheeks not to burn.

My eyes landed on Annabelle's patterned skirt. She'd coupled it with an embroidered shirt and looked sumptuously hippyish. In contrast, Hannah wore tight black jeans, ankle-boots and an oversized jumper that made less than subtle allusions to the 1980s, a period in fashion that had not yet returned to the likes of Topshop and H&M.

Lucy, a tiny blonde woman swathed in coloured silk, was explaining how she chose each bead. Something about the karmic energy, I think. I watched her mouth as she talked for a while, but quickly turned my attention to her husband, Graham, who wore ripped jeans and sat with an air of boredom on the sofa next to Matthew. He and Lucy had a son two years above me at school, but Graham looked a bit like a floppy-haired George Clooney so I figured it wasn't too bad to have a crush on him. I sat on the floor next to his feet and asked him about his motorbike, giggling when he said I should come for a ride one day.

'If your mum says it's all right, that is.'

I flushed with excitement and tried not to notice how old

Matthew looked beside Graham, how his leg rested effeminately upon his knee and his shirt fell over a muscle-less torso. It wasn't that I didn't love him or that I didn't want to repeat what we'd done this afternoon, but something had changed today and I felt a new kind of energy coursing through my limbs, one that drew me instinctively towards the Grahams and Lucys of the world.

I wasn't the only one, though, and before the evening was over, Hannah was sat tipsily in Graham's lap and Annabelle was fawning over Lucy's earrings, brushing the skin on her neck as she fingered the green gems dangling from her lobes. My mum and Valerie were deep in discussion about the treatment of mental health patients in 1975 and James's head rested heavily on his arm as Lydia spoke of the difficulties of getting out to do the gardening. On the way home, James growled at my mum that he'd never be forced to go to one of those things again and she muttered a reply along the lines of, 'I don't know why you have to be so antisocial; Nat seemed to enjoy herself.'

3

On dreary country days, when the air choked with the pitiful mediocrity of small town life, old ladies wheeled their trolleys through town to collect their pensions from Nicky at the Post Office and Ray listened to people natter about haemorrhoids in the chemist before dispensing Preparation H, I would sit in Matthew and Annabelle's open-plan kitchen, playing cards and drinking tea from a pot. Sometimes I'd curl my legs under me on the awkward unpadded chairs while Annabelle doodled flowers beside the crossword in the *Telegraph* and Matthew consulted *The Racing Post*. He sat at the head, with the two of us on either side; these were unarticulated but set places and it was always odd when Annabelle was away and Matthew set my place for dinner at her chair.

During term time, I spent six out of seven nights there and, on holidays, most days too. Eight front doors and eleven cars separated their house from my mum's. The Grays, the Smiths, the Popels, Mrs Pratt, Mr Davis, Oliver and June, Beatrice and the Roberts lived in between. Our immediate neighbours, the Grays, had retired to tend their immaculate garden and always said hello when I passed them on the pavement, but would become more reserved in a few months once I moved in with my dad and my

44

mum began muttering up and down the street about my being an 'awkward teenager'. Mrs Pratt had been a teacher at my primary school and, although she asked kindly about my exams and future plans, I was still a little afraid of her and mumbled nervously whenever I encountered her on my way to the house on the end.

Matthew's study lay behind the street-side window, so I could always tell before I arrived whether he or Annabelle would answer my knock first. Their post-box-red front door encased in its black frame now looms overly significant in my memory. Stepping through that doorway I would shed the unhappy teenager living in a deadly dull town that haunted me on the outside and enter the safe place of art, poetry, philosophy and love.

A kingfisher I had drawn in pastels at the age of eight hung above their stove, the Piglet I had won Matthew at the fair was pinned to the whiteboard in his study, my cribbage board had found a permanent home on the shelf with his chess set, and Juno, Annabelle's cat, paid no attention to my comings and goings. Towards the end, I might even have had a key, and, of course, volumes of my angsty diaries lay in a locked drawer of Matthew's bureau because we'd agreed early on that this was safer than having them only perfunctorily hidden beneath my mattress.

The three of us played cards, drank wine and sometimes smoked weed acquired from my friends at school. Matthew and I would touch feet under the table and sneak a kiss when Annabelle ran upstairs to fetch something. Sometime after 10pm Annabelle would pour herself a tiny glass of port and wish us goodnight. I would stay, wrapped in Matthew's arms as we whispered secrets to each other or dared ourselves to forget Annabelle was only upstairs, until it got late enough that I worried a parent might come looking for me and I let myself out, arrived home and calmly watched some television repeat with my unquestioning family.

* * *

45

My first memories of Matthew and Annabelle hardly involve Matthew at all. Annabelle and my mum were introduced through Ruth, a woman who had had her first marriage annulled and convinced a Methodist priest, despite her four grown children, to perform her second attempt to a childhood friend. When my parents were ending their messy though marriageless relationship, Ruth was the witch who stole my mother from me when she cried, but Annabelle was the angel who gently entertained my brother and me; she turned packing up our family home into a game of make-believe pirates and princesses.

Annabelle's husband was just one of those shadowy figures of husbands you remember from playing in the garden while your mother gossiped with her friends on the patio, drinking cups of instant coffee. He must have been in the background and I must have known him, but the squiggly jigsaw pieces of his identity in my mind didn't slot together until our conversation at his birthday party. From that moment, though, it was like someone flicked a switch and swapped the direction of the escalators in a department store. As Matthew became a fleshy figure, a father, mentor, Uncle and lover, and I spent more time with Annabelle, building the friendship I'd craved as a child, the haloed idol of my youth slipped away and was replaced by her altogether more self-assured husband.

I didn't, don't and probably never will know what Annabelle knew about what was between Matthew and me, but she was my friend. I'd loved her in a childish way and still adored spending time with her, but I never felt guilty about sleeping with her husband. The larger difficulty was sneaking around. Matthew and I were conducting an affair in a small, gossipy town where privacy didn't come easy. I had to sneak along the street, invent reasons to go into town, dart through his door when the coast was clear, tell my mother I checked my email five times a day because of school projects, leave notes under a plant by his door, pin myself to the wall until he'd drawn the curtains, worry about his aftershave

46

on my coat and secretly wash my expensive lingerie in the bathroom sink.

Communication was the most difficult: frequently I would arrive at his door expecting intimacy only to be greeted by a booming, 'Oh look, it's Nat, how unexpected. We haven't seen you in ages! Barbara and Richard are here, do come in. Have you come to borrow that book?' and have to endure an afternoon of personaed small talk instead. Or I'd wait all day to visit at the appointed time, but discover Annabelle had changed her plans and run her errands in the morning.

Mothers and brothers and fathers and in-laws, neighbours and doctors, shopkeepers and postmen all thwarted our arrangements, left us tapping out frustrated messages from separate computers, compelling us to dream of a mythical time and place where we could be free to love in the open.

Sometimes we'd plot elaborate Bunburys and, to our surprise, they'd come together: we'd escape for a night in my half-term holidays to return to Swindon, or I'd skip my Wednesday afternoon Psychology class to drive to Rye for a cream tea and a hunt through the second-hand bookshops. But more often than not, these secret passionate or plebeian encounters would be spoilt or at least dissipated by unlucky coincidences.

A favourite free-period picnic spot was the Beachy Head car park in Warren Hill, where Matthew and I would share flasks of coffee and flaky pastries as well as more incriminating things. But two terrifying incidents marked an end to those visits. The first was Felicity Roberts, daughter of Mr and Mrs Roberts who lived next door to Matthew and Annabelle, passing our parked vehicle with her dog Bobby on the way to the footpath while Matthew and I were in the middle of one of those incriminatingly passionate things. I convinced myself she hadn't seen or hadn't recognised me and was persuaded to go back the following week, but returning from a lazy amble into Holywell, we found the passenger-side window of Matthew's car had been smashed and my school-bag stolen. I had to sit in the back avoiding shards of glass on the way home and we developed a flat along a country lane, but none of that was as scary as having to explain to my parents how I'd lost my wallet, house keys, new glasses and a piece of coursework and why I didn't want to try to claim them on the house insurance.

Much safer options for seeing each other were under cover of larger groups, where we could steal glances and share knowing laughs. We arranged cinema trips with my mum where I sat in the middle and tentatively touched Matthew's knee during dark scenes, group outings to the races where Matthew paced seriously, studying form and winking as he told me to put my allowance on a 30-1 outsider, and neighbourhood picnics at Pevensey Bay where I pranced in tiny bikinis only to notice my neighbour Bob ogling me as well as Matthew. But these half-moments together often left me missing the Matthew I knew even more than when we were apart.

One Saturday in the spring, two weeks after Matthew's birthday, four months since I lost my virginity and thirteen weeks until my AS exams, I followed Matthew into his study after a silent greeting. With his back to me, he took something from the desk, and then turned around to present a carrier bag.

'I bought us phones,' he grinned and waited for my response.

'Huh?' I managed after a pause and took the bag from his outstretched hand.

'They're on the same network, so as long as we put ten pounds on each month, we can text each other for free.'

I pulled a box the size of a *Roget's Thesaurus* from the bag.

I'd had a phone before. My best friend Alicia had been promised one for her fourteenth birthday in August and, with the insane jealousy known only to teenage girls, I'd begged my dad to beat her parents to it and get me one for mine in July. At the last minute, he'd acquiesced and bought me a pay-as-you-go Vodaphone brick that I'd diligently lugged around for three months, receiving approximately two phone calls per week, generally from my mum to see what time I'd be home, before conceding that I didn't really have a use for it and kicking it under my bed along with the ancient Mega Drive and the broken personal CD player.

This was a third of the size of my old phone, red plastic encasing the minuscule screen. It weighed less than my house keys and already had a screen-saver message saying, 'Hello Kitten'.

'Look, mine's the same,' continued Matthew, pulling an identical handset from his inside jacket pocket.

I smiled.

'To activate the SIM you'll need to call this number,' he pointed to a white sticker on the box. 'I chose us the same PIN number: 1661.'

'Okay,' I murmured, concentrating on finding the Unlock button.

'It's our ages,' Matthew chuckled. 'Also the year Newton got into Cambridge.'

'Fascinating,' I drawled precociously and kissed him on the lips.

Despite the precedents of Anna Karenina, Lady Chatterley and other pre-twenty-first-century literary examples, affairs and mobile phones go together like stockings and suspenders. Six months into ours we had passed the incidental lying-in-the-name-of-love period and were ready for the cold, premeditated deception-for-the-sake-of-debauchery stage. The jumble of plastic and circuits in my hand meant, without a doubt, Matthew was mine: my illicit lover, my shocking secret, my erotic exhilaration – my man.

4

My mum stopped eating when my dad left her. She told me later that a couple of times she went to bed with a carving knife. I was eleven at the time and we were close. We went swimming most days, and, driving along the dual carriageway with our costumes in the back and tears staining our cheeks, she'd tell me about the separation. She explained my father had found another girlfriend before he'd even told her he wanted out; described his shock that she'd changed the locks one morning when he returned from Katie's to collect clean socks before work; and told me he wanted to keep the house, meaning we would have to move. She recounted the names he'd called her, sobbed about promises he'd broken and raged at how much she'd sacrificed for the relationship.

Some would say I was too young to hear this and my mother must have contributed to the lousy relationship I had with my father through my teens, but I adored being told these things. Her confidence in me assured me I was her best friend and provided me my first taste of the contradictory pleasure of intense pain.

When she told me my dad had suggested I live with her and he take James, I threw myself into hating the father who loved me less than my brother. When forced to spend the weekend with him, I would scream an explicit response to his, 'Would you like to cut my lawn?' and stomp back down the road into my mother's arms.

That kind of intense closeness with a parent is exhilarating, but exhausting. My mum's friends would comment that I seemed insecure because I insisted on telling her I loved her a dozen times an hour. And when I was old enough to stay at other people's houses, I'd feel guilty for breaking up our family unit for an evening.

By the time my second life began, my mum and I were already clashing like any teen cliché. So, when, half a dozen months after my first Bunbury at Swindon, she screeched up the stairs, 'WHY DON'T YOU GO AND LIVE WITH YOUR FATHER IF YOU FEEL LIKE THAT?' I did. While she sobbed that she hadn't meant it and couldn't understand why I was doing this, I dragged suitcases across town and moved in with the man I'd hated for the past five years.

Living with my dad proved convenient. He was out a lot and didn't ask where I was going. Over months of microwaved rice and washing-up stand-offs, my dad and I began to rebuild the relationship I'd treasured as a little girl. However, my basic lack of respect for him as a parent meant conducting an affair under his nose was purely mathematical; uncomplicated by the guilt I'd felt when lying to my mother. My biggest shame, even now, out of everything I did and everyone I deceived, was allowing my mum to think I left because of her. My brother would update me on how many times a week he found her crying and how, for years afterwards, she would periodically tell him she still didn't understand why I'd gone. After our initial anger had worn off, we tentatively made up, but our closeness was lost. We never spoke of me moving out and she told me she would be my friend from now on, but no longer my mother.

At sixteen, I'd achieved what I'd set out to do and what most teenagers long for: I'd shed parental guidance and found autonomy. But it felt awful.

I turned to Matthew and Annabelle. Matthew was not only my lover, but my father and mother too. And eating roast dinners around their table or helping them do the crossword on a Saturday morning let me pretend I had a functioning family.

However, when my dad took his campervan to raves or visited one of his girlfriends for the night, my functioning family became less Brady, more Bovary.

I'd wait in the hall, peering through the glass front door. The transparency of my father's bay-windowed house freaked me out when I was alone at night and I'd imagine faceless strangers standing on the lawns, watching as I climbed the stairs and walked in and out of uncurtained rooms. On nights like this I'd worry the couple in the manor house across the road could see everything I did. I'd turn off the lights.

From the dark, I'd watch the curved front path bathed in orange streetlight. I'd jump at every shadow and tap my foot nervously when an old lady pulled her Fiat Punto to the other side of the street to stuff an envelope into the post-box.

I'd be wearing the knee-length suede coat my dad had bought me as a reward for getting straight As in my GCSEs. I'd have on the one pair of heels I owned, purchased for a tenner from New Look, and, underneath the coat, an intricately detailed lace thong or a complicatedly clasped suspenders set.

A black-coated figure would make his way up the path. He'd climb the porch steps and trigger the sensored light. We'd both panic. I'd let him in and shoo him away from the window. We'd go directly to my bedroom.

The walls were a deep red that my grandmother had warned would look like the lining of a womb. With candles flickering shadows to the ceiling and Norah Jones lilting softly, I felt it had the appropriateness of a theatrical set. The bed flaunted itself in the middle of the room, not beside a wall or tucked into an alcove, but centre stage. Around it were no stuffed toys, stacks of board games or cheesy 'Best Buds' photo frames, as featured in my friends' bedrooms, but instead: white canvas furniture; bookshelves divided into novels, poetry, reference and erotica; a leather armchair with *Steppenwolf* resting upon it; six or seven kohl pencils beside the mirror; and a bottle of baby oil on the bedside table.

My silver-haired guest would unlace his shoes and place them together before neatly removing his clothes and folding them in a pile upon the chair. I'd keep my coat buttoned and he'd come to me. He'd coyly ask what I was hiding and I'd giggle.

At some point, the coat would fall to the floor and he'd push me, still in my heels, onto the bed. It had posts, to which I was sometimes delicately laced with silk scarves or violently chained by handcuffs. Other nights, however much I gripped the bars and moaned that I wanted him to take control, he wouldn't be in the mood.

He'd direct his attentions beneath the lingerie, glancing at my face regularly to gauge his success, before methodically wetting himself with oil and spilling two drops on the beige carpet but not apologising. He'd manoeuvre my limbs as he wanted them, concentrating on his angle as he entered. He'd look at me briefly, searchingly, angrily, perhaps even accusingly, but eventually say, 'I love you.' I'd reply and the hardness in his eyes would return.

'Do you?' he'd demand as he twisted me over and pressed me to the sheets. I'd feel the weight of his wrinkled hand upon my back, but my crotch would respond and he'd split my thighs further with each thrust. I'd reach underneath to touch myself and, seeing me, he'd quicken his pace, clutching my hips to guide his strokes. I'd utter low, gravelly responses to his questions: did I like that? Could I feel him? Was he deep inside me? Was I bad? Did I need to be punished? Did I want to be fucked? He'd continue talking not looking for a response; my stifled cries enough. He was fucking me, he'd tell me, and he wasn't going to stop, he was going to fuck me until I came, until my cunt was sore and I begged him to stop. I was a naughty little girl who needed to be taught a lesson, he'd growl. He had my legs split and was fucking me with his thick cock, he'd say, he was filling my hole, was right up inside me and wasn't going to stop however much I wanted him to, was going to give me the best fucking of my life, was going to ruin me, was . . .

The deep thrusts would melt into frantic and sloppy jerks as I felt a hot liquid smear between my legs and begin to trickle. For a moment, I'd stay in the same position, still locked to the bed though his hand had gone. I'd become aware of my arse waving in the air and shyly roll over, reaching for a tissue. He'd be lying down already, drifting into sleep. He'd reach out his arm for me and we'd lie stiffly, avoiding the wet patch, until he roused himself and said it was late, he should leave.

My sixth-form life was thus divided between sordid trysts and a desire to fit in. I'd ruined a relationship with my mum, my dad was out four nights a week and my friends at school were so alienated by my jumble of lies that there was a rumour going around that I'd made up an imaginary boyfriend that I actually believed in, meaning I was probably certifiably crazy. Instead of spotty boys and impossible algebra, my head was filled with poetry, Uncles and how I could next see the man who told me I was special.

Every day after school, most weekends and all holidays I'd snake down the garden path and fall onto the street. I'd pace across town, and, hurrying past my mum's house, I'd worry vaguely about the Grays and the Roberts as I darted through Matthew's wrought-iron gate, noting whether Annabelle's car rested beside his. I'd press the doorbell, plus bang the knocker if the chipped red door failed to open immediately, and my foot would tap anxiously before a face peeked from behind the draught-excluding curtain, checking over my shoulder for witnesses and whispering hurriedly about Annabelle's mood or how long we had alone. Once inside, those familiar smells of incense and coffee, cat and perfume. The hallway full of Indian patterns, net curtains and antique lamps, stairs leading upwards and doors to my left and one to my right. If Annabelle was home, a quick shuffle to the right and softly close the study door. A kiss and an embrace between the solid fire-proof door and the light blue curtains, drawn above the leather chaise longue, banishing the street outside, separating Uncles from others; us from them. I'd lean back on the dark wood of the ancient desk, absently fingering the knob of the locked drawer where my diaries were kept. I'd smell the familiar scent of the books on the shelf, twisting with too much Jovan Musk in the air. My ancient lover would be clean-shaven, wearing a soft pink shirt, or stubbly and sick-looking, padding about in a dressing gown and repulsing me with his weakness. The whiteboard would be scrawled with names like Southern Star, Kieren Fallon, Monty's Pass and John Velazquez, and a picture of me from the previous summer was taped discreetly to the back of the door, along with a calendar dotted with the word 'Baba'.

Following prudent 'hellos', we'd venture back into the hall and seek out Annabelle. Though she rarely sat in there except to watch television in the evenings, I'd poke my head in the living room and survey the formal couches, the locked bookcase of first editions, the china cats guarding the wedding photograph on the faux-marble mantelpiece and the real feline, Juno, gazing at me from a cushion on the rocking chair in the bay window. I'd follow Matthew along the hall into the extended kitchen and wait for my eyes to adjust to the light pouring from the south-facing veranda windows. Through them I could see their long, overgrown garden, and the tips of the trees in the wood beyond.

Annabelle would be sat at the chunky table twirling a pencil above a shopping list, or standing by the counter pouring water into the teapot, or kneeling by the boarded-up fireplace painting a mural. Or the kitchen would be empty and I'd wander to 'my seat' and grab a pack of cards from the bookshelf, begin shuffling while Matthew filled the kettle, glanced in the fridge and stepped onto the patio to check Annabelle was safely engrossed pulling weeds. He'd kiss me and we'd giggle naughtily about 'doppelgänger' and 'kitten' as we played cribbage and Matthew let me win. After a while, Annabelle would amble slowly up the garden path and we'd shuffle our chairs apart. We'd all discuss Mrs Roberts's new decking, Lydia's latest DIY dream or Hannah's new boyfriend.

After a cup of tea, Annabelle would say they needed bread for the morning and something to eat for dinner, so perhaps she'd drive down to Sainsbury's. It'd be another half hour of desperate anticipatory glances between Matthew and me before she'd actually leave. We'd act nonchalant as she finished her list, hunted for a lost glove and telephoned her mother to see if she wanted anything picking up, but as soon as we heard the Yale click into place, we'd spring from our seats. Matthew would lead me back along the hall and up the staircase lined with laminated collages of cats and fairies. We'd sweep past the first landing, which always had two closed doors. As I always did when I passed through this floor, I'd try to imagine Annabelle's bedroom, picturing a mass of ancient teddy bears piled on cotton sheets and books like *Jane Eyre* beneath a lamp. I never saw inside, though. The other door led to Annabelle's equally mysterious office. For all that she welcomed me into their unit and was 'kind' to us by finding excuses to leave us alone, there was a tacit understanding that this floor was sacred; that I belonged in the attic. So I'd follow Matthew up another, steeper flight of stairs with nothing adorning the walls.

The room in the attic was sparse, an old B&B offering with an en-suite shower room and two twin beds under the eaves. One was always unmade, a chiropractic pillow resting beside striped pyjamas and thick reading glasses. The other had just a navy fleece blanket and one pillow. This one was for me. At the foot of the second bed sat a desk piled with hardbacks overflowing from the two bookcases: evidence, should anyone ask, that I belonged up here 'sorting books'. Matthew would drape a piece of gauzy fabric from two nails either side of the window as a makeshift curtain, then unlace his shoes and remove his socks. We were usually in a hurry, I suppose, but I'd still hesitate until Matthew asked if I was being coy, then I'd remove my jeans to reveal an expensive thong he'd bought me or Primark hold-ups or nothing at all. He'd make love to me on his side, always looking for the 'love-light'. He'd try to make me come and tell me what his friend in the 'industry' had said about the percentage of women who can't reach orgasm, but we'd inevitably end with a stickiness between my thighs and his penis shrivelled contentedly back into place. He'd disappear into the bathroom and return smelling of baby powder, then I'd go to pee and clean myself. We'd lie together for a few minutes, speaking of love and poetry, but soon grow restless and pull on our clothes, anxious to be back playing cards before Annabelle returned. Sometimes we'd hear her key before our underwear was in place and he'd hurry down in his dressing gown to tell her he'd suddenly 'felt funny' and I'd gone home, before ushering me silently out the door while she put the shopping away downstairs.

Back on the street, I'd breathe the daylight air or skulk into the starry shadows and wonder if my cheeks were flushed. I'd miss him instantly and suddenly want to cry. Sneaking back past my mother's house, I'd take a detour via the empty park, sit on a swing and reach in my bag for my diary. I'd scrawl about how life was unfair and the bitter irony of true beauty. Eventually, I'd return home and begin boiling pasta, chat to my dad if he was home and absently make up a lie about doing homework with Claire. He'd only half listen while watching *Stargate* anyway, and I'd lock myself in my room with Tori Amos and the latest book Matthew had instructed me to read.

5

On 20th October 2001, I walked to Matthew's after school as usual. My dad was still at work so it was easy to sneak away and I left a note saying I'd be out for dinner. Annabelle was visiting her mother for the evening, so Matthew wrapped his arms around me as soon as the door was closed. We kissed as if we hadn't seen each other yesterday and the day before. With hours before us, there was no hurry. Matthew was making shepherd's pie and there was an Eccles cake waiting for me with a pot of tea ready to be poured. We played cards and talked about books until my foot beneath the table aroused enough interest for Matthew to pull me from my chair and shoo me upstairs.

In the attic, we fucked. I don't remember how. Perhaps that was the day he bent me over the bed and I cried as his cock dug painful holes in my abdomen. Or perhaps it was the time I knelt to suck his dick and guided my hand behind his balls only to find shit on my finger when I was done. Or perhaps I enjoyed it, despite not orgasming. Either way, we finished and dressed and padded downstairs to shovel potatoes and gravy onto our tongues. Annabelle came home at some point and we divided a bottle of wine before retiring to the living room. When *Friends* ended, Annabelle made a show of yawning and said she was going to bed.

I scurried to the other sofa and folded myself into Matthew's arms, flicking to the music channels hoping to find the Britney Spears video that turned me on. As Matthew was slipping his hand beneath my T-shirt and fingering the fabric of my bra, knuckles rapped at the front door.

Matthew snapped his hand away and stood up in one motion, then strode into the hall, smoothing his hair.

'John!' I heard from the other room.

'Um, hello Matthew. Is Natalie here?'

'She is. Would you like to come in?' Matthew's voice was liquid, subtly patronising yet unquestionably friendly.

I moved into the hallway. My dad looked distracted, annoyed even.

'Nat, I've been trying your phone for hours.'

'Oh, sorry,' I muttered, realising my bag was in the kitchen and I probably hadn't turned my profile off silent since school.

'Your mum called. Nana's in hospital—'

'What?!' I shrilled, as if shoving all the concern I should have felt in the past few hours into one short sentence.

'She seems to have collapsed in the supermarket. Your mother says it's possibly a stroke. I've been trying to get hold of you.'

'I'm sorry, I left a note. My phone's on vibrate,' I muttered guiltily. 'Is she going to be okay?'

'I don't know. I don't think it's looking good.' My dad looked apologetic. 'James is at ours, will you come home?'

'Of course.'

I darted along the hall to get my coat and bag, and then left with only the briefest of waves to Matthew, hovering helplessly in his study doorway.

As we walked back to the house, I begged my dad to drive us to the hospital immediately. I imagined my mother all alone in some waiting room as blue-suited nurses rushed in and out of an operating room, my nana lying on her back, her face as pale as

59

her permed hair and today's carefully selected jewellery gleaming rudely against a dishevelled hospital gown.

Trying to calm me, my dad explained it would take thirty minutes to get to the hospital and that my mum had said there might not be that much time, that we should wait for news; that it didn't bear thinking about, but there was no point making the trip if she was going to die in the next half hour.

I cried of course. I could hardly see the tiles on the floor as we stepped into the house. My brother was a smudge as he offered a shy hello and asked if I wanted a glass of water.

The phone rang at 11.46.

'Sweetie, Nana's passed away . . . No, it's okay, there was nothing you could have done anyway. It would have happened before you got here . . . I'm fine . . . I have to sort some things out here and go back to her house, but then I'll come home . . . Don't wait up . . . Honestly, I'll be okay . . . Goodnight darling . . . I love you too.'

I crawled into bed and saw a strobe of images in the dark. I saw my nana falling in the bread aisle, reaching out for the handle of her trolley and crashing into a display of muffins. My mum struggling for breath as the paramedics wheeled her mother into the ambulance. The blinking of a sad coffee machine opposite plastic chairs in the relatives' room. A man in a paper suit and white shoes telling my mum they did everything they could. Her hand wrapped around the payphone, the dial tone buzzing from the receiver after I'd hung up. The walk back to her car, seeing Nana's coat on the passenger seat, entering the house where the afternoon teacup still bore lipstick, the fridge still hummed and the VCR had kicked in to record *Midsomer Murders*. I saw my mum pacing around the house, flicking switches off and trying to avoid looking at knick-knacks. Locking the door behind her and sitting in her car, resting her head upon the steering wheel and wondering how she could drive down the dual carriageway with so many tears in her eyes. Finally getting home at almost two in the morning and looking in on my brother, tangled in his sheets and snoring lightly. Glancing at my old room and wondering if I too was sound asleep at my father's house. Turning to her own bed and sobbing quietly into her pillow because her mummy was gone and nobody was there to hold her. Then I saw myself, writhing in Matthew's sheets and laughing at a sordid suggestion. My foot sliding up his trouser leg as we ate and his lips nibbling my ear while I selected a CD. I saw my phone vibrating furiously in an empty room and my tongue forming a lie for my father about playing cards.

As I slept, my sheets turned to chains; I felt my lies wrap themselves around my limbs and imagined my nana in a sterile room, watching me on a projected screen, seeing my thoughts and knowing my crudest acts. I woke in a sweat and cried as I stared into the bathroom mirror.

I called my mum as soon as it was light and offered to help her sort everything out, but she told me to go to school, she'd be fine. I ignored his emails and didn't return to Matthew's for a fortnight.

6

There were other times I doubted our relationship too. When Simon Shaw asked me out in the common room and an image of a normal teenage relationship involving cinema dates and second and third base flashed before my mind; when my English teacher asked what I wanted to be when I was older and which universities I was looking at; when the kids in my Philosophy class finally learnt about existentialism but moved on to Foucault and post-structuralism the following week; when I tried to imagine myself in ten or twenty years' time; and when I turned up at his house and his unshaved jaw, tatty slippers and complaints about sciatica made me imagine Matthew's death. One way or another, though, he always brought me back to my safe places between the pages of books and the sheets of his bed.

From: Matthew Wright <theoutsider@worldopen.co.uk>
To: Natalie Lucas <sexy_chocolate69@sweetmail.com>
Sent: 4 November 2001, 08:27:31
Subject: O me! O Life!

I hear you, my darling. Why, if we are built to feel, do we construct a society that cuts off feeling? Why, if our loins ache with longing, do we instil in children guilt and fear of intimacy? Why, if we value learning, are we afraid of those with knowledge? Why, if your teachers want you to think philosophically, do they punish you when you ask questions to which they know no answers? Why, if truth and honesty are the highest virtues, is it necessary to lie to those who are close to you? Why, if humans are taught generosity, do thousands die in poverty? Why, if we are taught to be individuals, are those who raise their heads above the parapet shot down? Why, if love is pure in all forms, are those who feel it outside the heterosexual, mono-generational, singularly racial norms punished? Why, if you feel passion in your veins when holding a book or mouthing a verse, do others pierce your reverie with mundane expectations? Why is the world so sad? Why does your Ma not understand love? Why does your Pa run away from commitment? Why does your brother turn everything into a mathematical equation? Why does Annabelle want only a hand to hold? Why do people discuss the weather when Shakespeare lies on the shelves? Why, Why, Why, what good amid these sad questions? O me, O Life?

The Answer:
That you are here—that life exists, and identity;
That the powerful play goes on, and you may contribute a verse.

Yet, throughout my bizarre yo-yoing of passion and guilt, happiness and misery, I maintained some element of teenage normalcy. Despite my devotion to Matthew, alongside sitting exams and applying to universities, I flirted with boys at school and wove myself into such difficult situations with Nathan, David, Stephen and Pete that I was branded a cock-tease. Sometimes I felt guilty about Matthew or about the boys themselves, but my actions were not deliberate, just gestures of self-preservation to keep me from going insane in my unreality. I felt the only part of school and the teenage Nat I pretended to be that connected to the real me, the one only Matthew knew, was my continued attempt to drunkenly seduce sixth-form girls.

Though Matthew hadn't made me come, I enjoyed sex with him and adored the secret eroticism of my life and the power I felt it endowed me with. But there was an ache. A hole beneath my intestines that throbbed when I watched pop stars gyrate in music videos. I'd lie for hours on Matthew's couch, demanding deep tissue massages while I channel-hopped through Britney, Beyoncé and B*Witched. My fantasies were fed by Matthew's stories of threesomes in his past, our mutual appreciation of Helmut Newton and his promises to find me a girl so he could watch me enjoy her. I ached from the beginning to the end of the school day, barely able to check my desire to ogle the popular girls in their skin-tight jeans and navel-rising tees. I wondered if they could see into my head and blushed when a male friend jokingly sought my opinion on Suzie's behind. My one saviour was the regularity of house parties. I rarely got very far, but alcohol and a lack of parental supervision made everyone more open and I managed to content myself throughout Years 12 and 13 with periodic lesbianism.

After the parties, of course, I heard whispers in the common room like, 'Hey, that's the "keeno" girl who gets drunk and becomes a lesbian.' But, thinking of Matthew and how all these people were just plebs watching the wall of the cave from their chains, I shrugged off their ridicule. I tried not to be discouraged by the popular girls who avoided me and regularly punched my male friends with whom conversations about my fantasies always ended: 'But of course you're bi, though.' I attempted to develop a collection of witty responses behind which to hide my feelings of isolation. When Steve slouched beside me in the common room as I was eating a granola bar and asked, 'Is that a dyke bar?' I responded calmly, 'Yes, and I'm about to shove it up my cunt.' He ran out of the room in shocked disgust and I laughed to myself on my lonely couch.

I tried to live on the glory of each drunken party for as long as possible, but was always looking for another opportunity. Kissing Jenna before she passed out at my birthday bash saw me through the summer. Spin-the-bottle at Ruth's house party made September bearable. In October, at Holly's Hallowe'en do and with my best friend Claire's encouragement, I whirled around the Lambrusco-littered rooms in search of a girl called Leah. She was the year below and only slightly pretty, but I'd heard she'd properly come out as bi and I was totally in awe. I found her downing Becks and we kissed with tongues on the couch until she deserted me for a rugby player. Sipping more fruity alcohol, I returned a skinny ginger girl's gaze and idled up to her with what I thought was a flirtatious line about getting another drink. She admitted that I was the first girl she'd kissed and I cracked lame jokes about popping her lesbian cherry, feeling almost experienced. On the way home with Scott, the boy who gave me flowers for my birthday and would eventually be my platonic date for the sixth-form ball, I invented a story about dating a secret older woman that I couldn't tell anyone about. I elaborated on my lie, making Matthew younger, female and a supremely attractive teacher stuck in a loveless marriage, until I began to believe it myself. I fell asleep with my clothes on, dreaming about Radclyffe Hall.

When, some months later, I had become so disheartened by the heteronormativity of my small town surroundings that I decided lesbians were just a myth, I contented myself with reading *Oranges Are Not the Only Fruit* and writing imaginary love letters about 'unrecognised social conditioning' to Claire. Matthew and I spoke of Virginia Woolf and Marlene Dietrich, and while my friends at school laughed that my latent lesbianism was a harmless quirk, I privately lamented the plight of the outcast in society as if it were still Victorian England. After rereading *Tipping the Velvet*, I came to the conclusion it would actually have been easier to be gay *then* than it was now.

At a New Year's Eve party in Year 13, I drank disgusting cocktails and teamed up with Toby to form a terribly clever club called 'Ibs'. With an air of superiority, we perused the party declaring ourselves Ibs, until someone politely informed us that it was pretty obvious what we meant, and were we aware that we'd just announced our dubious desires to the entire sixth form?

Frustrated and with nothing more to lose, I focused my hopes on the one girl who might have been desperate enough: Kate. Kate was the sort of outsider of the group who imagined she had her own fashion sense and turned up to school in a mixture of checked lumberjack shirts and fishnet tights. Tonight, she had arrived with a new haircut that made her look like a member of a bad eighties girl-group.

Toby and I found Kate throwing up in the bath because someone had dared her to down half a bottle of vodka. We cleaned her up and asked if she would like to join our club. We sat on the kitchen tiles and attempted a three-way kiss, before I shamelessly stole Kate's lips for myself and spent the rest of the night bouncing between my friends' hysterical laughter and Kate's vomit-tinged breath.

When Matthew read about this episode in my diary, he said something had to be done. We had never spoken in detail about these teenage parties where I pretended to be normal. I'd never asked his permission, but I felt free to do what I liked at them. Still, I never told him our games of spin-the-bottle involved me locking lips with boys as well as girls, that some nights I tasted the saliva of up to ten of my peers and that James Huntwood had managed to thrust his hand into my jeans as I lay almost passed out on Ruth's kitchen floor. I only told him about the girls because he smiled and talked of 'tight little pussies', whispered in my ear during sex that if any of them were here right now we could

66

change their stubborn little minds, tease them until they creamed and begged for more. He seemed to enjoy these things as much as I did, so I continued attending my promiscuous parties and never worried too much about issues of fidelity.

But, though he brought mention of her into our bed once or twice, Matthew was decidedly unimpressed by the idea of Kate.

'You need a real woman. You deserve something far more sophisticated than these drunk idiots. It's probably the answer to your orgasm problem too. We will have to find you someone.'

I was terrified, but titillated.

His plan was to create a profile on a dating website using our combined details to attract someone to join not just me but *us*.

In April, we discovered Gaydargirls.com. The profile we made featured just me, as did the picture. 'You can't say you're a couple because then they don't trust you. You'll have to meet them first and convince them I'm not a sex fiend,' Matthew winked.

'You'll also need another name. You should have one anyway, for other things,' he added vaguely.

We spent three hours perfecting the description of me (us) and what I (we) wanted to find. By the evening, we were ready to make it live and Harriet Moore, the 'sexy Literature student looking for fun', became a reality.

'Harry Moore. I like it: both androgynous and greedy.' Matthew kissed me excitedly and I felt the familiar anticipatory ache between my legs.

In June, I received an email from I<3ellen16@sweetmail.com. She described her interests as shopping, flirting and playing football; Tori Amos and Aimee Mann were listed under her musical favourites; and her profile picture showed a roundish face with a choppy blonde bob, pink highlights and startling blue eyes. I imagined love.

Her email asked me if I wanted to 'chat' and offered her MSN Messenger addy. Sitting at my dad's PC in the downstairs study,

I keyed her into the Add New Friend box. When the sand-timer had finished rotating, a little green figure appeared beside her name, indicating she was online.

Chat with I<3ellen16

Harriet_Moore101:	Hey
I<3ellen16:	Hey, u found me!!
Harriet_Moore101:	Yep
I<3ellen16:	Howz uz 2day?
Harriet_Moore101:	I'm good. How about u?
I<3ellen16:	OK. I had a REALLY boring day at school, but apart from that everyfins peachy
Harriet_Moore101:	Tell me about it, I can't wait for the weekend!!
I<3ellen16:	Me either. Wot u up 2?
Harriet_Moore101:	Not much, it's pretty boring where I live.
I<3ellen16:	Me too. Tunbridge Wells's so lame. There's like one gay night at one club, and they've started getting pretty tight about ID.
Harriet_Moore101:	That's one more night than where I live. Quite seriously, I'm the only gay in the village!!
I<3ellen16:	Lol! You're hilarious. You should come see me sometime.
Harriet_Moore101:	That'd be cool. Would you show me around?
I<3ellen16:	Sure.
Harriet_Moore101:	Cool
I<3ellen16:	g2g, chat 2 u l8rz
Harriet_Moore101:	Oh, ok. Bye.
I<3ellen16:	bye sweets xxx

On the third day after the end of my last ever term at school, I set out to begin my destiny as an enlightened Uncle lesbian by making up an overly complicated story about going shopping with Claire in Hastings because she needed to find something to wear to her third-cousin's wedding as her sister had already claimed the colour blue and all of Claire's favourite clothes were blue, plus it was her boyfriend's birthday and she needed to buy him a present and he'd seen everything in the shops around us so she had to go somewhere else and needed my opinion because she was rubbish at making decisions. The intention was to bore and confuse my dad so much that he wouldn't notice that I'd asked for a lift to the wrong station to get to Hastings.

One of the first rules of Bunburying is to keep your story as close to the truth as possible – i.e. never change the place you are going to. You have to think about eventualities: What if a bomb goes off and your parents try to contact you? What if someone tries to rob a bank while you're in it and you end up on national TV, proving you're in London rather than Liverpool? What if a car breaks down and you can't get home, but you've said you're just down the road? What if Hastings turns out to be closed due to freak flooding and you don't see the news until you've waltzed through the door and said you had a fantastic day's shopping there?

I knew all of this and pondered the possibilities nervously as I plonked into my firm window seat in an empty carriage. There was no excuse; I should have been more careful, and, considering the complex duplicity I'd successfully woven into my life over the past two years, I really should have been able to pull off a simple blind date. But I was nervous. I'd changed six times this morning and had another panic about my casual jeans and T-shirt decision as I left the house. I'd put my hair up, then brushed it over my shoulders, then tried pigtails and half-up, half-down, finally settling back on a ponytail with a few loose strands that I now began to worry. I'd tried no make-up, then just eyeliner, then full face, then scrubbed it all off and stencilled a thick kohl line beneath each of my eyes and dabbed green mascara on my lashes.

Heather, aka I<3ellen16, was to meet me outside the station. She hadn't been impressed that I didn't know where her favourite coffee shop was and that I wouldn't be able to make my own way to the town centre (she'd typed 'omg, wtf, wot planet r u from?!'), but she'd seemed quite jovial (she'd typed 'lol') when she'd finally offered to just pick me up from my train and show me around.

She was late. I fingered a hole in the sleeve of my jacket with annoyance. When a girl vaguely resembling the photo I'd studied sauntered nonchalantly up to me, though, I of course replied: 'No, I just arrived.'

'Cool,' she muttered, making no effort to hide the fact that she was eyeing me up and down. 'So, you want to go shopping?'

'Sure,' I smiled, realising I must have blinked and missed the 'Hi, hello, how are you? How was your journey? It's good to finally meet you. Hey, we might even hug at this juncture'-part because Heather was already waiting by the traffic lights at the end of the road.

Still, her distance gave me a chance to subtly assess her in person. She was shorter than I'd imagined, but still about an inch taller than me so that was okay. Her hair had been cut since the picture I'd seen and she seemed to have a sort of natural sourness to her face that had not shown in the soft, posed smile of the photograph. I was a little repelled, but my nervous, desperate excitement won out and I began to picture us meeting like this throughout the holidays, going on picnics, holding hands and kissing by lakes.

The first stop was Gap.

'You know, I go shopping all the time, so I don't really need anything. What do you want to buy?' Heather stood by the security gates at the door with her shoulders slumped and her hands in her pockets.

'Uh, I don't know. Whatever I see I guess. I don't think I'll

70

spend forty quid on a cardigan, though.' I fingered the item on the rail in front of me and attempted a light smile.

Heather sneered and muttered something along the lines of, 'Whatevs.'

Next stop, Fat Face.

'Like, what do you wear if you don't wear designer stuff?' I glanced down at Heather's baggy jeans and it dawned on me that she'd bought them with those rips already in place, that someone somewhere had artistically torn that denim just so she could look like the sort of person who wears out her clothes but still looks cool.

Don't get me wrong, I was a seventeen-year-old with an allowance. I bought masses of crap myself. When I think of the money I wasted on shoes I never wore and a collection of forty-six handbags in my teens, I wonder if I could have halved my student loan. But I shopped at New Look and Primark and Mark One. I even snuck into charity shops if I thought nobody from school would see me. I'd kicked up a fuss in primary school when I hadn't been allowed Adidas tracksuit bottoms for PE, but ever since I'd agreed with my mum that paying five times the price for a logo measuring less than an inch was not just stupid, but actively insane.

We abandoned shopping and tried lunch.

'I won't eat anything with olives and I can't touch the salad garnish,' Heather explained in the queue. 'But I'm really good at counting calories – you're not really thinking about chocolate cake, are you? You know that has like twenty grams of fat in it?!'

Ten minutes of diet discussion later, I tried to change the subject. 'So, are you looking forward to getting your results?' I asked as I tore my mozzarella and olive-stuffed panini and eyed the chocolate cake beside it excitedly.

'Whatever, I don't really care. I didn't try very hard because it's not like I need A-Levels to do what I want to do.'

'Oh, what do you want to do?' I asked, angling for something Heather might be enthusiastic about.

'Well, like, work with abused teenagers and, you know, on like Pride things.'

'Oh, cool,' I smiled. 'That sounds so much more useful than anything I'm heading for. I'm really excited about going to university, but I feel a bit guilty with my subject choice – like the world needs another English graduate.'

'Yeah, exactly. And I've, like, experienced homophobia and stuff, and it's something I feel really passionate about,' she deadpanned.

'Good for you.'

'Yeah, anyway, I've gotta like meet my mate at four, so I should, like, get going.' Heather stood up, grating her chair against the floor.

'Oh,' I said, standing too, surprised by her sudden departure.

'You can make your way back to the station from here, can't you?'

'Sure. Look, it was great meeting you; I've had a really nice time.'

'Yeah, ditto.'

I took a step around the table, hoping for a goodbye hug, but Heather instead clasped my bicep in her hand and sort of patted me like I'd seen American fathers do to their softball-playing sons in crappy Hollywood films.

Then she turned and yanked the café door, making the bells on top jangle excitedly, and stalked down the street with her hands in her pockets.

I sat back down and stared without enthusiasm at my chocolate cake.

Before I left Tunbridge Wells, I returned to Gap and paid £40 for a cardigan. On the train, I mulled over everything that had been said. I recalled Heather's eyes and lips, arms and legs. I even thought about the Billabong bag she'd been carrying and wondered if I should use next month's allowance to buy one like it.

By the time I'd reached my stop and called my dad for a lift home, muttered some rubbish about Claire finding the perfect maroon halter-neck in Hastings and scuttled to check my email, I'd convinced myself that, though the day had been a little awkward, that was natural for a first date and Heather and I still had a sweet Sapphic summer before us.

So I emailed her.

And when she hadn't replied after two days, I emailed her again.

Then I tried to IM her. But her status seemed permanently set to busy.

So I emailed her again.

A week later, I emailed her once more, just in case the others had been sent to junk.

Then, finally, I think I got the message.

And I cried, alone into my pillow, for a girl with a sour expression and a stick up her bum who'd bored me for half a day and not had the courtesy to hug me goodbye.

Matthew told me not to worry. Gaydar was impersonal. A meat-market. I would find someone – a beautiful girlfriend for us both to share – at university. He was sure of it. I smiled through my tears and wondered if a girlfriend to share was what I wanted; wondered where this wrinkled old man would slot in to my student life.

7

My mum drove me to Durham. She hates driving in traffic, so we left at four in the morning. The journey was fine, though I can't imagine what we talked about for six hours. When I take long car rides with her now, in my third life, we tend to discuss Matthew, my most recent counselling sessions and whether I'm still writing about him (of which she disapproves). But back then we must have nattered less freely, at least on my part. I had a mountain of secrets hidden from her, yet still managed to play the best friend and hard-working daughter.

We probably sang along to Annie Lennox and Tina Turner, neither of us thinking much about the lyrics 'I've got a wall around me', then perhaps we talked about people, psychoanalysed her group of friends, laughed about the woman she knew who began sentences with things like, 'When I was an airline pilot . . .', and most likely we moved on to Matthew and Annabelle. My mum often admired their separate sleeping arrangements, commenting: 'I think it's much healthier for a couple to be able to *choose* when to sleep together.' In most ways, she said, she thought they were the ideal couple.

Depending on my mood, I would gossip with her about them, criticising Matthew's bad breath if we'd had a spat the day before, or defending his bizarre behaviour as 'artistic temperament' if I felt she was being overly cruel. In this way, we conducted mother–daughter bonding sessions, slowly repairing the jagged holes I'd ripped in our friendship by sewing a new patchwork of lies, moderate untruths and blatant deceptions. Such things tripped off my tongue by now and I hardly registered as my lips structured stories about visiting a friend last night when I was lying in Matthew's arms and enjoying camping in the New Forest last week when Matthew and I had been sharing a hotel room in Brighton.

While I burbled to my mum about insignificant and unreal things, I thought about the previous evening's complicated goodbye. As had become usual since the beginning of summer, I'd had dinner at Matthew's. Annabelle had left us alone after washing the plates, muttering about wanting to watch a programme on TV and giving Matthew a look that he later explained meant he'd promised to take her to Pevensey Bay this weekend if she'd give us some privacy tonight. I played with my table mat and mouthed the words to the Leonard Cohen CD, wondering what I'd be doing this time tomorrow, who I'd be speaking to and how I would feel about the grey-haired man before me.

Matthew was sad. I think he cried. I suspect I did too. I was much more upset than I thought I'd be. This was what I'd wanted after all. Matthew was weeping because I'd imposed this artificial ending, forced it upon him; but my tears were tinged with the contradictory knowledge that I had the ability to make it all better. I imagined my lips curling around an apology, a 'let's give it a go' or 'I can't do this without you.' Part of me wanted them to and longed to fall into his arms and talk of for ever. But another part had already floated miles from my sadness and was dancing on an imaginary plane, cartwheeling with nervous glee that in just a few hours I would be free.

I'd told Matthew in mid-July, just after my meeting with Heather in Tunbridge Wells, that I wanted to go to university without him. It had been two years and we'd had a fantastic time. I had no regrets, I told him. But living a secret life and maintaining such intensity was driving me crazy. I wanted to see if I could be normal. Perhaps he was right and the world of Uncles would be the only place in which I could exist, but I needed to find out for myself. I would go to Durham and try to be a regular teenager, perhaps get it out of my system, or perhaps find some sense of harmony. A little part of me hoped university would be different. Matthew said Uncles were scarce, that they lived in the shadows and had to stick together; but I wanted to believe there were more of us. I thought maybe I'd find other passionate Literature students, other kindred spirits ready to see beauty in the world, other people I could share myself with, and this time of my own age.

Either way, I said, I'd still be his best friend, and we'd see where we stood in three years. But I didn't want him to wait for me. I no longer wanted to be responsible for his 'needs'; and he needn't be for mine.

We hadn't spoken about it much through the summer. Perhaps he thought I would change my mind. I almost had as we'd touched salty lips behind the curtain by his front door. But I'd stepped onto the concrete outside and looked back only once to see him hesitating to slam the latch, then swung the gate, breathed the autumn air and tripped along the pavement to finish packing.

'Uh, hi.' I stepped tentatively through the heavy blue fire door into the sterile kitchen. 'I'm Nat – 112 I suppose.'

Three teenagers and two adults looked up from the circular table. The tall guy with a mini afro who was standing nearest to me put his mug down and offered me his hand.

'Tim,' he said with some kind of accent. '19 – I think that's below you, or below you but one. I'm not sure how they managed to number sixteen rooms on three floors between seven and a hundred and twenty-two, but hey.' His spotty cheeks stretched into a shy smile and immediately I wanted him to like me.

'Dave, but everyone calls me Horse – long story!' said a shorter boy with a stockier build and a sort-of cheeky flirt in his eyes. 'I'm opposite Tim. This is my girlfriend Jade; just helping me move in.'

'These are my parents,' added Tim and I stretched across the table to shake hands politely with two nervous-looking adults, trying to give them my best I'm-responsible-and-a-good-influence-on-your-child smile.

We chatted awkwardly about what subjects we were doing, where we were from and how long it had taken us to drive here, wincing each time someone's chair scraped on the tiled floor. I found out Tim was from Liverpool and studying Biology, but he also really liked cars and football. 'Horse' got caught up in a conversation about Manchester City, but finally explained he was from Leeds and taking Chemistry. His girlfriend told me she was taking a gap year and doing something or other, but I didn't listen because she'd only be staying one night and I'd already decided I didn't like her. She and Horse disappeared up to his room after half an hour or so and were replaced by a heavily made-up girl with highlights named Jane, who demanded we choose and label shelves in the fridge and gushed that she was from Surrey, studying Psychology and couldn't wait to join the netball and hockey teams – wasn't it great our college was right next to the gym?

Another Dave arrived, this one with a deep voice and a receding hairline that made him seem twice as old as the rest of us. He was from Hull and studying PPE, hoping to become a Labour politician. Next was Anna, a giggly, mousy-haired girl from Skegness who was taking Chemistry like Horse, but was really just looking forward to going clubbing every night: 'Nobody can party like us Skeggy slappas!'

A rugby boy named Will poked his head in, but left with some similarly bronzed and Lacoste-wearing boys he'd found living next door. Mike, a gruff guy from Wigan who looked like he'd be happier covered in grease beneath his car than speaking to us, introduced himself and his dad, grunted that he was doing Computer Science and returned to the kitchen after moving just two boxes of possessions into his room.

The last two to appear were Lizzie and Chrissy, neither of them freshers. Lizzie snuck into the kitchen and sat quietly in the seat nearest to the door with a big smile on her face before I noticed the white stick folded in her lap. Nobody mentioned it, but we all stiffened a little until she giggled nervously and explained that she was starting her second year but was living on campus because she knew her way around and the university had kitted this house out especially for her. After that, we spent a good fifteen minutes playing with the talking microwave and asking her what other gadgets she had. I instantly liked Lizzie and shuffled into the seat next to her when Anna got up to go to the toilet.

Then Chrissy bounced into the kitchen and introduced herself as if she were our tour rep and we were all embarking on a coach trip around Prague. Within half an hour, she was sat on Tim's lap and telling Dave Two, whose room it turned out was next to hers, that her boyfriend was visiting next weekend and she was sorry, but she liked loud sex. We discovered Chrissy was a third-year with some kind of medical reason to stay on campus for the entirety of her degree. I asked her a few questions, but she always turned her attention back to the boys, so Lizzie and I began chatting about the Freshers' Week schedule.

After a while, my mum popped in and reluctantly said hello. I followed her up the puce-carpeted stairs to my new bedroom, where she'd been busying herself re-cleaning the bathroom, making the bed and arranging my textbooks on the one shelf.

'You didn't have to do all this, Mum.'

'Oh, I didn't want to intrude on you downstairs, and I wanted to at least know you had somewhere to sleep.' She gave a weak, awkward smile.

'Thanks.' I gave her a hug, realising she was about to go and suddenly nervous.

'I think I'll set off now, leave you to it.'

'Don't you want something to eat first? Or a cup of tea?'

'Oh, Natty, that's sweet, but I can stop at a service station. I think it's important I let you get on with it alone. Anyway, I'd like to be back before it's dark.'

'Oh.' I'd forgotten Matthew and wanting a new life and needing to untangle myself from the fishing-net of lies I'd thrown over the whole of Sussex; right now I just wanted my mum – the woman who'd plastered my knees and brought me grapes when I was ill – to stay for ten more minutes.

'Don't look so scared,' she laughed and patted my arm. 'It'll be okay.'

'I know,' I forced a smile.

'It really will, love, I promise. I know meeting new people is hard work, but you're going to have so much fun. You're starting a whole new part of your life, completely your own.'

'Ring me to let me know you're back safe?'

'Really?' she grinned. 'You sound like *my* mother. But, fine, I will. After that, though, I'll leave you to telephone me when it's convenient. I don't want to intrude on your life. And don't worry about me. I love you very much, darling.'

'I love you too.'

I plodded down the stairs behind her, asking again if she wanted me to make her some sandwiches. We walked across the landscaped quadrangle, passing other parent and children couplings in various states of moving-in. I noted the fashionable and the shy, the grungy and the scared, the sporty and the already popular. I hugged my mum a couple more times before she ducked into her Fiesta, and tried not to cry as she reversed out of her space and headed for the exit barrier. I waved at the car a couple of times, then felt self-conscious and fingered my plastic keycard instead. What to do now? I was free. This was what I'd wanted. This was the beginning of the best years of my life, so everyone said. So why couldn't I bring myself to cross back over the quad and breeze into the kitchen where those whose parents had already left were finishing with tea and bringing out bottles of Bacardi?

Two litres of rum, 500ml of vodka, a 24-pack of Carlsberg and 12 cans of Coke later, my 15 new housemates and I wandered en masse to the Welcome Reception. We were guided by our second-year 'parent', who had turned up around five to teach us how to play Ring of Fire and to write the numbers of the best all-night takeaways on our communal whiteboard. His name was Ross, but after this first night, in which he quickly deemed us all 'unfuck-able', we wouldn't see him again. Still, for now he directed us perfectly competently to the grand, listed building opposite the cathedral.

Inside, freshers from all the colleges were clumped in groups roughly reflecting their newfound living situations, making nervous small talk and excitedly sipping the complimentary glasses of wine. There were a couple of speeches from heads of years or Provosts or someone, but my predominant memory of that event was the endless repetition of one question:

'So, where else did you apply? Oxford? Cambridge?'

And the defensive replies that, though they might have applied, they were glad they hadn't got in because Durham would be way more fun or everyone at Oxbridge had a stick up their arse or their drama society wasn't as good or it was only their parents that had wanted them to go.

Though the room was full of academic rejects who had dreamt of donning gowns much further south, but finding themselves here in the cold North, they seemed determined to make the most of it. And who was I to break the mould when the final scholar shut up and our now-wobbling 'daddy' Ross stood on a table and hollered, 'After-party in Collingwood?'

So that was how I came to be playing drinking games with a group of strangers on the lawn outside my house.

'I have never had sex outside.'

A few people sipped their beers and the rest of us looked long-ingly into our cans wondering why we hadn't done something so vanilla.

'I have never played strip poker.'

When this game had started, I'd wondered briefly whether it was such a good idea for me to play – should I admit to the things I'd done but omit the details? Or should I pretend two years of Matthew hadn't happened, in which case I might have to explain why I'd been living like a nun throughout my teens?

'I have never kissed someone else's partner.'

I opted for the former and drank, but silently cursed that, even hundreds of miles away from my old life, I still had to lie. Maybe Matthew was right, maybe I'd never be normal; maybe those two teenage years were utterly formative and I'd now dug myself such a humongous hole I'd never be able to shout to the ground for rescue and I'd just have to keep scratching at the earth hoping to find some other lost individuals for company.

'It's your go, uh – Nic?' said a dark-haired boy opposite me.

'Nat.'

'Sorry!' He smiled embarrassedly.

'No problem. Oh, um, I have never, um, had sex while watching TV.'

A few people sipped and everyone's attention turned to the person on my left. The boy who'd got my name wrong held my gaze for a moment and scrunched his nose up disapprovingly as if to say he'd been hoping for a juicier confession.

'I have never watched a porn film.'

I noticed Tim gulping his Becks three people to my right.

'I have never *made* a porn film.'

Everyone laughed and nobody drank.

'I have never had a cheeky finger shoved up my arse during sex.'

A couple of girls on my left made confused noises and the game paused while the person who had spoken tried to explain what he meant and how it had, in fact, happened to him during a one-night stand.

'Ew, in keeping with grossness. I have never had an STI test.'

A few people slurped and when someone elbowed one of them, he replied defensively, 'Having the test is not the gross part; the gross part is all of you who haven't been tested wandering around with diseases between your legs.'

There was a pause.

'Well, that killed the mood a bit. How about a nice simple, I have never been naked in public.'

With relief, we began sipping again.

'I have never done it doggy-style.'

Most people pressed their cans to their lips.

'I have never bought a vibrator.'

Sip. A few raised eyebrows, but Chrissy made such a show of downing her drink that I went mostly unnoticed.

'I have never touched a dildo.'

Sip. All eyes still on Chrissy.

'I have never swallowed semen.'

Sip.

'Haha, all you girls are busted.'

'I have never woken up and not been able to remember the person's name.'

A couple of guys jostled each other and gulped.

'I have never broken a bed.'

Sip. At this point I noticed the eyes of the dark-haired boy were on me again and wondered how long he'd been watching my quiet confessional.

'I have never given a strip tease.'

I blushed as I sipped and looked at his hazel eyes over my drink.

'I have never kissed a member of the same sex.'

Sip. I took a curious glance around the group.

82

'I knew you would have, Chrissy,' slurred some rugby-looking guy. 'You dirty lesbian.'

'Whatever, I'm not gay or anything.' She batted her mascaraed lashes. 'It's just fun to do at clubs – I kiss all my friends.'

'Well that's all right, but have any of you noticed how many gays there *are* around here? It's a bit weird, like it's fairy Mecca or something.' That was Jane, my netball-playing neighbour, and most of the boys in the group belched out loud, manly laughter as she flicked her highlighted hair in distaste.

'Hey, it's getting cold, can we go inside?' asked one of the generic girls on my left and a few people grunted agreement.

As everyone stood up to leave, the dark-haired boy held out his hand to help me from the grass.

'Hey,' he smiled.

'Hey.'

'Nat, right?'

'Yep. Sorry, I've already forgotten your name.'

'Rupert.'

'Hi Rupert.' I held out my hand and he took it.

'So, do you want to go inside and play more games with these people?'

'Not much,' I grimaced. 'But they're heading into my kitchen, so I'm not sure I have much choice.'

'Uh, you could come to mine if you like. I'm only over there and I think my housemates are at the bar.'

'Oh, um.' I wondered what the correct answer was.

'Hey, don't worry, this isn't my sleazy way to pick up girls. I'm just kinda bored of these sports-types and you seem like you don't belong either. I could make us tea – I even have Hobnobs!'

I laughed and nodded.

We walked in silence to his building, which was newer than my own and had spacious kitchens surrounded by glass on every storey. Rupert let me into his third-floor flat and showed me to a plastic chair, then flicked on the kettle.

'So, I noticed you didn't explain any of your drinks,' he said with his back to me.

My cheeks were growing warm. 'I was hoping nobody was watching me.'

'Everyone else was too boring and predictable to be worth watching.' He pulled two teabags from a box on the counter.

'I'm not even sure if that's a compliment or not.' I smiled in spite of myself.

'I think it is.' He handed me a steaming blue mug. 'Na, but I'm curious about the kissing girls questions.'

'Why?' My grin disappeared.

Rupert lowered his long limbs into the chair next to me. 'Just whether your reasoning is like Chrissy's or not.'

'Um, not.' I shrugged. 'But it doesn't really matter because that blonde girl, Jane, lives next to me.'

'What's that got to do with it?' he frowned.

'Well,' I paused, wondering whether to try to explain the tornado of thoughts that had passed through my mind since arriving this afternoon. 'I'd kind of hoped I'd come to university and everyone would be really liberal and it'd be okay to be bi or whatever, but I've been here less than a day and there's already as much homophobia as in my small little school in the countryside.'

'Where are you from?' Rupert looked at me kindly over his mug.

'Sussex, near Kent,' I intoned with my poshest English accent. 'You?'

'London,' Rupert laughed. 'But it's not much better. My parents are really conservative.'

'Oh, are you . . . ?' I trailed off, embarrassed.

'No,' he replied matter-of-factly. 'But I went to a boys' school, so some things are kind of inevitable.'

'Really? Wow.' I was impressed by his honesty and unsure what to say next.

'Anyway, I think you should ignore that Jane girl and anyone

84

else who says anything. It's perfectly acceptable to be "bi or whatever", he winked as he gestured air quotations, 'at university.'

'Thanks.' I blushed again.

'Just be for real, won't you, baby, be for real, oh, baby,' he sang-whispered.

'Hey, you like Leonard Cohen?' my voice brightened.

'Of course,' Rupert replied. 'Do you?'

'Yeah, a lot.' I ignored an angry buzz beginning in the back of my mind.

'I'm thinking of forming a Last Year's Man society,' he said seriously.

'Cool, what's it going to do?'

'Oh,' he shrugged. 'Sit around drinking whisky and listening to The Man of course.'

'Of course.' I returned his grin.

'What's your favourite song?'

'Yikes, I don't know.' Matthew's face flitted through my mind before I could stop it. 'Maybe "Suzanne".'

'Sure, classic,' Rupert responded in an authoritative tone, 'but not as poignant as things like "Fingerprints" and "The Partisan".'

'I'm not sure I know "The Partisan",' I admitted sheepishly.

'No way! You *cannot* be a Leonard Cohen fan and not know this song. Come with me.' He grabbed my hand and dragged me gently to the door, along the corridor to his bedroom, then hesitated. 'Sorry, there's no CD player in the kitchen. I'm not being presumptuous.'

'It's okay,' I smiled and stepped into the narrow room.

Rupert hovered over his computer for a moment, then played me 'The Partisan' while I perched on his bed. When the song ended, we sang along to 'Suzanne', 'Bird on the Wire' and 'Sisters of Mercy'. When 'I'm Your Man' came on, Rupert stood up and made a show of miming actions to the lyrics. He knelt before me with his hands on his heart and a grin on his face, punched in the air, placed an imaginary stethoscope on my chest and

85

manoeuvred an invisible steering wheel. I was giggling uncontrollably when he touched his lips gently to mine.

'Is this okay?' he whispered with concern.

Still unable to speak through giggles, I kissed him back.

At every stage he asked again if this was okay and I kept saying yes. I wondered about the strangeness of making out with a boy of my own age while listening to the music introduced to me by my sexagenarian ex, but kept kissing Rupert's elastic skin and running my hands greedily over the muscles on his back.

With precision that belied his sensitive-boy image, he slipped on a condom and eased himself into me. Again asking if it was okay, he picked me up off the bed and held me on his cock, smiling and whispering through butterfly kisses into my neck that he'd always wanted to do this. He rested my back against the wall and I looked down to see my hair falling over my nipples, his taut stomach slamming into my own, the muscles in his slightly bronzed arms and legs straining to hold me up and his chiselled, stubbly jaw set in excitement and concentration. This is normal, I thought, as my body responded; this is hot, meaningless sex that I wouldn't mind someone walking in on; this is two attractive people responding to animal desire; and it feels good.

Rupert came and set me on the bed, wrapped the condom in a tissue and threw it in the bin. Shy, I put my underwear back on.

'Are you going?' he asked as he emerged naked from the bathroom.

'No, yes, maybe,' I stuttered.

'Stay if you like,' he smiled and stroked my back.

'No, I should probably go. It's like four in the morning and we have to go to that nine-fifteen Introductions thing.'

'Yeah, I guess.'

He wrapped a towel around his waist and saw me to the door, kissing me softly on the mouth.

I walked back across the now-quiet college and slipped into my building. Alone in bed, I wondered what I should be feeling right now. That had been fun, but I sort of wanted to cry. Already I was wondering if Rupert would want to see me again, if I should have stayed, if leaving made me seem easy, if calling him tomorrow would be too needy.

I didn't call Rupert and Rupert didn't call me. But on the first day of classes, when our livers waved happy goodbyes to the end of Freshers' Week and we plodded our way through the ancient buildings looking for the right lecture rooms, Rupert and I saw each other again. We were in the same seminar group. Rupert, me and six other eager little Lit students would be meeting to pick apart the intricacies of *Mrs Dalloway*, *Beowulf*, 'The Rime of the Ancient Mariner' and *The Last of the Mohicans* twice a week, every week, for the rest of the year.

'Hey Suzanne,' Rupert brushed up to me after our first class.

'Hi,' I mumbled, no idea how to act.

'So, I haven't seen you all week. I guess Freshers' Week's been pretty crazy.'

'Yep, I guess.'

'I hope this isn't awkward.'

'Me too. I mean, it shouldn't be, right?'

'No, listen, do you want to get a drink later?'

'Sure.' We'd reached the library and I gestured that this was me, so he gave a little wave and strode off after Lucy, another girl from our seminar group.

What to wear, what to wear? What was this? Drinks. But drinks what? I-want-a-repeat-of-the-other-night drinks? I-want-to-let-you-down-easy drinks? I-want-to-get-to-know-you-better-and-possibly-date-you drinks? I-have-a-girlfriend-so-please-don't-mention-this drinks? I had no idea.

And I also had no idea whether it would be weird to wear underwear Matthew had bought me with the intention of showing it to someone else. And if it was, what was I supposed to wear?

All my underwear had been bought *by* Matthew, *for* Matthew or from BHS by my mum, and my instinct told me the latter was worst of all.

I opted for jeans and a snug T-shirt but with a lot of eyeliner and a sexy bra but plain pants. We met at the bar and Rupert bought me a Corona. Then a Jägerbomb, then a shot of tequila.

We stumbled back across to my building and I found my bottle of £3 Aldi red wine in the back of the cupboard. We took it to my room, fumbled to uncork it and poured the blood liquid into mugs while simultaneously undressing each other. Rupert spilt some on the carpet and I giggled. He unclipped my Gossard bra as I fingered his belt and pulled him to the bed.

'God, you're sexy.'

I smiled and thought of being tied up by Matthew.

'You seem kind of shy when you're in public, but you're so, I don't know, confident in bed. It's such a turn on.'

I slithered down his chest and kissed the tip of his penis, noticing for the first time that it was circumcised.

'Is this okay?' I whispered with a smile.

'Wow, yes,' he breathed.

I kissed his cock and tried to rub it with my tongue, but there was no movement. I brought my hand to meet my mouth on his skin, but my fingers just slid, then stuck with the lack of friction. I tried whirling my tongue over the top as Matthew liked, but got little more than a sigh.

After what felt like hours of pure humiliation, Rupert stroked my hair and said, 'It's okay, it's you I want anyway.'

He pulled me up to the pillows and propped himself above me, then looked around expectantly.

'In the paper bag in the drawer,' I muttered, still embarrassed.

He reached around and found the white sweet bag full of condoms a nurse had thrust upon me at the Freshers' Fair. After a few seconds, he was splitting my legs with his thighs and sliding into me. I gasped at the friction, wishing he would slow down but eventually getting into it. I wrapped my legs around his back and rocked with him as he thrust backwards and forwards, staring at a point on the wall above my head.

As I reached the familiar plateau I knew would provide no release yet still longed for, I heard myself whisper, 'I love you.'

Rupert said nothing and I wondered if I'd said anything at all.

He came quietly and rolled to his side, removed the condom and jumped out of bed to wrap it in toilet paper and place it in the bin.

It probably wasn't quite as blunt as it felt, but essentially he got dressed and told me he had to go home to finish the reading for our class tomorrow. He kissed me, still naked and clinging to my duvet for a modicum of self-respect, on the forehead, then left. I suspect I cried. I definitely showered. I swept my underwear from the floor, thinking of the two men who had now seen me in it. I finished the bottle of wine and lay in bed touching myself, rising to that plateau, then sliding unsatisfactorily back down again. I hugged my tattered childhood teddy bear and fell into a lonely sleep.

'Hey.' Rupert caught up with me the following morning on my way to our seminar. 'Do you have a sec? It's only quarter to.'

'Uh, sure.' I smiled weakly, wondering for the tenth time this morning if he'd heard me last night.

'So.' He looked down. 'I don't want to be a jerk. I've had fun, you know?'

'Yeah, me too.' I tried to sound nonchalant.

'The thing is, I'm not really looking for anything right now. I mean, I broke up with someone quite recently and I'm a bit messed up in the head and I think uni should be about having fun and finding yourself, so . . .'

He trailed off.

'Right, yeah, me too. I wasn't looking for anything either.'

'Oh, that's a relief. I was worried you were going to hate me.'

'Don't be silly.'

'Cool, then we're friends?'

'Sure.'

'I guess we should get to class then. Did you read *The Yellow Wallpaper*?'

'Uh yeah.'

'Yikes, I didn't. I just looked on SparkNotes.'

8

The following weeks passed in a lonely blur. I signed up for a LOVEFiLM account and became a member of the independent cinema in town. My days tumbled into a routine of watching half a foreign language film over breakfast while agonising over what to wear and wishing I could pull off French chic like Eva Green and Emmanuelle Béart, followed by hiding in the back of a lecture hall and absently scribbling angrily atomic doodles resembling the EUR tower from Antonioni's *L'Eclisse* beside my illegible notes, wandering through the streets alongside an imaginary Jules and Jim to watch an afternoon film in an empty cinema, then returning to college to cook pasta for a non-existent extended family of boxers called Rocco, finishing my film from earlier while my dream-world brother and lover waited for me in the bath, scanning the books for tomorrow's seminar while sipping wine and imagining myself an academic version of la femme Nikita, and maybe watching some TV in Tim's room while we swapped stories from our days, muttering fantasies of less mundane lives spent with more sophisticated peers.

This monotonous but artistically stimulating existence was broken by an email from my childhood boyfriend Todd. The son of one of my dad's flatmates from college, we'd played together since we were kids and 'gone out' for a month when I was fifteen and he was seventeen. He'd lived in Northampton, though, and we'd soon decided a long-distance relationship consisting of little more than pecks on the lips even when we saw each other was rather pointless. We'd stayed friends and he'd often email me saying something reminded him of me. Usually these messages plunged me into guilty feelings towards Matthew and drove me to send frosty replies. But now my fingers hovered over the keyboard. Todd was studying German in Birmingham. His message said it'd be fun to meet up. My head was forming excuses and brush-offs before it had even processed the request. I paused. Why not? I was free now. And a normal teenager. A normal university student. What could be more normal than a weekend trip to see an old flame? He might not even be single, of course. Perhaps he just wanted to see me as a friend. But even if he was and even if he wanted more, what was wrong with that? It might even be fun.

A week later, Todd met me at Birmingham New Street and carried my bag for me as we took two buses to the messy terraced house he shared with three other pot-smoking students. I saw little of Birmingham that weekend or in fact much of Todd's house beyond his bedroom. It was not the sexy booty-call I'd been picturing, nor was it the usual awkward disaster I'd come to expect of my life. There was an issue with Todd being unable to use a condom and, blotting out the voices of school nurses, sex-ed teachers and responsible friends, I gave in to his moans about 'loss of sensation' and 'so much more intense'. Even after that, we had problems manoeuvring into all the positions he'd 'always wanted to try' and mostly settled for short bursts of missionary. But Todd made me feel good about myself and I realised it was something I'd been missing since Matthew. He told me I was the sexiest girl he'd seen, whispered about my 'tight pussy' and 'amazing arse'. When he kissed me goodbye at the station on Sunday, he looked sheepish and apologised for some unnamed thing. I smiled and pressed my lips to his cheek before saying 'Thank you' and squeezing my way onto the too-crowded carriage.

* * *

Returning to college, I found a series of emails from Matthew with the subject heading 'Urgent', and one from someone called Rose.

I'd heard of Rose before. She may have been Suzanne's daughter. Or possibly niece. Or had Matthew boasted of having kissed three generations of her family? Or did I remember that having to do with his being in love with his primary-school teacher?

Actual blood ties and familial relations were easily confused in the world of Uncles. Rose may not have been an Uncle, though. I did remember that the jury had been out for some time, deciding whether this psychology-trained porn star could be admitted to the secret club.

Either way, she knew about Uncles, and she was writing to me because Matthew had a problem. Matthew's preceding emails explained this problem by telling me I needed to visit a clinic. He'd sent me two pages of dense, single-spaced prose about what to tell the nurse, about the painful bend that had developed in his cock shortly after I left, and about the probable herpes diagnosis that would mean I could only safely have sex with other carriers for the rest of my life.

I read Rose's email alone in my gross mint-green bedroom, crying to myself after calling the University Health Centre and being told, 'We don't deal with *that*. You have to try the GUM clinic.'

From: Rose Shaw <ladyred@sweetmail.com>
To: Harriet Moore <harry_moore@sweetmail.com>
Sent: 13 November 2002, 09:47:32
Subject: A message from a friend

Dear Harriet

You do not know me, but I am a friend of Albert's. I fear you might see that and delete this email immediately, but please read on. I am a friend of Uncles. I have known

Albert my whole life and I have seen him struggle against the world for all of that time. But in the last couple of years I have seen something different emerge in him. He has told me about you. He rang me when he first made love to you, worried you did not bleed. Do you remember getting cross about that? He says you have always been feisty. He has contacted me every time you have fought and every time you have told him you'd prefer a 'normal' life. He has worried he's done the wrong thing by you and is always asking me whether he should block his own fears and allow you to fly away.

He asked me the same last night. I told him it's out of his hands. You will fly if you need to. But, if you're a real Uncle, as he has told me you are, you will return with love in your heart.

He's asked me to give you some advice about getting tested at a clinic. He fears if he tries to help you himself you will say he is meddling, but given my line of work I might be able to help. I'm a sex worker, by the way. I trained as a psychologist, then got bored and got into porn. I'm a bit old for it these days (36, groan!), so I only do a bit and am trying to redefine myself as a sex thera-pist. My manager Damien is helping me out with that – he has contacts in Hollywood, so with any luck I'll soon be listening to the likes of Tom Cruise moan on my couch.

But anyway, you need to get yourself checked out and I've attached a document with a list of questions you need to ask the nurse. There's also a bit of information there about herpes and the like. Don't be scared baby, it's not the end of the world. Even if you're positive, there's no reason you can't have a healthy sex life with Albert.

He's told me so much about you and I'm desperate to meet you. Have you found any girls yet on your little hiatus from Albert? I hope so, though I'll also be jealous. Albert makes it sound like you're totally ripe for a girly encounter. I keep telling him I'm more than happy to hop in a car and oblige, but he refuses to let me. Jealous you'll fall for me instead if you ask me!

If you need anything: if you want to talk about Albert or girls or ask about the tests or just say hi, I'm always around.

Take care, babycakes

Rose xx

Rose's attachment calmed me with medical facts and instructions about who to see and what tests to ask for, but I was confused by the rest of her email. A friend of Uncles? A healthy sex life with Albert? What about without him? What if I didn't want to be an Uncle any more?

I walked to the clinic across town the next day, only to be told I needed to go away and phone to make an appointment. I returned to halls and ran into my housemate Tim as I came through the front door. Seeing I was upset, he put his arm around me, boiled the kettle and began distracting me with impressions of our other housemates. I hiccupped giggles through my trembling lips and considered Tim. He wasn't an Uncle, that I knew: he studied plants and wasted his free time on computer games. But he was kind, he noticed when I wasn't okay, and, more importantly, he was my friend. Perhaps my only one.

Later, holding my hand, he escorted me back to the clinic. After my tests; after bursting into tears in front of the unsympathetic nurse, after entirely omitting Todd from my sexual history because I thought she might force me to phone him from the premises once I had my results; after I dithered about writing the name of my real doctor because he was a family friend and might put two and two together if he saw both mine and Matthew's results; after they forgot about me for an hour and broke three needles trying to take blood for the procedural HIV test; after they gave me the all clear on everything and told me to be more careful in the future; and after Tim took me for fish and chips and I cried into my mushy peas, I stumbled back into my bedroom and replied to the mysterious Rose.

From: Rose Shaw <ladyred@sweetmail.com>
To: Harriet Moore <harry_moore@sweetmail.com>
Sent: 16 November 2002, 11:22:13
Subject: RE: A message from a friend

Harry, I'm soooo glad you replied.

I know it's difficult working out what to do with Albert. I hear your cries for a normal life – that's natural – but take a look around, babe, do you see any of those kids leading normal lives that are happy? You and Albert have a beautiful thing, something most people never EVER find. And you're going to give it all up because you want to kiss boys and girls that won't call you back and only care about the price of the next beer they're going to buy? Remember the poetry, babycakes.

Sorry, I don't mean to lecture you. All of these are your decisions to make. I just find it hard to sit back and watch two beautiful Uncles who could be so happy together throw it all away. I'm not an Uncle, you know. Albert said I could have been once, but I chose porn and all that rough sex stuff instead. It's great, don't get me wrong, but you have to switch yourself off. It's not like you and Albert. You guys can have the mucky sex stuff, but it's infused with the purest of love. God, you two could go so far. Has he spanked you yet? I used to beg him to spank me, he's so good at it, but the bastard was stingy. I wish he'd let me meet you. I get wet just thinking about the fun the three of us could have. Not that you'd probably be interested in an old bag like me. Get Albert to show you some of my pictures and we'll see. If you're only half as amazing as he makes out, you'd have us both as your slaves. And we could get you other little girls if you liked, do your bidding . . . Uhm, I must stop. Sorry if you're shocked. I'd like to tell you everything I want to do to you, but I don't want to scare you off. Perhaps you don't like reading about this stuff. I just can't help it. I've never met you, yet I think I've already fallen for you.

I'll leave you to your studies babycakes.
Rose xxx

And, lonely the following night, I found myself pausing *Manon des Sources* and replying again.

From: Rose Shaw <ladyred@sweetmail.com>
To: Harriet Moore <harry_moore@sweetmail.com>
Sent: 17 November 2002, 21:06:51
Subject: RE: A message from a friend

Wow! You really are as amazing as Albert says. And ripe as plums in August for a girl by the sounds of it. He should have found you one by now. If you were mine, I would have done your bidding a long time ago.

I'm glad my email made you horny. There's much more of where that came from. And, no, I don't think it's too weird that you and I are emailing like this while you and Albert are on a 'break'. I won't tell him if you don't. ;) In all seriousness, maybe a friendship with me could help you work out your feelings for him. And if not.. well, we can have fun trying! I know, I'm wicked, aren't I?

Soooooooooooooo, you and Albert haven't tried proper spanking yet? Well, babycakes, you are missing out. Perhaps I'll have to introduce you to it instead. There's nothing better than a good raw hiding to get your pussy juicing. We'll have to start gently to build you up to it. Perhaps just a playful bend over a kitchen counter and some light palm contact. Three or four strokes, then some feathery kisses over your pink flesh, trailing a tongue down between your thighs to lap up the sweet nectar of your peach . . . Later, we could try a paddle, or a leg divider, to get your butt nice and taut. I'm not sure I want Albert to do this at all; I want you all to myself. Or maybe I'll do the spanking and watch you juice with longing while I make Albert sit on the other side of the room. Then, when you're nearly screaming with desire, I'll allow him to slip his cock in you from behind and feel you spasm around him. Well, maybe, or maybe I'll just be incredibly selfish and rut you myself with a strap-on.

Oooh, do you know about frotting? I want to teach you everything.

Your slave

Rose xxx

Rose emailed a couple of times a day, usually once about all the things she wanted to do to me and once to tell me how much I was hurting Matthew, how ill he was getting, and how much of a saint he was to still be willing to take me back. I replied hungrily to the former, my mind swirling with all the things I felt I couldn't admit to my peers and revelling in the idea that one person in the world didn't think I was a freak because I reached for my vibrator every night and found good literature erotic. The latter emails, however, froze me to my cheap desk chair, turned my skin ashen and made me want to smash my third-floor window and scream into the night. I was not functioning. I looked like a regular student from the outside: I drank cheap cider with my housemates, learnt how to burp the alphabet and even helped Tim steal an entire footpath sign, post and all. But, behind my bedroom door, Matthew and I had nightly rows on the phone, followed by 'I still love you' or 'I need you' texts each morning.

After almost a month of this rubber-banding, he booked a night at a nearby Travelodge. It was late November and he'd told Annabelle he was visiting his mother. We cried together in the cheery blue-and-yellow room before having sex. I apologised for being a child and for hurting him, telling him I'd never leave him again, and he wrapped me in his arms, promising to protect me from the dead-eyed plebs I lived amongst. If I remember correctly, that was also the first night I presented my new digital camera and allowed him to photograph me.

After the reconciliation, Rose continued to email. She told me about her experience as a sex worker and her new job as a sex therapist in LA. I told her about growing up in Sussex and how disappointing everyone in Durham was. I moaned that Tim never wanted to do anything but watch football and that people in my seminar groups didn't even bother to read the books. She told me her regrets and how special I was. Soon, she was ending emails with 'I love you, babygirl.' We swapped up to a dozen messages a day: some loving, some horny, some explicit. She told me about the sex woes of the casts of HBO series and impressed me with Hollywood rumours days before they hit the newspapers.

To explain my absences, Matthew and I revived the pretence that I worked for him, and I began talking casually and a little proudly about 'my gambler' and 'my porn star'. Some of my house-mates gave me odd looks and a wide berth, but Tim, especially, seemed impressed.

'Is that her?' he asked, pointing with his toe at the TV screen where some big-busted blonde was welcoming a beefed-up plumber into her home.

'No!' I scoffed in disgust, thinking, *I hope not, anyway.* It was a Tuesday and Tim and I were sat on his bed drinking Lambrini and watching the bonus extras of the Paris Hilton sex tape. A week or two ago I'd plucked up the courage to tell him I liked girls, to which he'd shrugged and said, 'Me too.' Since then, we'd spent each evening locked in Tim's room, shutting out our bitchy house-mates and grumbling about our mutual disappointment with university. Tim's parents had announced they were getting divorced less than a month after we'd got to Durham, but so far I was the only person he'd told. Even with me, he sidestepped the subject and turned our conversations back to my worries. Sex, porn and innuendo became our go-to modes of communication, providing cathartic escapism from the heavy thoughts plaguing each of our brains.

'What's her name again?' Tim asked as the camera focused on the blonde's left nipple.

'Her professional name's Lady Red,' I replied importantly.

'So she's a ginge!' Tim stopped watching the screen to grin in my face. 'Does she have ginger pubes as well?'

I elbowed him violently back to his side of the bed and stuck out my tongue. 'I'll have to let you know,' I said coyly.

I was supposed to meet her on a couple of occasions. She was flying back from LA for a conference and could see me for a few hours at a private airport, or she would be in Newcastle that same weekend Matthew was coming to visit me, so we could all go out for a meal or something. One way or another, though, each plan fell through and all I had to connect the mass of emails I received to a real person were an ancient magazine with a woman in a blonde wig and an old grainy video cassette with a brunette being eaten out by a red-head with freckled shoulders. I tried not to think too hard about how unsexy these out of fashion porn clips were and how many years it must be since she looked like that, and instead imagined a sophisticated woman wearing black and smoking cigarettes; a woman who would take control and teach me about myself, who would be able to do what she promised and what Matthew, Rupert and Todd hadn't: make me come.

In November, a gender performer came to Durham to run a drag-king workshop. Though too shy to bring my own prosthetic and join in, I went to the performative lecture that followed and left buzzing with gender-bending excitement. I rushed back to my bedroom to email Rose about how inspiring the speaker was and how I wanted to move to New York and make superbly queer performance art on street corners and discuss Judith Butler and Eve Sedgwick in bohemian cafés.

Within a couple of hours, Rose wrote back. The message was short and lacked her usual flirty warmth:

> God, so you've met that bitch. What she doesn't tell anyone is that she was born a hermaphrodite, the crazy freak. I tried to write about it in the *Village Voice* once and she slapped a law suit on me.

For some absurd reason that perhaps only keen little freshers from small towns who find themselves in big cities asking homeless people with Rottweilers and gangs of hoodies for directions can understand, what I did next was hunt through Google for an email address.

> Dear Ms P---
>
> I attended your lecture in Durham today and wanted to tell you how thoroughly I enjoyed it. Also, I spoke to a woman I know as Rose or 'Lady Red' and she says she had some dealings with you in the *Village Voice*, but I can find no records in my library's archives, so I was wondering if you have any idea what she's talking about.
>
> Once again, thank you for a hugely inspirational lecture today.
>
> Yours
> Natalie

From my university email no less. I had no response for a few days and, just when I was beginning to chew the inside of my cheek with recognition of the sordidness of emailing a public figure about a porn star you've never met and wondering whether I would now be blacklisted by the whole international gender-performing community, I found a reply.

> Natalie
>
> I do not know and never have known anyone by the name of Rose or Lady Red and cannot help you with your line of enquiry.
>
> P---

Okay, so no obvious anger and perhaps no blacklisting, but what did this mean? Was Rose lying? Or P--- covering up? Why did it matter? Because something outside of the world of Matthew, intergenerational love and endless strings of lies had made me feel passionate and had been instantly tainted by someone related to that very world.

9

Three weeks before the end of my first term at university, an email arrived in my inbox.

From: Office of International Studies
To: First-Year English Literature Undergraduates
RE: North American Study Abroad Programme
Date: 2 December 2002, 13.07

Dear Undergraduates

An exciting opportunity has arisen within our North American Study Abroad Programme (NASAP). As you will know, for many years, we have been offering a select number of students the opportunity to spend part or all of their second years at institutions across the USA, including Columbia, UCLA, UC Berkeley and Northwestern.

The deadline for these schemes was last month and we are busy reading the applications and selecting candidates for interview. However, our international liaison team has recently secured another unique initiative for one more individual.

Unlike the other placements, this one will be run as an exchange programme with Rosella Liberal Arts College in Delaware County, NY. Beginning in September 2003, it will last one year and, on condition of relevant courses being studied and grades achieved, will count as the student's second year of study with full credit.

For more information, click <u>here</u>.

Applications to be handed in to the Office of International Studies by noon on Friday, week 10.

Yours

Sandra Pilson
The Office of International Studies

Having ignored a dozen previous emails about NASAP, the ERASMUS study abroad programme and opportunities to build schools in Namibia over the summer, it was for no particular reason that I read this one. But I did. And I clicked the link for more information.

I scanned the details about paying fees to Durham and having to maintain appropriate credits, being an ambassador for the university and agreeing to participate in promotional activities upon your return, and with only a vague idea of where Delaware County could be found on a map, I filled in the application form. I didn't read about the college and I didn't tell anyone I was applying, but on the last Friday of term, I found the Office of International Studies and handed my four neat pages of block capitals to the pregnant lady at reception.

Sitting on the train heading south, I felt tired. Not the sleepy tired that might have enabled me to snooze despite the woman with her three-year-old child in the seat across the aisle, but the tired that made me want to draw my knees up to my chest and cry. I had made it through my first term at university.

I had played at being normal: I'd had paranoia-inducing, not-very-satisfactory sex with two boys my own age; I'd got an A- for an essay about Virginia Woolf; I'd felt my shoes stick to nightclub floors on three occasions; I'd thrown up at my college's winter ball; I'd watched my first full-length porno with Tim; I'd established a regular *Neighbours*-viewing schedule; I'd formed a first-names bond with the Costcutter staff; I'd avoided consuming the pink and blue mould that had festered in our kitchen throughout November; I'd slept in for a 9.15, and I'd winged a presentation on *Paradise Lost* after three hours of sleep and six espressos.

I had also filtered stories about my 'gambler' and my 'porn star' into conversations so that my housemates naturally accepted I was disappearing to Newcastle for the weekend or had to take an important phone call about form and odds; I'd lied to NHS employees about my sexual history; alienated a drag king; told Tim I'd got back together with my fictional nineteen-year-old boyfriend from home; filmed myself masturbating and emailed it to a sexagenarian; allowed – nay begged – said sexagenarian to spank me as atonement for the sin of thinking I could live a normal life without him; chosen a Camus module for my third year not because of a teenage interest in existentialism but because I truly believed the sixties doctrine and used it to justify the quirks in my life; lied to all around me; and applied to move 3,000 miles away for nine months without uttering a word to anyone.

One term at university and I was exhausted.

My mum met me at the station and helped me load my bag into her boot.

'How was your journey?' she asked with a smile as we ducked into the car.

'Okay. Just a few screaming children.'

'It's good to have you back.' She touched my knee before turning the ignition. 'I've missed you.'

'I've missed you too,' I ping-ponged as we reversed out of the space.

'You sound sleepy.' She flicked the indicator before pulling out of the car park.

'Yeah, I guess I am. How's James?'

'Fine. He's looking forward to seeing you too. I've made up a bed if you'd like to stay with us,' she said in the meek half-whisper she still adopted for all references to my having moved out.

'Oh, that's sweet, but all my stuff's at Dad's,' I replied, feeling a twang of guilt but thinking I could pop in to see Matthew before heading across town if I opted for my father's house.

Familiar roundabouts and concrete buildings began to zip by my window and after only a brief hurt pause my mum launched us into chatter about Christmas plans, the latest episode of *ER* and which shops in town had closed since I left.

It had only been a few months since I'd left, but with my bedroom mostly empty and my CD collection a few hundred miles away, I already felt that I only half-belonged at home. As if to underline this, I woke on Christmas morning to find my dad blasting techno through the walls. Though we shared our inability to play music in just one room without turning the dial to ensure it could be heard halfway up the garden, my father and I had little else in common in terms of music, popular culture or social conformity. After a quick shower to a noise no one should be subjected to before breakfast, I exchanged hastily wrapped presents with him over coffee from his expensive espresso machine. I gave him six different types of Thornton's chocolate and Stephen Hawking's latest hardback. He handed me a card with a penguin on the front and a wad of £10 notes, as requested. We made stilted conversation as he ate muesli and I munched toast with olive oil because he'd forgotten to go shopping, then he wandered off to his computer.

Having fulfilled my duty to spend part of Christmas Day with him, I pulled a coat over my woollen dress and sparkly tights and left him to his Christmas DIY rituals. I shouted a goodbye over the music and crossed town to knock on my mum's door, which, despite her yearly threats 'not to bother with Christmas this time', had an actual living wreath attached to the knocker. As I waited, I checked my phone for a message from Matthew. Nothing.

My mum opened the door in a floaty black jumper and a festive scarf. 'Merry Christmas, sweetie!' She closed the door behind me and I gave her a thick, guilt-ridden hug, wondering if I'd be able to sneak over to Matthew's before this evening and whether he'd be able to get away from Annabelle's parents, if he'd like the DVD I'd found for him and if we really would be able to stay in Swindon for New Year's.

Peeling myself from the embrace, I placed the bag of presents I'd brought under the tree in the living room. James sat cross-legged on the floor assembling some electrical-looking contraption. They'd exchanged one present each but were waiting for me for the rest. My mum handed me a cup of tea and we began.

James opened a mini pool table while my mum unwrapped a heavy wooden chopping board and I tore open a companion to English Literature; James got a PlayStation game, my mum an Anita Shreve and me a scarf; James a computer mouse shaped as a rodent, my mum a collection of pens, me a jewellery box; James money, my mum chilli-flavoured olive oils, me a vegetable steamer; James chocolate, my mum bookends and me earrings; James a fart machine, my mum pillowcases and me a visual history of the twentieth century.

The last presents we opened were in dark blue paper that was dotted with moons and stars. I recognised the loops of our nametags before I opened my card and saw the neat 'Love Annabelle and Uncle Matthew x.' I smiled and fingered the writing. James ripped his unceremoniously and found a collection of funny postcards. My mum undid the paper neatly along the Sellotape lines and exposed a cardigan in green and brown velvet. When they were done, I tentatively tore into a thick volume of poetry.

With a pile of multi-coloured wrapping paper now sitting in the centre of our triangle, we paused. The tree looked sad.

'I'll make another pot of tea,' my mother said and wandered out of the room.

'D'you mind if I play my new game?' asked James.

I nodded that it was fine and turned to my pile of gifts. Lifting the anthology, I fanned my thumb over the pages and chose a random poem. After doing this a couple of times, I came across a small pencil mark beside one of the titles. My mum returned with the tea and, seeing James firing at some zombie-like creature on the screen, took her cup into her office and booted up her computer. Left alone with my book, I searched the whole volume for Matthew's selections, mouthing the words and imagining his arms as I read.

At 7pm, guests began to arrive. The previous year, which had been the first Christmas since my nana had died, I'd complained to my mum that Christmas was depressing in a nuclear family and that it should really be about friends – the family you choose – rather than locking yourself up with blood relatives. She agreed and we'd tentatively started a tradition of a friends-and-family meal.

Our doorbell began to ring and in trickled Beatrice, Valerie, Hannah and Lydia, Barbara and Richard, Dick and Jemima, and, finally, Matthew and Annabelle.

'What lovely table decorations.'

'Your turkey is divine, not at all dry.'

'Did you see the Queen's speech?'

'Thank you, Richard gave it to me. Doesn't he have good taste?'

'I'm not an *EastEnders* fan, but I do like to watch the Christmas episode.'

'We're going to the Cotswolds for New Year, just a quiet one, you know?'

'Matthew's got to work tomorrow unfortunately.'

'I bought *Dinner for One* on video if you fancy a viewing after we've eaten?'

'How on earth do you get your potatoes so fluffy, Heloise?'

'Oh, I've probably had too much already, but why not?'

'Red please.'

'Mmm, coffee sounds lovely.'

'We're hoping to get to Italy again this year, but it depends on work.'

'Who made this trifle? It's gorgeous.'

'Oooh, choccies. The diet starts tomorrow!'

'Yes, let's adjourn upstairs.'

'Thank you so much, Heloise, you're a wonderful host.'

'Yes, I'll give you a ring about the theatre.'

'Goodnight.'

'Merry Christmas.'

'Sleep well.'

'Thanks again.'

'Bye.'

The evening was ordinary except for a few stolen glances and a brush of toes beneath the table. I drank every glass of wine poured for me and accepted a challenge from Matthew to give up coffee for New Year's, deciding to get my fix in advance and drinking a cafetière to myself while everyone passed around the Matchmakers. I fell asleep leaning against an armchair while the rest giggled to Freddie Frinton and May Warden's black-and-white antics, then stumbled up the stairs. Finding my bed, I opened a text message that read 'My darling, you were wonderful tonight,' before collapsing fully-clothed into a half sleep, leaning over the edge of the mattress and regurgitating dark-red, mint-flavoured vomit onto my mum's copy of *I, Claudius*. Then sleep found me.

A few days later, before departing for university once more, I lay in Matthew's arms and then on his chaise and then in my own bed cradling the phone, each time whispering 'I love you' and promising I'd got my desire for normalcy out of my system, that I would be true to him forever more, that I knew how awful I had been, that I was sorry, and had I mentioned I love him? He still had a slight bend in his penis, a broken blood vessel that could no longer inflate, perhaps from too-ferocious fellatio he told me, but it was no longer painful. I emailed Rose constantly over the holidays, and Matthew and I spoke of meeting her, of the incredible sparks that would ignite our shared bed. We spoke of girls again and he asked about the students I lived with, enquired whether Chrissy could be bent over a banister or if Jane would kneel to receive a thick cock while I lapped at her cunt. These were normal conversations and made me laugh as well as moan, but they also filled me with despair at the impossibility of being bi even at university.

With my mum waiting in the car with my suitcase while I 'dropped off a book I'd borrowed', I kissed Matthew passionately in his kitchen.

He grabbed my wrist firmly and growled in my ear, 'You're mine. Don't forget it.'

I giggled nervously and pecked butterflies on his cheek in reassurance. 'I'll call you tonight. I miss you already.'

Back on the street, I slithered into the passenger seat and my mum asked how Matthew was.

'Fine.'

'He seemed distracted at the meal; I do hope he and Annabelle aren't having problems.'

'Yeah, me too.'

'They're such a lovely couple.'

111

'Yep.'

She drove me back to the train station and I hugged her before the ticket office.

'Thanks for a lovely Christmas, Natty.'

'No, thanks for having me. I had a great time.'

'Yes, it was fun doing it with friends, wasn't it?'

'Yeah, we should do that every year. Bye Mum. Safe drive back.'

'I don't want to be a neurotic mother, but do give me a quick call just to let me know you arrived safely.'

'Sure. Love you.'

'Love you too, darling.'

With a wave, I turned to find my platform. Exchanges like that made my stomach churn. I hadn't lied; I had had a great Christmas and I did love my mother, enormously. There were just a hundred other things woven between those words, clinging like the most vigorous ivy and poisoning any light, true sentiment with their tar-like deception. I was a bad person. Lying to everyone had become second nature and I viewed it as a necessity for survival, but lying to my mother still left a bitterness on my tongue. I felt she still looked at me with incomprehension; whenever we were tender, she'd search my face questioningly, asking what had happened to the little girl who would tug her jumper to whisper 'I love you' and who asked to be read *The Tale of Peter Rabbit* over and over again? I couldn't answer her. I didn't know myself.

By the time my train pulled into Durham, I'd mulled my way through such thoughts and justified my guilt away with quotes from Uncles, images of Matthew and, of course, the anthology of poetry in my handbag. I stepped into my city with an armour of persona protecting my flesh and a curl on my lips betraying my conviction that I knew the truth about love and life and that those around me were mere ghosts, floating aimlessly beneath the parapet.

I marched through the city, dragging my wheeled suitcase over cobbles and kerbs, up the hill to my college. Relieved to find no one in my kitchen, I raced to the third floor, fiddled with my lock, slammed the door and opened my laptop. I was feeling confident. I was feeling sexy and in control. I was feeling debauched and desirous. I logged on to Gaydar.

10

I waited for Gemma in a pool of lamplight on a cobbled corner, imagining that the atmosphere was so charged this *must* be the night I'd fall in love. After sifting through profiles, rejecting the sordid, the butch, the old, the couples and the frankly weird, I'd been left with a petite girl with vociferous opinions about gay rights and a love for Grace Jones. Seeing she studied in Durham too, but on the Stockton campus, I'd sent a nervous email suggesting we meet, imagining she wouldn't pick it up for a week, but hoping she'd like my artistic black-and-white profile picture.

She'd replied immediately. She was online. She'd love to meet me. How about tomorrow?

I'd gone to bed dreaming of yellow days holding hands in parks and scarlet nights under silk sheets. I wore Doc Martens and an elastic rainbow belt. She was late, but that was okay; she'd have a perfect excuse. Every time someone approached, my heart beat faster as I imagined their shadowy lips on mine, then slowed as they passed and turned the corner.

Finally, as I was fiddling with my bag in the hopes of feeling less stupid for standing there doing nothing, I heard someone squeak, 'Harriet?'

A 'Yes' was out of my lips in an anticipatory pant before I'd even managed to look up. My eyes settled on a girl who looked about twelve; my heart found its way to my socks.

She was a good three or four inches shorter than me – quite something as I'm only 5'1". And her arms somehow reached to her knees, making her look like a primate.

I could imagine Matthew's cruel laugh in my ear: 'Oh Baba, what are you doing with *that*?!'

Feeling terrible for having such a shallow reaction to her appearance, I followed her to a pub. It was full of students she knew and I was paraded around, mortified to be introduced as her date, especially to the dozens of truly attractive women that seemed to be swamping the bar.

I made excruciating small talk for the duration of one pint, my horror mounting exponentially as I noted her hideous leather jacket, 1980s mullet and single stud earring. With an over-the-top yawn, I lied that I had a 9.15 seminar and bolted to the door before she could offer to walk me home or hug me goodbye. On the way back, I flicked from guilt to amusement to despair and back again. Matthew would laugh and I might even tell Tim that I'd seriously thought monkeys were invading, but for all the future entertainment the night might provide, I was still heading home alone, still stuck staring at women in magazines and never getting close to them.

Term started a week later, and logging-in to my email at 8am on the first Monday, I found a message from the Office of International Studies asking me to attend an interview for the Durham–Rosella exchange scheme.

The porter directed me through a narrow door and up a shadowy staircase to a long corridor of academic offices I'd never seen before. Four minutes early, I knocked nervously at Professor Beck's door.

'Come in.'

I turned the metal knob and stepped into a cramped but

well-lit office with bookcases on three walls, a solid desk by the window and two worn yellow armchairs filling the rest of the floor-space.

'You must be Natalie.'

'Yes,' I smiled. I hesitated, then held out my hand.

Professor Beck was in his late fifties; a skinny, suited man with a white beard and white hair, both flecked with their original black. 'Thank you so much for your application. I don't know if you know, but we didn't get a huge response. In fact, it's just between you and one other girl.'

'Oh,' I was surprised. My pride at being selected for interview plummeted, but the simultaneous realisation that my odds were as good as a coin toss balanced my nervous excitement.

'Yes, quite disappointing really, but no matter. I'm just going to interview you very informally about what you'd like to get out of the exchange and what you think you can bring to it. Then we hope to have a decision within a couple of weeks.'

'Great.' I smiled dumbly once more. My mind was rebelling and dredging mortifying memories of my Cambridge interview, reminding me that despite all my As and my perfection on paper, I had never actually won anything I'd been interviewed for. What would it be like to be rejected even when the odds were 50:50?

'The first thing I need to ask you is how much you know about where you're going?' Professor Beck began.

'Oh, well, I looked on a map of course, um, and I read some of Rosella's website,' I lied, thinking those were exactly the sorts of things I *should* have done and realising I'd probably blown it already.

'Oh good,' Professor Beck smiled. 'Because one of the things we're worried about is how the student will adjust to the location. It's very rural, not like being in Durham at all. How do you think you'll cope with that?'

'Oh, not a problem. I grew up in a tiny town of 5,000.' *You hated growing up in the countryside*, I argued silently with myself, *do you really want to apply for this?* 'I mean, I like being in Durham, being in a city, but I certainly don't need it, especially if there's a campus full of activities going on.'

'Right, excellent. And how do you think you'll cope with being at a women's college?'

You what?! How did you miss that?! 'I-I don't think it will be a problem.' I swallowed. 'I get on with both sexes anyway.' *Not really true. All your friends are boys; you just wish you got on with girls so you could date them.* 'And I think it would be interesting to see a different kind of academic environment.' *It's probably going to be horrific and bitchy. Full of prissy public school kids with rich parents. Do you even like Americans? You've never wanted to go to America before. What if they're all like Kirsten Dunst in* Mona Lisa Smile? *You haven't thought this through at all.*

'Yes. Very good. And academically, you'd have to do some classes that would relate to those you would be doing if you stayed here in your second year.'

'Of course, that's fine.'

'Our students who study in America tend to find the workload is much heavier there, but perhaps not as vigorous – there seems to be less onus on you to do individual research, but you'll take up to four classes per semester. The school day at Rosella runs from 8am to 9pm and you'd probably have one or two classes every day. How do you think you would find that after the schedule here?'

Christ, eight in the morning?! 'Oh, I'm sure that would be fine. I enjoy the personal research assigned here, but I'd also enjoy a wider range of subjects. I think I'd like taking four classes a semester.'

'And they wouldn't all have to be in the English department, or even necessarily at Rosella. As I'm sure you've discovered in your research, there's a free bus connecting Rosella to a neighbouring college. There's some kind of alliance, so students can study at both. There really are many benefits to the Liberal Arts system.'

117

'Excellent.' *You have no idea what he was just talking about, do you?*

'Do you have any questions for me?'

'Um.' *Shit, you should have prepared something; they told you that in the careers workshop. You're crap at this.* 'Well, is there support for getting out there? Applying for a visa and such? Because I've no idea how that works.'

'Oh yes, should you be successful, you'll work closely with the Office of International Studies to sort all of that out. Part of the terms of the exchange dictates that the student must use a specific medical insurer, and we'll sort it out so the candidate pays tuition fees and accommodation here in Durham, plus probably a stipend for food for the exchanging student because over there you'd be on a meal plan. So, really, most of it is laid out for you.'

'Great. As long as there are people to talk to.'

'Yes, and you'd have a liaison while you're out there. We don't want you just running off and never getting in touch.'

'Sure.'

'We also have to ask you to prove you can afford it.'

'Right.'

'Though most of the fees will be paid to Durham, there will be other expenses like flights and things, so you'll need a little more than you'd require for a year here. Do you have the funds?'

'Um, yes, I mean I have student loans and everything, but I've also got some savings from an inheritance from my grandparents.'

'Great. Well, should you be successful, we'll need to see a bank statement just to prove you won't run out of money halfway through the year and not be able to afford your flight home.'

'Of course.'

'Okay, well I think that's sufficient for now. I'll be in touch in the next couple of weeks.'

'Yes, thank you. Goodbye.'

I left Professor Beck's office feeling deflated. How bland could an interview be? Had I said anything remotely intelligent? Surely the other girl would shine and prove her perfection. Would it matter? Did I really want to go to a place in the middle of nowhere full of spoilt girls? So what if I just stayed at Durham?

But, as unprepared as I'd been for the interview and as little as I knew about Rosella, part of me was truly disappointed. For some reason I wasn't telling myself, I really did want to go. I wanted to fly a long way away to a place no one knew me, a place I could start again.

'Hiya,' I said softly, knowing only Matthew, my mum and my dad knew my halls phone number and that neither of my parents ever called unless I rang them first.

'Natalie?' It was a man's voice but not Matthew's.

'Yes,' I tried to rectify my previous informality by standing up straight beside my desk, flattening my pyjamas over my stomach.

'It's Professor Beck.'

'Oh, hello.' *It's only been two days*, I thought. *He must have hated you and decided to reject you already.*

'I have good news. We've made a decision and you're going to America next year.'

'Oh.' It slipped out before I could form a thought. 'Wow.' *Shit. What are you going to tell Matthew?*

'Yes, I hope you're pleased. Listen, I won't keep you long. Why don't you pop in to see me during office hours tomorrow and we'll discuss what needs to be organised first.'

'Uh, okay. Thanks.'

'Congratulations, Natalie. See you tomorrow.'

And with that, I was alone in my bedroom, holding a dial tone to my ear and wondering what I was meant to be feeling.

'Wow Natty, that's great. I can't believe you kept that a secret. I'm so happy for you,' my mum trilled into the receiver.

'New York State, that's where I worked for a few years back in the eighties. Very nice,' my dad's voice betrayed a sense of pride that his words did not.

'You what? Are you fucking with us? What about housing for next year?' muttered my housemates collectively.

'That's cool and everything, but I'll miss you,' said Tim, squeezing my knee.

'Cool. By the way, I got past the robot at the end of level four last night,' my brother responded via email.

'When were you going to tell me?' This was the conversation I had been dreading. 'Did nothing you said over Christmas mean anything? You knew this might be happening, yet you came into my house and told me you wanted to be with me always. You can't even cope with being on a campus a few hundred miles away without me ringing you every night, what do you think you're doing moving to America? Do you have no regard for my feelings at all? You selfish little child. I keep beginning to think you might be an Uncle, then you go off and do something like this, or fuck puny little Rudolph or whatever his name is. Are you ever going to learn?'

He went on. We argued for days and he sent me regular updates about how our fight was affecting his health, how he'd spent the afternoon in bed because his back had seized up through stress, how Annabelle was wailing at him to see a doctor.

Rose joined in. She told me I was selfish and disrespectful, hurtful and cruel. Among her chastisements, however, were smatterings of excitement, including: 'Rosella? I've heard of those places. Along with Smith and the other girly colleges. They're meant to be full of hot little lesbians. God, you're going to have an amazing time, you'll be eaten alive. I'm so jealous – you're still a little bitch, though, and you should have thought about how this would affect Matthew.'

Of course, eventually we made up. It took another trip to the nearest Travelodge and a few more digital pictures of my vagina flashed from beneath a pleated mini-skirt, but Matthew forgave me and we began to plan how we could spend my holidays hiring a car and tracing Jack Kerouac's route. Obviously it would be difficult for Matthew to leave England for a whole year to be with me, but he would shuffle things and find a couple of months in the summer, perhaps a few weeks over Christmas too. Rosella wasn't far from Manhattan: we could stay there and see shows, then jet off to LA to meet Rose and hang out in her plush showbiz world.

Making plans was exciting. We told Rose. She repeated that Rosella would be full of little girls gagging for me, and Matthew laughed that it was okay as long as I saved some for him. I was quiet at these moments. I wasn't sure if Rose meant what she was saying. I couldn't imagine any place having open lesbians like she described and, anyway, on the map I'd finally consulted, the college was in the middle of a bunch of fields and forests, so it seemed more likely to resemble Treyford than *Tipping the Velvet*. I talked myself out of believing her, but I still fantasised that she might be right; that at this strange place I might find a girl to touch lips, hold hands and play under duvets with.

11

The rest of my term was spent filling in visa application forms and discussing payment plans with the registrar and the housing office. I handed in an essay about Keats and Shelley, then headed home for the long Easter break. Thinking about the flights I'd soon have to book, I got a job at the local pub. My holiday would be spent serving IPA to sad saggy old men at 11.30 in the morning before they plodded off to their factory jobs, glasses of house red to the secretaries being bought lunch by their bosses and Smirnoff Ices to kids who might not have been eighteen but looked older than me.

For my first day off from the pub, my mum booked tickets to see *Hedda Gabler* in London. Early in the morning, five of us piled into her red Fiesta. Matthew and Annabelle were meant to come and we would have taken two cars, but Matthew's back had played up in the night and they'd called off. Instead of perching happily in the back seat of their car, gossiping about the neighbours or making crude comments about the people in passing cars, I found myself sandwiched between Beatrice and Valerie, while Bob occupied the passenger seat.

We probably had lunch and maybe saw some art; it'd be safe to say Bob ordered a large glass of wine and Beatrice joined him;

and perhaps we discussed what a shame it was that Matthew and Annabelle hadn't come and whether we'd be able to give their tickets to the box office for resale. But none of that really sticks in my head. What I remember from the day is climbing the plush stairs to the dress circle and peering through the half-light at the letters on the sides of the seats, then picking my way to the centre of row B and briefly meeting the eye of a wavy-haired blonde as I lowered myself into my seat.

The play was fantastic. I sat forward in my seat as the actress languished across the stage and offered Løvborg the pistol. I caught the eye of the blonde girl next to me again in the interval. Sitting alone while the others found the loos and more wine, I merged in my mind the blonde's curls with Hedda's heaving bosom and felt the muscles tense pleasantly in my thighs.

After the bang from backstage, I peered through people's shoulders as we filed down the stairs, trying not to lose the bobbing blonde head. On the street, a decision was made to turn left and I cheered silently as I noticed the denim jacket on the same girl's back as she walked a few steps ahead of us with someone I presumed to be her grandmother. I muttered responses to the others and applauded the costumes, lighting and set, all the while thinking *we must keep pace, I need to know where she's going*.

We followed them halfway down the main street, but Valerie was lagging and Beatrice was staring longingly at the wine lists in the windows of the bars we were passing. Eventually we stopped, choosing an outdoor table. Everyone was jolly and I joined in the amateur critique, feeling more excited and alive than I had for months, yet also crushingly deflated by the anticlimax of the whole event. I thought of Matthew and wished it had been just he and I in the theatre, wished he could have seen the girl and encouraged me to say hello. *No*, I didn't wish he was there. I liked the purity of it as it was. The girl had been mine to watch, not in a sordid way, but in the beautiful, poetic way that Hedda takes her own life and Mrs Dalloway buys the flowers. This was my moment and, though I'd liked to have sat in that bar with Matthew describing and analysing the literary eroticism of living above the parapet, I was glad I hadn't had to share it.

The following day, Matthew and I sat at his computer scanning a list of Fringe theatres in London. I was looking for addresses; I'd already drafted a letter.

Dear Sir/Madam

I'm an English Literature undergraduate, just coming to the end of my first year, and I would like to enquire as to whether you have any work-experience opportunities.

I'm interested in pursuing theatre, eventually as a director, and am looking to gain as much experience of the industry as possible. My summer break runs from 30th June until 1st September and I could be in London for some or all of this time.

Thank you for taking the time to consider my query. Please don't hesitate to contact me if you require any further information. I have enclosed a copy of my CV.

Yours faithfully,
Natalie Lucas

Hedda Gabler had been the first play I hadn't fallen asleep in. I'd attended the theatre with my mum as a child, mostly with my nana, who liked to see adaptations of things like *Wuthering Heights* and *Sons and Lovers*, but even if I was enjoying the play and I cared about the characters, something about the soft seats and the darkened auditorium always lulled me into a light snooze after the interval. But having finally understood an ending by piecing the third act to the first and second rather than to the first alone, I was convinced this was the world I wanted. I longed to be in charge: to be the master of the beautiful puppet-like actors, to choose the colours and the set and to own the audience's imagination for those brief hours. It was an industry of Uncles; it had to be.

Matthew was supportive. He said his tenants' contract ran out at the beginning of July, so he could keep his flat in Kew empty over the summer. I could live there and he could visit me a few days every week, juggling his betting and Annabelle. We would be together and alone. We could go food shopping and spend afternoons in cafés where no one would know us. It'd be perfect.

I sent my letter to thirty theatres in London. With a little more hesitation, I also wrote an email to the secretary of Durham's Student Theatre asking how I could get involved.

In the first week of the new term, I was assigned to stage manage a production of Michael Frayn's *Clouds*. The director was a tall, friendly, ex-public-school boy, the producer a short and bubbly Literature student, and the designer a tiny, beautiful, brunette vegan. I ran around arranging poster printing and finding props, but also began following the production team to college bars after run-throughs and laughing with people my own age.

I told Matthew on the phone I'd finally found people at university with passion. Unlike the English students who partied all night and rolled out of bed for their nine-fifteens without having opened the books, here were people offering their time for free, willing to paint sets until four in the morning, then return to their bedrooms and finish writing that paper on John Donne that needed to be handed in at 10am, grab some sleep before rehearsals at noon, then do the whole crazy thing all over again. Matthew quietly replied that he was happy for me.

With a week and a half until our get-in, I received a letter from the Blue Box Theatre. I keyed it into Google and found it was right there on the District Line, just a dozen or so stops from Kew. They said they had a good internship programme and, if I could make it down to London for an informal interview, they could probably offer me six weeks in the summer. They needed a 'deputy stage manager' for a new play.

I told Lee, one of the actors in *Clouds*, first and he jumped around with me in excitement, then took me for a picnic to celebrate.

'So, you want to be a director?' he asked, passing me the brie.

'I think so. What about you?' I lay back and propped myself on my elbows, careful to avoid the duck and goose shit covering the grass.

'I like comedy. Stand-up and stuff.' Lee's long legs were crossed and he was turned to me, focusing intently. 'I mean, acting's okay, but I get stuck with all the supporting roles here, you know – the token black guy in a white university.'

I snorted a giggle and immediately wondered whether that was inappropriate.

'So I'd really like to be a comedian,' he smiled.

'Cool. How do you get into that?' I tore some bread for something to do with my hands.

'Just do it I guess. I'm going up to Edinburgh this year, and I'll spend the summer at home in London trying to get some gigs at clubs and such.' He was still smiling his half-goofy, half-sexy grin.

'Fun.' I smiled back.

'Hey, you should come. You'll be in London. We could go out.'

'Oh.' I looked at his chocolate eyes and wondered what exactly he meant. 'Yeah, maybe.' An imaginary something poked me in the stomach: *Isn't London meant to be just you and Matthew? You and Matthew living in his flat, living together, living like a normal couple who don't have to worry what people think of them?*

'Where are you staying when you're there?'

'Oh, um, my uncle has a place in Kew that's going to be empty.' *Is he flirting? Are you?*

'Cool, Kew's *really* nice. You must be close to your uncle.'

'Yeah, I guess.'

126

'We could go to the botanical gardens. Or Hampton Court. You'll have to have a day off, right? I could show you round my city.'

'Sure. Well, I probably won't know my schedule until I'm down there, but maybe.'

The conversation died as we ate and later it turned to making up silly rhyming songs. As Lee made me laugh until Coca Cola came out of my nose, my muscles untensed; this was just two friends having fun, he wasn't interested and neither was I. It was fine.

12

'Scarlet Jean? Natalie Scarlet Jean Lucas? Ha ha ha ha!' The slightly balding guy sitting behind the shabby desk with a half-smoked cigarette dangling from one hand and my CV in his other collapsed into loud, honking laughter. 'Your parents didn't like you much, did they? Sounds pretty pretentious!'

I blushed, partly because of his good-natured ridicule, partly because I was realising how out of place I looked in the carefully chosen black trousers and button-down shirt that at nine this morning I'd thought made a perfectly appropriate outfit. Far from the frighteningly formal interview I'd expected, I was now sat on a chipped wooden chair on the first floor of a corner building filled with over-stuffed files, pots and pots of paint and an ancient electric kettle balanced precariously on a fridge that needed a copy of the *Yellow Pages* to keep it shut.

'Well, put the kettle on and we'll see if you can handle the job.'

I hesitated, unsure whether he was serious, then fumbled to obey.

'I have two questions for you,' he continued. 'Can you make a cup of tea? And, do you mind passive smoking? Because, if you do any work here, there will be a lot of both.'

I smiled. I was beginning to like this odd guy with his cheeky smile and slightly Northern accent. His name was Raoul. He'd agreed to meet me this weekend, the first after *Clouds* had closed, so I'd forked out for the train down to King's Cross and was doubling it as an excuse to stay in a hotel with Matthew for the night. We were going to see Mark Rylance in *Hamlet* at The Globe this evening, his treat.

After I'd made Raoul a satisfactory cup of tea, he showed me around the theatre, which didn't take long: it was a small black box above a pub that had made the Fringe lists because of its reputation for championing new writing. The stage was no bigger than my college bedroom and the temporary seating could fit a maximum of fifty in the audience. Backstage consisted of the office, which doubled as prop room and stage-left entrance, and a small dressing room with two mirrors and shelves full of wig heads.

By the time I left, we'd arranged for me to start attending rehearsals as soon as my term ended. The stage manager would handle everything alone until then.

Back in Durham two days later, I was buoyed by the thought of my summer plans. Matthew and I chatted excitedly about what we would do with my days off, how amazing it would be to have our own space and how we could construct Bunburys for Annabelle and my parents.

There were still four weeks left of term, but with *Clouds* over and most of the drama students preparing to take plays to Edinburgh, I found my social life dwindling. I agreed to design a set for WomanSoc, who were putting on *The Vagina Monologues*. I found them less sociable than the theatre crowd and grew rather miserable painting flats alone in a borrowed studio.

After chatting to Rose online one evening, feeling frustratedly horny, I logged on to Gaydar for the first time in months. My inbox was full. Among the predictably crude and weird, I found a series of emails from NJ26, desperate to meet because we were in the same city. I clicked to her profile and saw a pretty dark-haired girl who described herself as 'seeking fun'. Her profile said she was from Egypt, doing a Masters in England and 'hoping to make the most of my time here'. I clicked back to her latest email, sent two days ago. My mouse icon hovered over the reply button. She was attractive. She was in Durham, probably in the graduate college, just a few hundred yards away, perhaps only steps from where I'd spent the day constructing my set. If I contacted her, we'd probably have an awkward coffee, and then she'd make an excuse to leave because she found me utterly repulsive and I'd never see her again. But, on the other hand, the potential for humiliation was limited by the fact that I was leaving soon: I had little to lose.

Something stopped me, though. I saved her email and signed out of Gaydar. I heard Tim and Dave's crass laughter in my mind, their drunken, manly warnings to each other about 'shitting on your own doorstep'. I masturbated in bed and fell asleep.

A couple of days later, I dragged my housemates to *The Vagina Monologues*. As we queued to enter the lecture hall in which it was being performed, the girl who had orgasmed over and over before me during the dress rehearsals the night before walked by us. A couple of people ahead wished her luck and – because I had gone home to replay her moans as I lay in bed – because I had thought of nothing but her in my lectures that morning – because I had left the auditorium sure that the wetness between my thighs must be visible to all – because I had ached miserably all night for a girl with blonde curls who wore leather and screamed for more – because I was totally besotted – I stopped her too. I stuttered out a, 'You were really amazing yesterday, break a leg tonight,' and went bright red as she smiled sweetly and my friends giggled. She walked away as I swallowed my mortification.

After the play, Tim and I trudged back to our college. I slammed my door and punched on my computer. Attacking the keyboard with more vigour than was necessary, Harriet Moore sent NJ26 a reply.

'By the way, my real name's Natalie,' I blurted in embarrassment as we sat down. It was the following evening and we were in a college bar, in plain sight of students and staff. An immediate flirt, she'd bought me a beer and put me at ease.

'Nadiyya,' the girl shrugged. 'It's Arabic, it means delicate. Are you Italian?'

'No, why?'

'Natalie. It's Italian, I think.'

'Oh yeah, sorry.' I blushed. 'No, I suppose my parents just liked it.'

'You could be Italian. Or maybe French. You have gorgeous eyes.' Gazing into Nadiyya's wide, clear smile was like looking at a bottle of Evian after completing a city-wide bar crawl.

My life transformed into a scene from *Better than Chocolate* as she led me back to her room. I had little idea what was going on except a vague voice in my head chanting: 'This is it, this is it!'

As she pulled me through the doorway of her spacious double room, she wrapped her hands around my waist and kissed me lightly on the mouth.

'Are you okay, baby?' she drawled.

'Uh huh,' I managed.

'I'll put some music on.' She paced across the room and turned the dials on the stereo until a lazy melody began to play low. 'Hey, relax.' She returned to me and shrugged my jacket from my shoulders, brushing her lips along my neck. 'I hope you don't think me too forward.'

'Oh, no,' I managed to choke out.

'It's just I don't have much longer left in England, and I like to live.' Her fingers brushed their way beneath my T-shirt.

'Uh huh, that seems, um, fair enough.' I self-consciously began to nuzzle her neck.

'I've met quite a few people from Gaydar, but you're by far the most beautiful.' Her hands ran over my stomach and up my back. 'You're so sexy and you don't even know it.'

I smiled into her hair.

'You also seem quite open and true, which is good,' she paused. 'I should have told you something in the bar, I hope it doesn't change the way you feel about me.'

I stiffened and wondered what she had to say, but murmured, 'I'm sure it won't.'

'I have a fiancé. Hugh. Back in Egypt. He knows all about what I do here and gives me his blessing. I'm allowed to love girls here, but I'm going to be his wife when I return.'

'Oh.' My nose was still in her hair and I didn't remove it.

'Is that okay with you, baby?' Her fingers tickled my spine. 'I'll understand if it's not, but it really shouldn't make any difference.'

'Um, I guess not.' A messy feeling crept into my gut, but I thought about Matthew and whether the half-truths I'd told Nadiyya in the bar counted as dishonesty. Sure, Matthew had warned me against becoming caught up with couples and getting in trouble, but if the fiancé was in Egypt, he couldn't pose a threat, could he? And I could hardly accuse her of misleading me when I'd revealed nothing about my secret life and pretended only to be a normal first-year student.

Nadiyya manoeuvred me to the bed and kissed me harder now. She purred 'baby's and 'beautiful's as she undressed me and slid her tongue down my belly. She pulled her own clothes off and I saw she was shaved. The first girl I'd truly seen naked.

Nervous and giddy, I don't remember much. Nadiyya asked me to stay the night, but I told her I needed to remove my contact lenses. I left her curled in blue sheets and walked into the night. I wandered along the river, staring at my mucky reflection with coy smiles.

I woke up thinking of Nadiyya and found her online.

Chat with NJ26

NJ26: I missed you this morning baby.

Harry: Sorry.

NJ26: I want to see you again.

Harry: Okay.

NJ26: When? I have a girl from Leeds coming over tonight, but I'd rather see you. Are you free?

Harry: Yes, but if you have plans.

NJ26: No, no, she won't mind. She sounded relaxed in her profile.

Harry: Oh. What profile?

NJ26: Gaydar, silly. I'm sorry, obviously I wouldn't have arranged it if I'd known you were going to contact me, but it's a little late to cancel it now. I have to be polite.

Harry: I suppose.

NJ26: But you could come too. We're having dinner, then maybe going out to a club. Please please come. I want you there.

Harry: I don't know. I think I'd rather not.

NJ26: Really? Are you mad at me?

Harry: No, why should I be? We could see each other tomorrow.

NJ26: Yes, but I'd really like you to come tonight. I miss you so much already. Will you come to my room this afternoon? I have to study, but I'd like you here.

Harry: Okay, maybe for a bit.

NJ26: Yay! I need go now. See you later beautiful.
xxxxxxxxxxxxx

After Googling 'cunnilingus' and reading an article about tracing A–Z with my tongue, I showered. I tried on three different pairs of knickers before deciding on a black lace thong Matthew had given me last Christmas.

After lunch, I headed over to Nadiyya's room and we lazed in bed, interspersing making love with reading critical theory.

'Can I take your photo, baby?'

'Like this?' I was naked on top of her sheets.

'Sure. You're beautiful. I told Hugh how gorgeous you are, baby, and he wants to see.'

'Um, I don't think so.' I pulled the duvet over me.

'Oh baby. I'm sorry. I won't if you don't like it, but I really want to. Maybe you'll let me another time.'

I ignored that feeling in my gut again and turned back to my essay.

A few hours later, Laura arrived. She had scruffily bleached short hair and a nose piercing. Her face was blotchy and her stomach squidged over her jeans. She said she was thirty-two. She had a seven-year-old daughter and a partner who didn't mind her seeing other men as well as women as long as she only had anal sex with him. I found this out over fajitas in Nadiyya's communal kitchen.

After we'd eaten, I said I'd leave them to it. But Nadiyya re-filled my wine glass and begged me to stay a little longer. We finished two bottles before the pair of them dragged me to the club. Laura ordered me doubles and it wasn't long before I was gyrating with Nadiyya on the dance floor. In the bathrooms, she drawled that she wished she was just going home with me tonight and wouldn't I join them – it would be fun.

'Noooo,' I slurred. 'I think I should just go home.'

'Please.' She pushed me into a stall and slid her fingers into my jeans.

Two more drinks later and I was stumbling up Nadiyya's stairs with the two of them. Once again, I declined an invitation to stay the night and managed to depart before Nadiyya put her water-proof sheet on the bed and opened her cupboard full of strap-ons, but not before her camera came out and, bullied and drunk, I posed next to Laura's sagging nipples, arched my back and allowed the two of them to crouch between my thighs.

I cried on the phone to Matthew the next day. He laughed and said at least I seemed to be having fun. Rose asked if I'd orgasmed with Nadiyya yet. Matthew added, 'Perhaps your friend can visit us in London.'

I scrubbed my skin in the shower and refused to check my email all day.

That night, Nadiyya called my room phone. She'd looked it up in the college directory.

'Where have you been today, baby? Will you come over tonight?'

'I don't know.'

'I'm sorry; you didn't like Laura did you?'

'It's not that.'

'I'll cancel everyone else. Would that make it better?'

'I don't know.'

'I only want to see you. I know it's just been two days, but I'm crazy about you already. Please come. Let me make it up to you.'

'Maybe.'

'Please.'

'Maybe.'

'Please.'

'Okay.'

For the following two weeks, I camped out in Nadiyya's room. In the mornings, she made us large mugs of sweet black coffee before we left for lectures. I stopped eating during the day, just so I could arrive at her door hungry and watch her make me a 'super sandwich', towering lettuce on mustard and cheese and meats and beans until the thick bread was toppling from the plate. 'Eat, baby.'

On the fourth day, Nadiyya told me she loved me. I didn't say it back, but I stopped being shy about her reaching for her camera and, towards the end, we set up my digital video recorder on a tripod facing the desk chair.

It wasn't all sex in every corner of her room. We went for walks along the river and she introduced me to some of her friends from her course. I took her to my college once and showed her my room, then felt foolish when she turned to leave and whispered that we should return to her comfy double bed.

Eventually, too, I told her about Matthew, though not his exact age and not any of the details that might have left an acrid taste on my tongue. She kissed me hard, saying, 'I'm sooo glad you have someone, baby. Like me and Hugh.'

I handed all my essays in and Nadiyya checked out from the library the books she would need to finish her dissertation back in Egypt. She was returning to Durham in August to hand it in, but wanted to spend July with her family. Her flight was in two days. I was leaving in three, skipping the final day of term so I could be back down south in time for Glastonbury Festival.

The thought of Nadiyya leaving was crushing, but I was excited about Glastonbury. Rose was supposedly part of the entourage for Garbage and, not only were we planning to finally meet for the first time in those muddy fields, but also she'd promised to introduce me to the band's frontwoman, Shirley Manson.

'You should come and visit me, baby – come to our wedding, you could stay with us.' Nadiyya grinned with that smile I no longer thought like water.

I kissed her and pulled her to me.

'I'm going to cry when you leave,' I whispered.

'Me too. I love you, baby, even if you won't say it back. You're incredible.'

And with those words, or some like it, my first girlfriend packed up her belongings, secured her hard drive full of pornographic photos and left the country to return to her Muslim fiancé.

13

'You don't know why I'm angry? That's the typical selfish little child Natalie, isn't it? I don't know why I expect more. You prove me wrong time and again.'

I sighed into the phone. 'I'm sorry, I really don't understand what I did.'

'You don't understand what you did?'

'No.'

'You don't understand what you did?!'

'No, I'm sorry.'

'YOU DON'T UNDERSTAND WHAT YOU DID?' he roared. 'I set you up with women and listen to your pathetic little stories about why you can't even hold hands with them. I bend over backwards to accommodate your needs and to do everything for you in bed. And when you *finally* get a girlfriend, you ring me up telling me how wonderful it is to lap the cunts of the dirty little slut and probably her disease-ridden friends – "*Oh darling*, I love you and I'm having such fun" – "*Oh darling*, I miss you so much and I wish you were here, but while you're away I'm frotting with this Egyptian bitch and sending her fiancé photographs, *Oh darling*, isn't it great?"'

'I'm sorry, I thought you were okay with it.'

'Okay with it? Okay with it? I've been waiting for it for three fucking years. But it's fucking insulting. You sent Hugh photographs and you hardly found a spare moment to even phone me. I was here, waiting by the phone, ready to leap in my car and book a hotel for the three of us as soon as you said "jump", but it didn't even occur to you that it might be polite to share. YOU DIDN'T EVEN THINK OF MY NEEDS, DID YOU?!'

'I'm sorry, I'm sorry, I'm sorry.'

'And it's not even just me. You've upset Rose too and she really doesn't need it right now. She thought you were an Uncle – she's so disappointed.'

'Is that why she's not coming any more? She emailed me last week saying "Glastonbury's off".'

'No, you selfish little bitch, it's not always all about you. Rose didn't want to worry you or spoil your happy little cunt-sucking mood. She wanted to protect you, but I don't think you deserve it any more. So here goes. Rose's got cancer. That's why she's cancelled every meeting, because she's woken up vomiting blood and she doesn't want you to see her in a wig and with bags under her eyes. She was feeling better, which is why she was going to pull everything out to see you at Glastonbury. I told her she shouldn't exhaust herself, but she said she wanted to, for you. But with all the stress of your behaviour, she's relapsed. She's flying to LA for more treatment – that was why she went in the first place. The Hollywood job was secondary. So now she's on a plane not knowing whether she'll live or die and worrying about you and me because she's that kind of person.' He fell silent.

'I'm sorry,' I eventually whispered. 'I didn't know.'

'No, I'm sorry,' he replied more softly. 'I shouldn't have told you like that. I'm just hurt, supremely hurt. I'm worried about my friend and sick of Annabelle nagging at me and the one person I thought I could turn to has been off frolicking with her girlfriend and forgetting about me. It's too much. I can't cope with it right now.' I heard his voice break and wanted to say something to heal the man I loved, but he cut me short: 'I can't talk any more. Goodbye. Enjoy your festival.'

I stared at my mobile. Call ended: 13.41. I was standing between a pair of tyre tracks behind a caravan in the quietest place I'd been able to find when Matthew called. The Thrills would be playing on the Other Stage in twenty minutes and I would need to make my way to the Pyramid Stage at least an hour before Radiohead's eight o'clock set to ensure a place by the barrier. I was hungry and slightly stoned. I hadn't pooed in thirty-six hours and the mud was squelching beneath my boots. I kept seeing things I wanted to point out to Nadiyya. There was a Henna tent that had caught my eye this morning that I thought I might go back to. I was surprisingly taken by Idlewild. R.E.M. had been incredible. And Rose had cancer. And Matthew was disappointed in me. And I didn't know it yet, but I had a bacterial infection that would need antibiotics. And Rose had cancer. Rose had cancer and she hadn't told me. Rose wasn't coming to Glastonbury because she had cancer and might die. Rose was angry with me and she had cancer. Rose was flying to LA because she had cancer. Rose, my Rose, my friend and everything-but-lover, she had cancer.

14

Arriving at the Blue Box, I was greeted by a frenzy. The producer squealed that she was glad I was here because the stage manager was sick and rehearsals were already running behind. She put me on book and assigned me the jobs of making prop lists, reporting script problems and noting down the blocking – a task that, I was informed, would be somewhat thwarted by Raoul's 'organic' way of directing plays. I nodded, took the offered pencil and clipboard and sat in a plastic chair trying to translate my instructions into English.

Returning to Matthew's cosy Kew flat after my first day, I lay in his arms and told him I already loved it. We had made up, once again with me apologising until my tongue was numb and submitting to his will in the bedroom while his eyes hardened and he told me he would teach me a lesson. Also, I'd emailed Nadiyya and she'd agreed to visit us both in Richmond when she was back in the country to hand in her dissertation. Matthew was content. I was nervous.

I immediately loved living in Kew, though. Matthew showed me a pretty route back from the station, pointing out the enormous houses celebrities supposedly owned. His flat was on a picturesque, tree-lined street. It had a gravelled parking space, treasured in

London, and an imposing white front door. The curved hall, where every day I hoped not to bump into real residents because I wasn't sure who knew Matthew as Albert and who didn't, led to the less impressive door to the flat. Panicking a little, I'd fumble at waist height for the keys and finally fall into the narrow entrance, coat rack to my left, cramped bathroom ahead. The toilet didn't flush too well and when Matthew and I fought that summer, he'd call me a 'constipated bitch'. The shower was functional but not pleasant; I didn't look forward to languid latherings so much as hurried hops in and out before wrapping myself in a scratchy towel and passing quickly into the main room to seek warmth in my clothes.

The main room was why the flat was lovely. If I turned right from the front door I faced an enormous bay window. As a ground floor flat, all I could see was the car, the pavement and the town-houses opposite, but the net curtains maintained our privacy and the flood of daylight from that much glass made the place feel larger than it was. To my right would be a narrow staircase that led to a fairly decent sized kitchen, half sunk underground, its ceiling jutting into the main room with a good two feet of wooden banisters that spewed natural light onto our scrambled eggs and fruit bowl. We didn't cook much that summer; the flat contained only the basic equipment landlords provide for tenants and, anyway, Matthew enjoyed uncomplicated meals. We ate ham and eggs, mashed potatoes and banana sandwiches; salads were simple, served in breakfast bowls and offered only with a jar of Colman's Mustard. There was a door from the kitchen so small that even I had to duck; through it, bare stone walls lined a narrow passage and cracked paving slabs offered stepping stones. Around the spooky corner, where one bulb glowed a faint yellow, lay a washing machine and cleaning equipment, including an ancient vacuum cleaner. I tried to avoid this room. I did my washing only twice and, each time, propped the door open in case it automatically locked and I became trapped down there where no one could hear me scream. I'd heap the damp bundle in my arms and hurry back to the light, up the stairs to drape it in the main room, remembering again that this was what I liked about the place, what I liked about the intimacy of living with Matthew. Beneath the bay window sat a small dining table with just two chairs. They were not comfy, but it was a nice place to read or to boot up my laptop. There was no other furniture; it wasn't our place. We sometimes talked about how we would decorate it if we were to stay, musing that one day – once I was done with university and we no longer had to worry about parents and wives – we could move here.

If I stood before the window and turned to face the room, I could view the whole flat. I could see three deep steps in front of me, framed by long white banisters. The tops of the banisters continuing from the kitchen below formed a railing around the bedroom above. Taking the steps in one leap, I would be in the left corner of the room, which was raised above the rest and held the queen-sized bed, a mahogany wardrobe and a mostly bare bookshelf. Flopping on the sheets, Matthew would join me and we'd stare at the ceiling, speaking of how wonderful it was to be alone.

'You know what to do, right? It's hardly rocket-science!' The American twang in my ear projected the girl's boredom and superiority to the task at hand with crystal clarity, despite its thickness betraying her blocked nose and evident illness.

I hadn't met Becky yet, but I'd heard a few (not especially favourable) reports from the actors and now tried to picture the bolshy international student on the other end of the phone. I assured her I had it under control, staying quiet about the fact that while Becky herself might find writing rehearsal reports tedious unskilled labour, I – having never written one before – was petrified.

When we finally met, it was in a whirl at the beginning of a rehearsal the following week. Becky breezed into the rehearsal room wearing torn jeans and a bandana around her hair. She dumped her backpack on the floor and sank into a plastic chair, her long legs spread either side of the bag as she unzipped it and removed the props she'd collected over the weekend. When I entered, the gangly girl looked up vaguely and mumbled a hello as she went back to the task at hand. Once she was done, she explained in an authoritative tone that almost masked her Philly accent what each prop was for and that she hoped I was able to manage because she had to help paint the set and wouldn't be in rehearsals for the rest of the week. 'Okay?' she concluded, impatient to be off.

'Okay,' I replied, wondering whether I'd be able to get on with this gruff girl for the weeks ahead.

By opening night, I had my answer. The only backstage crew who had to be at every rehearsal and performance, Becky and I developed a ritual of racing each other silently down the stairs after the play. One of us ordered two Coronas while the other claimed a pair of stools in the corner of the bar. In silence, we poked lime slices into our bottles and raised them to a perhaps immature, but nevertheless satisfying toast of 'FUCK'.

Then we collapsed in giggles and proceeded to gossip into the night. Becky was studying performing arts in London and filling every waking hour with theatre, bar work, art classes and lovers. Over the next few weeks we became friends, often talking cynically about the latest diva-esque actions of the actors. The eldest and more widely known of the two was a rather large, flamboyant man in his seventies. He never tired of telling us of the old days, name-dropping directors and stars to remind us what a step down this play was for him. One night, he even turned up with a break-a-leg card from Paul McCartney and handed it around while applying his face. Far from star-struck, Becky would cruelly imitate the old man and mock-vomit at the fact she'd seen him in just underpants in the dressing room.

Press night happened to be my nineteenth birthday. My mum came up to see the show, bringing along my brother and a couple of friends. I was excited and a little nervous for them to see it, but the cast and crew were all in a good mood. Raoul had made a few last-minute changes to the technical running of the show and I was frantically going over my notes in the little tech booth. The house was filling up and I knew the audience contained representatives from *Time Out*, *The Times*, *The Guardian* and *The Telegraph*.

As I brought down the house music with the lights, switched to the new show CD and set my levels for the next cue, the play began. On the first scene change, I hit play and pressed the light cue. The music blared out much louder than I'd expected and, panicking, I tried to subtly bring it down. The same happened with the next cue and the next. Checking and rechecking my notes and the soundboard, I could find nothing wrong and decided it must sound different in the house and perhaps I was just paranoid.

However, I watched one of the actors flinch as I gave the next sound cue and a second later a scrawled piece of paper was shoved through my window: 'SOUND LEVELS WAY TOO LOUD! DO SOMETHING!'

I panicked. I checked everything again and saw it was all as we'd set it during the technical run and as I'd executed it in the previews. Muttering uncertainly to myself, I cautiously turned the main volume down three notches. For the next cues I would just have to guess. But at the end of the play, there was what was supposed to be a nuclear explosion, which involved me frantically pressing five buttons at once, fading bombs out and repeating, all to cues in the script. If I guessed wrong for that, the heart-pounding bombs and shatters would either be laughably quiet or so loud they'd cause permanent damage to the audience's hearing.

Perspiring, I cued up for the final scene. The first bomb went off and the audience jumped. Good. But now the actor had lost his flow and was jumbling up his lines. I had to improvise with my cues and looked up at one point from my frenzied button-pushing and knob-twisting to see I'd left him bathed in light. I swore and willed him to hurry up and get this disastrous night over with.

After the show, Raoul came up to ask what had gone wrong.

'I've no idea; I did everything as we'd agreed. The only difference was the new CD.'

'Shit, we didn't do a sound check to make sure the levels were the same as the old CD.' Raoul slapped his hand to his head.

'Oh God, was that it?' I asked, half relieved that it wasn't something I'd done, half pissed that I'd been made to sweat for someone else's mistake.

'Yeah, I'm sorry, totally my fault.'

The actor wasn't so forgiving. He glared at me as I tried to say sorry for the lights at the end.

'Just get it right tomorrow,' he boomed and turned away.

Becky shoved a glass of champagne into my hand and, after we'd cleared the house, we descended to the bar. I introduced Becky to my family and, offering me more champagne, they all told me to forget about the tech and enjoy my birthday. Hungry, I asked at the bar if they had a food menu but all they could offer was a bag of crisps.

After an hour or so, my family said they had to drive back and bought me another drink as a final congratulation before heading off. Becky sat with me and asked if I was all right. Still a little upset but thoroughly inebriated, I said I was fine and continued chatting to the bar owner and theatre manager. They left me to buy more drinks and, sat on my own, I finally started to feel queasy. Closing my eyes, I realised I was going to be sick. I lunged towards the unisex bathrooms, colliding with Raoul on my way to the porcelain bowl. Becky followed me in and held my hair back as I hurled into the toilet, muttering apologies.

It was a while before we emerged and, upon everyone clapping at my re-entrance into the bar, I dashed for the sink and threw up again. Becky said she'd take me home. She pleaded with a bored-looking bus driver to let me on and I sat at the front with her shirt held tightly to my mouth.

I don't remember much else, but was informed the next day that Becky and her boyfriend had had to carry me up the stairs to her flat. I woke in my clothes and walked towards the bathroom holding my head. On the way I passed Becky's bedroom; the door was ajar and I glimpsed the naked back of Becky's boyfriend protruding from the covers, with her just visible beyond him. The sight upset me and, with my hangover pounding in my ears, I ran a shower and sat for a long time trying to erase the image of Becky in the arms of a guy.

Said guy later made me brunch and I thanked him profusely for looking after me the previous night, before returning to Kew to prepare for the evening's performance. It was a week before the bar staff let me forget that night, but Becky was sympathetic, only teasing me now and again.

She and I continued to have our post-show 'FUCK' and our conversations began to take a more intimate turn. Becky was by far the least bashful and, night after night, she made me hiccup with laughter as she related the gory details of her busy sex-life. While she was currently living with the Irish boyfriend I'd met, she had always had trouble with monogamy and seemed to constantly find herself in compromising situations with professors, strangers in bars, workmates and, currently, Raoul.

'I just *need* it, you know?'

In return, I told Becky modified versions of my own relationship history, painting Nadiyya as the tragically doomed love of my life and referring only vaguely to Matthew.

Becky's reckless love-life became a bit of a joke and, by the closing night of the show, two days before her twenty-first birthday, I was thoroughly entertained by my friend's disastrous relations with men. That night, a girl Matthew had been encouraging me to chat to on Gaydar had unexpectedly turned up at the play and asked for me after the show.

A little annoyed, I went down to talk to her. She bought me a drink and I nodded as she told me about her interests in theatre, but I kept glancing at the other end of the bar, where Becky and Raoul were doing shots and falling into each other's laps. With the bar staff giving me occasional funny looks, I grew more and more embarrassed by the sordid situation. At the first opportune moment, I excused myself and sent Becky a text from the bathroom saying: 'HELP ME!'

Five minutes later, Becky rushed up from the other end of the bar exclaiming, 'Nat, Nat, Raoul has just told me we need to start the get out tonight. It can't wait until the morning, we have to do it now!' Turning to the girl, she added, 'I'm sorry, another team's meant to do it tomorrow but something's gone wrong, it's going to take at least a couple of hours!' Before I could even shoot the girl an apologetic look, Becky clutched my wrist and dragged me out of the bar and up the stairs to the theatre, where we both collapsed in giggles.

'You're my hero,' I panted.

Three hours later, the bartenders had fed Becky multiple doubles, Raoul had tried to kiss her and I'd missed the last train back to Kew. Sat in a circle, the whole crew and various friends of Becky's swayed to the pop-music on the radio and hooted at only half-funny jokes. I perched on the arm of Raoul's chair and we both watched a boy of around nineteen try to chat Becky up.

'Shall I put him off?' Raoul asked.

'How?' I slurred.

'I'll kiss him,' he replied.

'You wouldn't!'

With that, he walked up to the boy and said, 'I've been looking at you all night and I just had to do this.' He took the boy's face in his hands and aimed his puckered lips at his mouth. The kid shrieked and ran back to the bar. Simultaneously, I grabbed Becky from her seat and took her to a different table.

Almost falling off the stool I'd planted her on, Becky looked at me and said, 'Everyone here knows I like you. Why haven't you kissed me?'

Digesting her spidery lashes, I swallowed.

After a long silence, I murmured, 'I should go. My last bus is in ten minutes.'

'Stay with me,' Becky purred.

I thought of Matthew waiting for me in Kew. Becky followed me outside, but I could say nothing except 'Sorry.' She shrugged and allowed me to walk away, shouting after me: 'Why don't you come to Philly for New Year's Eve?'

I looked over my shoulder and smiled, 'Okay.'

I missed the last bus, got stuck in Putney for an hour and fought with Matthew when I finally made it home, but Becky sent me an email saying she'd been serious, I should visit during my winter break.

With the play finished and my flight only a week away, I began to feel guilty about not seeing my family. Matthew and I decided to leave Kew at the end of the week. We would have to clean the flat ready for the new tenants, tidy baby oil, handcuffs and vibrators from the bookshelf next to the bed, and pack away the cards and Scrabble set permanently littering the fold-out dining table in the absence of a TV. My clothes would have to cease hanging beside his in the wardrobe, and our toothbrushes would need to be parted and returned to larger, cleaner, more luxurious bathrooms. Matthew would drive us both as far as Tunbridge Wells, where I would lug my suitcase onto a train and call my mum to pick me up from Battle an hour or so after Matthew pulled his Saab up to his house.

But before any of that could happen, I was to meet Nadiyya as she stumbled from the District Line.

'Baby!' She kissed me on the mouth and wrapped her arms on top of mine. 'Where is Albert?'

'He's at the flat.' I tried to smile away my nerves.

'I've missed you sooooo much.' She kissed me again as we walked. 'Hugh sends his love.'

'Oh, cool.'

'So, are you excited about tonight?'

'Yeah, of course.' I swallowed. 'We thought we'd get Chinese. Is that okay with you?'

We walked through lanes, past the tiny cemetery and up to the grand, converted building that had begun to seem like home.

'Hello?' I whispered into the gloom as I let us in. The curtains were drawn, which was not unusual for us during the day, but now struck me as shamefully seedy.

'Well, hello.' Matthew emerged from the one room, smiling and holding out his hand to Nadiyya. He was wearing his favourite dusty pink shirt and a pair of pale trousers. I saw his silver hair and the lines creasing his face, his yellowing teeth and his sagging earlobes. I noticed his old-man shoes and smelled his too-powerful Jovan Musk. I didn't dare look at Nadiyya, but wondered in horror what she was making of this bizarre situation. I felt a sick churning in my stomach, realising what a mistake it was to mix my worlds. Nadiyya, though a girl and part of something beautiful and unattainable I'd dreamt of in the sixth form, belonged to my student reality; she knew the nineteen-year-old, nightclubbing, beer-drinking Nat, not the ageless romantic Uncle who could sit with a sixty-three-year-old and cry passionate tears about his inevitable death. *This is a crazy mistake*, I thought.

But Nadiyya swallowed her surprise if she had any and launched into her characteristic 'baby's and 'darling's, telling Matthew she'd heard 'sooooo' much about him and touching both our arms as she spoke.

Our nerves quietened as we opened a bottle of wine and played some Aimee Mann. We sat around the table eating chow mein and kung pao with forks. Nadiyya asked excitedly about Rosella and quizzed Matthew on how he would cope with my absence. By the time we led and followed each other up the three stairs to the bed, Matthew and I were feeling sentimental and panicked. One of us set up a video camera on the bookshelf while the other two began kissing. I'd read that, in the majority of threesomes, the man gets left out, but as I thought more about leaving for America, I ached to be closer to Matthew.

The next morning Nadiyya gushed that she'd had a good time, but once alone Matthew and I giggled that she hadn't really got a look in. It had been a success I suppose: Matthew and I were closer than ever and I was sure we would make the long-distance thing work.

While Matthew finished vacuuming the flat and packing up the car, I walked Nadiyya to the station and lingered for a final stroll around Kew. My head full of love and Uncles, I dawdled through the streets, filling my stomach with bittersweet notions about the months to come. Passing an empty-looking tattoo parlour, an impulse rose through me like a fever.

Half an hour later, I skipped back up the hill with a small black ankh inked to my hip. Wriggling in the passenger's seat of Matthew's car, I grinned and peeled away the cling-film dressing to show my lover what I'd done.

'Wow,' he released the hand-brake and turned to the road with a smile. 'You really are mine.'

PART TWO

15

In a small office on the lower floor of the ugliest building on what I'd already come to believe must be one of the most beautiful campuses in America, Gregory Russell looked up at me from a desk of scribbled notes and hard-backed books ranging from Art History to analyses of the Russian Revolution. He had almost white hair and leathery tanned skin, but a clearly muscular body beneath his tatty T-shirt and jeans.

I stood nervously in his doorway.

'Hi,' I offered tentatively. After a pause, I continued in an apologetic rush, 'Um, sorry to disturb you. I wanted to talk to you about your directing class.'

There was blank silence that reminded me of the void of panic that catches your breath when a computer crashes in the middle of an essay you haven't yet saved. I waited for him to respond, but he merely nodded, studying me curiously. I had my hair pulled back into a low ponytail and suddenly felt conscious that my nails were bitten.

'I'm an exchange student,' I spoke to fill the silence. 'So, I don't have the credits to take the 200-level class, but they said at orientation to talk to the professor because I'm really interested in directing.'

'Are you?' He raised a messy eyebrow and stared at me some more. Ignoring my request, he said, 'Well, why don't you assistant direct my play this term? What's your name?'

I looked at him in surprise. With the offer hanging in the stuffy air, I felt that familiar pang of fear. As I had for most of my first week in America, I felt out of my depth: a child playing at an adult's game, convinced it would only be a matter of time before someone noticed that my masterpiece was simply a crayon drawing, worthy of no more than a place on the fridge.

I swallowed back my fear and told him my name. I vaguely tried to talk him out of his offer, admitting I didn't really have any experience, but he'd made up his mind and seemed quite pleased with his decision, no matter what I said. He told me it would mean a lot of watching him and taking notes, but some people would pay just to be able to observe a good director at work. Humbled and excited, I nodded. I was to go away and read the script and, if I liked it, come to the theatre at seven tomorrow for auditions.

I wandered slowly back to my dorm, thinking while I passed under the shadows of the impressive buildings and towering oaks of the ancient women's college that Professor Russell was the only person I'd met so far that hadn't immediately commented on my accent. He hadn't even blinked when I opened my mouth and had skipped any of the 'Where are you from? Oh, is that near London?' banter I'd grown accustomed to over the six days since my arrival in the US.

When I reached my dorm, I decided I couldn't face my empty room in the eaves and instead opted to sit in one of the wooden porch chairs. I took out the photocopied script Professor Russell had given me and curled up to read Mac Wellman's 'Twas the Night Before . . . in the late summer sun.

As I imagine it happening, at the very same moment, Jessica Hunt climbed out of her father's car and slammed the door shut with more force than was necessary. Her mom gave her an angry look and Jess suppressed the desire to roll her eyes. Her feelings about being back at Rosella for the beginning of senior year were, at best, mixed.

Today was her birthday and she'd just spent twenty hours in a car with both her parents. All summer, her brother and she had been planning a road trip as her transport back to school. They were going to chill out to some old-school nineties classics and stop at midnight diners and Taco Bells along the way. This way, the trip from Dallas to Delaware County would not be spent next to a crying child on a plane and, best of all, she would have her car for senior year. But the plan had died a solemn death when, on the way home from her sister's baby shower, Jess had rolled her vehicle off the road and into a ditch. Luckily unhurt, she'd clambered out of the dented mess and promptly burst into tears.

Now, heaving her suitcases out of the trunk as her father held the door open because of his back, she tried to muster some excitement. This was to be her last year of school: who knew where she would go after that and how amazing it would be to get away from this oestrogen-charged bubble?

It wasn't working. The last time she'd been on this campus was over a year ago and not an especially happy memory. Her senior year stretched before her more as a necessary sentence than an opportunity to sentimentally savour the 'final' everything and the power of being the oldest.

As a Sophomore, Jess had chosen to major in Theatre Arts and minor in German. Hoping to study abroad, she'd overloaded her Fall semester with language courses and impressed her professors with her extra-curricular reading. It was in 'From Hitler to Hesse' that she shone as the star student and secured her nomination for Student of the Year. Of course, it helped that the tutor – a PhD student from the neighbouring co-ed – was rated a ten out of ten for looks on the *Daily Jolt* website and had gaggles of first-years whispering about his chiselled jaw and toned body every time he walked past.

Unlike most of the giggling teenagers, Jess had spent quite some time talking to Mr Atlas and knew details such as where he'd spent his childhood skiing in the Alps to obtain such a physique and how he found it hard to understand why everyone walked around campus in their pyjamas. Jess was always the last to leave after class, not because she was deliberately dawdling – this happened in every class – but because she had an extraordinary ability to spread herself out. Even after the shortest of classes, she would have three notebooks and six pens, numerous scattered pieces of paper and various doodles, her phone, her glasses case, a couple of hair-ties, some Burt's Bees and possibly eye-shadow dribbled around her. In these minutes after the classroom had emptied, Jess would ask Mr Atlas seemingly random questions about language that she'd been mulling since their last session and grill him for information on regional variations in dialect. At first, her piercing curiosity had unnerved him. He had never taught a student who devoured syllabus and non-syllabus with the exact same attention. Jess seemed unaware of the fact she'd have to write a research paper and sit a midterm; she'd turn up five minutes late or early with the appearance of someone who'd been walking along the hall when it'd suddenly occurred to her to learn some German. She wanted to know everything she could and approached the language like a mathematical problem – 'If this rule works here, then what if I want to say this? And how does it change if this happens?' – coming up with the most bizarre of hypothetical situations in order to cover all possible circumstances.

In time, Atlas – as Jess soon began referring to him – began to look forward to these post-lesson chats, partly because they challenged his own knowledge and partly because of Jess herself. He became almost fascinated by her variations. His class was at 9.45am and, while with the other students he could predict which ones would stumble in bleary-eyed, which would be in full make-up and which would have the exhausted air of those who woke at 4.30 to get to crew practice, with Jess, every day was a surprise.

On the days when she wore enormous green hoodies and clashing baggy pants, he'd assume she didn't care about her appearance and sometimes wonder if she fitted the women's college stereotype and preferred girls. At other times, though, she'd strut into the room with her hair intricately knotted, her face made-up with blue eye-shadow and scarlet lips and three-inch heels transforming her slumped posture into elegant grace. On these days, he guiltily caught himself wondering if the effort was for his benefit.

It was because he knew he shouldn't be thinking this that he asked her one day if she would mind not applying her make-up actually in class as it gave the impression she wasn't listening. He hadn't meant this to sound as stern as it came out and immediately regretted it. Taken aback, she apologised and explained she'd always fiddled and doodled and it helped her concentrate, that she had never not listened in a single class and that his was her favourite subject this semester. He felt guilty and tried to make up for it. They were discussing the subjunctive as he locked the classroom door and, not wanting to end the conversation, she asked if he was free for a coffee. He didn't have another class until the afternoon and, though part of him thought it was a bad idea, he knew students and professors were often friends and seen having perfectly innocent coffees in the library café. He said yes. Over this hour-long latte, their conversation leapt from Texas to the Rhine, Oasis to Bon Jovi, dorm life to living alone in a foreign country. When it was finally time for them both to get back to their days, Jess, never having seen the point of subtlety, said she'd had fun and would like to hang out with him sometime. He ignored the alarm bells sounding in the distance and said he'd like that too. They arranged to meet in Albany at the weekend and said goodbye, each walking away smiling.

After that, they met regularly outside of class, never acknowledging anything more than a close friendship and always parting with excited promises to see each other again. When the weather improved, they went for walks around the campus and argued about the various merits of snow versus sunshine. On one particular afternoon, he'd driven them to Huntersfield Forest for a picnic. Jess was telling him she had only had one relationship at high school and it had been an awkward one; that sometimes she wondered if she wasn't just some freak destined to live alone. He looked at her and allowed some of the feelings he'd been suppressing for the past few months to seep through the dam of responsible teaching and the threat of losing his job. He touched her face and told her that would never happen, that she was the most remarkable girl he'd met. Without warning, he found himself telling her that he was scared of the feelings she aroused in him, that he knew they were wrong, not just because he was her tutor but because she was so young and he shouldn't be telling her even this.

It was Jess that kissed Mr Atlas rather than the other way around. But after that kiss, something shifted. Sometime between that first taboo confession of feelings and their final fraught fumblings, she shed her confident, Texan Lolita-meets-Natalie-Portman-in-*Leon*-and-perhaps-a-bit-of-Sharon-Stone skin and discovered something altogether more vulnerable beneath. She insisted everything was fine, but gradually stopped allowing Atlas to hold her, and he noticed she withdrew each time she saw even a hint of a rising in his pants.

In her dorm one night, Jess threw up four times in a row. She kept throwing up for two more days before dragging herself to the counselling service. In violent floods of tears she waited until they gave her an emergency appointment. Her parents were called and told their daughter had been having suicidal thoughts and it was probably best that she come home for the last two weeks of the semester. It was hell for about six months and Jess's doctors prescribed various cocktails of anti-depressants until one began to work. She spent her junior year in Texas, attending classes at the local college and working at Wal-Mart. It was quiet and simple and she got her life back together, trying not to think about Atlas and how she'd freaked out. Her family was supportive and Rosella made provisions for her grades to transfer. By the time she arrived on 3rd September 2003, she was deemed competent and happy, though still, of course, mildly medicated.

Once the car had been emptied of suitcases, boxes and last-minute remembrances that'd wedged themselves under the seat and into the glove compartment, and Jess's new room was stuffed with a disorderly pile of books, clothes and mostly green furnishings, she and her parents made their way down to the fluorescently lit dining hall.

Jess stood in the line for hot food wearing her pale green Rosella sweatshirt with baggy black combats spattered with paint from numerous get-ins and strikes. She'd shoved her strawberry-blonde hair into a messy ponytail and her feet were encased in beat-up Chuck Taylors. Before her was something claiming to be vegetarian lasagne, next to some rather anaemic-looking chicken, a bowl of broccoli, two different types of potato and some cold garlic bread. She picked out the least offensive bit of chicken while her mom, next to her, smiled broadly at the students working the kitchens and made faux-satisfied noises as she helped herself to the smallest possible slice of lasagne. Her dad whispered not very quietly in her ear that he'd seen a Cracker Barrel down the street and maybe they'd go there later.

She stood waiting for her parents to finish collecting their food and looked around for three free seats. She noticed a girl who'd lived on her floor in their first year. She asked if they could sit in the seats next to her and felt reassured by the slightly confused look of recognition on Stacey's face. She saved her the embarrassment of trying to remember where she knew her from by launching into a strained but chirpy: 'It's Stacey, isn't it? You lived in McKinley, didn't you? I'm Jess, I was Emily's roommate.'

Stacey smiled, relieved. 'Hi! You were away last year weren't you? Did you go abroad? Sorry, these are my parents, they just brought me up today.' Stacey's face was so genuine, Jess felt momentarily happy to be back at Rosella. The girl before her was pretty, but in the modest way of those who really don't know it. Jess remembered now that she and Stacey had spent an evening discussing Texas over milk and cookies (the one Rosella tradition Jess had missed) because Stacey's father was a pastor in Dallas, only a few miles from the church Jess's mother volunteered at. Jess was glad her mom and Stacey's dad were now sat at opposite ends of the table because she didn't feel like a merry discussion of religion that would undoubtedly end in her mother enquiring as to whether Jess planned to attend church on campus this year, 'Because she was rather slack in her first and Sophomore years and it really breaks my heart to think of the good Christian upbringing she had and, well, I worry it reflects badly on us as parents.'

Instead, her and Stacey's moms were politely discussing the nutritional value of the meal-plan and how they wished there was a larger salad bar. Stacey's mom was from Costa Rica and, sitting side-by-side, Jess could see where Stacey's genes came from.

Stacey smiled at Jess and she couldn't help returning it. *Stacey's sweet*, Jess thought. *Good and studious, happy and kind; she's not the type to make enemies, not the type to flirt with a professor then glue her head to a toilet. This is the sort of girl my therapist wants me to make friends with.*

'Are you taking any theatre this semester?' Stacey was asking Jess between tiny mouthfuls of salad.

'Yeah, I decided to major in it.'

'Cool, me too.'

'Really? I think I'm doing the *'Twas the Night Before . . .* practicum and I have to do a design course sometime this year. What about you?'

'Wow, what are you doing for *'Twas the Night Before . . .* ? I think I'll audition but I doubt I'll get a part. Greg told me I should try anyway.'

'You know him? What's he like? He wasn't here when I left and

I just emailed Lyn over the summer asking if she knew of anything coming up. I think I'm assistant directing, or possibly dramaturging, whatever that is.'

'Greg's really fun. He used to be an actor, then went into directing, so he has all these stories. He's a good teacher. I took his Acting 2 last semester. He doesn't give As, though.'

'Fuck, I need good marks in my theatre classes 'cause there's no way I'll get anything good in the physics requirement I still have to take.'

'Oh no, poor you, you still haven't done that? I got all my requirements out of the way last year; I guess that was one good thing about not studying abroad.'

'You stayed here? Who else was here?'

'Oh, some of the theatre people, like Alex and Hannah, but a lot went to London and Paris. Vic went to RADA, which is pretty cool. There was quite a big Sophomore group in the department so it worked out.'

The conversation went on. It was weird for Jess to think of Ruff Theatre having gone on in her absence. She'd worked on most of the plays it had staged since she arrived and had been close to a couple of the professors, both of whom had now left, one to finish his PhD and the other to teach at the neighbouring co-ed. She still vaguely knew the head of the department, Henrietta, but the only other people Jess would still recognise, according to Stacey, were: Carol, a tenured director from Michigan; Bill, the head technician; and Lyn, the department secretary. She was nervous to meet the new additions but excited too, sure the only way to survive this year would be to wrap herself in drama of a theatrical rather than a personal kind.

Knowing none of this yet, I stood awkwardly in the theatre lobby and wondered if I was meant to wait here or find the auditions for myself. Professor Russell had said 7pm and it was still only ten-to, so I decided to sit in one of the three chairs opposite the makeshift bar. I took out the photocopied script and read over the character list again. I knew I wasn't very prepared; even though I'd read the whole play yesterday on the porch, I couldn't have told someone what it was about and hoped Professor Russell wouldn't expect me to have anything too detailed to say. More and more, I felt like a fraud doing an English degree when I could quite capably read an entire novel while my mind danced through any number of thoughts and fantasies until I realised Jane Eyre, Silas Marner and Nicholas Nickleby were still no more than names and I'd have to Google them before class. Not only that, but I read slowly too, which felt like a punishable crime in academia, so I tried to keep it quiet, sitting up through the night and telling people the bags under my eyes were because I'd gone out and, yes, I too had just scanned the book an hour before the seminar.

Last night, I'd emailed Professor Russell saying I absolutely loved the play and offering some hopefully intelligent-sounding comments about absurdity and tone, but his reply had simply expressed curt satisfaction at my willingness to assistant direct and told me to come today. Now, I worried I'd sounded gushing and foolish.

'Are you Nat?' A kind-eyed girl with a clipboard poked her head out of a door I hadn't noticed. 'I'm Mel, the stage manager. Greg and the others are waiting in the theatre, come on in.'

I followed Mel back through the door and found myself at the top of the steep left-hand aisle of the auditorium. I could make out the dark shadows of two girls sat three rows from the back and saw a mess of notebooks around one of the middle seats. Professor Russell was moving plastic chairs from the stage to the wings and looked up when I entered. 'Nat! How are you? Take a seat, I'm over there, sit next to me.' I followed orders and Mel kindly pointed to the two girls, introducing them as Jackie and Jessica.

'Just Jess,' one corrected, smiling vaguely at me. 'So what you doing?'

'Um, assistant directing I think. You?'

'We're both assistant directors and dramaturgs,' Jess replied and, not knowing what a dramaturg was, I nodded and kept quiet.

'We're the Texan 'Turgs – We just made that up! Turns out we live like ten minutes away and we only just met! Are you a fresher?' This came from Jackie.

'Exchange student, I think I count as a senior.'

'Really?' Jackie's suntanned features fell into a frown. 'Probably just for registration and stuff, you don't graduate with us or anything, do you? I mean, that wouldn't be very fair. How old are you?'

'Nineteen.'

'Oh my God! And you're '06? That's kinda cool.' I quickly decided Jess was nicer; Jackie was looking really quite put out that I could be counted as a senior when I was only the same age as the first-years. 'I was twenty-two yesterday,' Jess continued. 'I feel so old!'

From: Natalie Lucas <sexy_chocolate69@sweetmail.com>
To: Matthew Wright <theoutsider@worldopen.co.uk>
Sent: 7 September 2003, 10:54:03
Subject: Hello

Hello darling,

How are you? I'm doing really well. I'm sorry I haven't emailed sooner – I still can't get the internet working in my dorm room, so I'm sending this from the library. There's a technician coming out this afternoon, though, so hopefully it'll be sorted by tonight. Maybe we can Skype?

How's England? How's Annabelle? Are you surviving?

I'm good. I'm going to be assistant directing a play, which is quite exciting. We had auditions last night and I got to know the other assistant directors and the director who is this professor called Greg who is really cool. I think you'd like him. He seems odd and tuned in, maybe Uncle material.

My classes haven't started yet, but I've been given my reading list for one of them. I'm meant to have started on it this morning, but I just got sidetracked for an hour reading the Wikipedia page about the Babylonian bible and Adam's first wife. Did you know the Christians just totally pinched the story for Genesis and cut out the coolest character? She slept with an angel and got kicked out of Eden and banished to suck the blood of small children and animals. There's something kind of awesomely sexy about that isn't there? I wonder if I can weave it into one of my essays this term.

Talking of awesomely sexy, I haven't exactly fallen into lesbian paradise like Rose told me I would. I've heard a few things, but the only people I've seen have been quite scary and butch-looking. And the first-years and international students on my floor keep shrieking and giggling whenever someone mentions anything that could be construed as even slightly gay, so I haven't really said anything yet. Maybe it's me; maybe I'll never find anyone. But still, the theatre stuff will be fun and keep me occupied until I can see you. And the campus is lovely – all old buildings and big trees in oranges and browns. There's a tiny town across the street with a bookshop and a café, but apparently you have to get a bus to go anywhere else, which I haven't tried yet.

I miss you so much. It's horrible not being able to just hear your voice or text you. I keep picturing you a million miles away and wishing we could just curl up on your chaise and read Whitman and send the rest of the world away.

Miss you with all my being,

Your Lilith

xxxx

One evening, after about two weeks of rehearsals, I sat with Jackie in Bobst café, the only place apart from the dining halls offering food on campus. We were savouring the late-night grease when she blurted, 'So, are you gay or what?'

'Excuse me?' I choked on my curly fry.

'Well, the cast have been placing bets and I said I'd try to find out. Because Mia noticed your rainbow socks, bracelet and belt, but Stacey thought maybe that meant something different in Europe.'

'Wow.' I felt heat reaching my ears. 'Well, um, I don't know, no one's ever asked me that before.'

'Really? 'Cos you're like a walking Pride flag with all that crap on. So are you?'

'Gay? Um, I guess, I mean I want to be.'

'Awesome. You certainly came to the right place then.' Jackie winked.

'Really?'

'Yeah. Only, lose the paraphernalia – rainbows are way obvious, you know?'

Over the next few weeks, I began to notice certain things about Rosella and the surrounding area. I noticed students walking to lectures and dining halls in their pyjamas, holding hands. I ventured onto the free bus to the nearest town and saw seven

165

female couples showing affection on the sidewalk and only one boy and girl sharing an ice-cream. And cycling by the sports centre early one morning, I witnessed the rugby team growling their terrifying motivational cheers.

I rang Matthew to tell him what I'd seen.

'So, Rose was right,' he mused with a hint of jealousy. 'How long until you find a little girl for us then, Baba?'

I didn't know. Rosella was beginning to feel like an upside-down world to me. It was suddenly queerer to be straight than gay, and people stared with curiosity at boys and girls in simple jeans and jumpers more than at transgender teens in leather jackets and lesbians with tattoos. My rainbows may have been too obvious, but I was beginning to notice a whole army of badges and signs, not hidden shyly beneath layers or worn as secret messages like I had, but presented proudly for the world to see, even by some of the teachers. I felt like a child in a sweet shop, frozen to the floor because, though the brightly coloured jars made my mouth water, I didn't recognise any of their contents and had no idea how to approach the counter with my order.

As I strolled through the library and lecture halls, I imagined myself part of each of the attractive fem-couples lolling on benches and carrying each other's books. Learning the lingo day by day, at night I dreamt of U-Haul clichés and a feline-filled future. Each time I left my dorm, I hoped that today I'd brush my Sapphic destiny, catch her eye and smile an apology. I pictured the two of us having coffee or agonising over flavours at the ice-cream parlour. I even scripted flirty conversations, followed by a first hesitant kiss and regular dates to hang out in companionable silence while doing our homework. After leaving my classes and finishing my errands, I returned to my dorm, deflated and angry at myself, wondering if my life might have changed had I worn a different sweater or eaten in a different dining hall.

I heard an element of concern in Matthew's telephone voice, but he continued to whisper about sweet, peach-like girls we could take to New York when he came to visit. I giggled and moaned in all the right places, but more than anything, his stories reminded me how different I was, how hopeless it was to imagine I might fit in, even here. I cried most evenings, wishing Matthew's arms were around me, wishing the world was full of Uncles. I talked enthusiastically about the play, but checked airfares daily and finally booked a flight to go home for Christmas. I told my parents I'd be spending the whole winter break with Becky in Philadelphia, but plotted a weekend in London with Matthew, followed by turning up on my mum's doorstep as a surprise on Christmas Eve. Knowing I'd see Matthew soon soothed my nightly loneliness and I stopped rushing home to Skype after rehearsals.

16

'Hey, Greg! Are you gonna invite us for dinner again?'

I gaped at Jess who was standing in her 'Don't Mess With Texas' T-shirt as if she hadn't just asked a senior faculty member to feed us for the second time in a week.

'Shut up, you asshole.' Greg glanced around. 'I'm not having the whole campus over.'

Jess shrugged and slumped into one of the red chairs on the end of a row, throwing her green sneakered feet onto the one in front.

'BEE! WHERE'S BEE?' hollered Mel and a skinny girl bounced onto the stage, still swallowing the remains of a bag of chips.

Rehearsals lasted another hour and a half, after which Jess and I dawdled in the lobby while the cast said goodnight.

Finally, Greg plodded out of the auditorium.

'Lucas, how old are you?' he demanded.

'Nineteen,' I replied sheepishly.

'You creep. I want to go to a bar.' He paused to look at me. 'You seem kind of like an adult.'

At that, he stalked past us and headed in the direction of the parking lot.

'Are you coming?' he yelled over his shoulder. 'I have an eggplant.'

Jess and I gathered our backpacks and scurried after him, childishly vying for shotgun.

'I'm reading a lot of Art History at the moment – T. J. Clark on Courbet, Kirk Varnedoe on American art after Pollock, the theorist Michael Fried.' As usual, Greg had refused to let us help and was crushing garlic with the side of a knife. 'I think my next play will be an Ionesco. Have you read *The Bald Soprano*?'

I shook my head dumbly as I always did when he asked me if I'd read something and he muttered what sounded like, 'Of course you haven't.'

'Where do you find time to read all this, Greg?' Jess was reclined on a dining chair, munching olives. I was still swilling my first stone, unsure what to do with it in the absence of a visible bin.

'I get up at five and read. It's the only thing that makes being here bearable.'

'What about us?' Jess spluttered. '*'Twas* is good,' she added.

'It's very good only because I'm a very patient and skilful director.' He winked. 'No, there are some good actors and I like having you two. I'm not sure about this dramaturg business, but it's good to have a number of assistants.'

I smiled to myself, remembering Jess and Jackie's rant in the green room earlier about how Greg just wants a scribe and won't let you do anything as an assistant director. The two of them were smug that they had dramaturg work to do as well and I was the one stuck making his rehearsal notes. I'd nodded in the appropriate places but felt rather guilty agreeing with them when I was still simply grateful Greg had chosen to give me a chance.

'Some of the others are a little shy, though,' Greg continued, adding things to a skillet. 'They don't know how to be with adults. There's something about this campus; it's very sheltered.'

Jess snorted but Greg ignored her, turning his iguana eyes on me. 'What are you doing here, Ms Lucas?'

'I dunno,' I shrugged, finally placing my olive stone on the edge of the tablecloth. 'I didn't know anything about it; I just wanted to get out of England.'

'You didn't get to choose where you went?' asked Jess, startled.

'No, they just advertised they were doing an exchange and I applied. They said it was going to be rural but that was it.'

'Ha, rural all right!' she hooted. I was beginning to piece together Jess's utter hatred of this place, but despite a nagging feeling that I should maybe hang around with more positive people, I realised I liked her.

'Is that eyeliner?' Greg had come over to the table in order to peer into my face.

'Uh, yeah. It's the only make-up I know how to apply.' I felt self-conscious and glanced pleadingly at Jess.

'It's a shame.' Greg's voice was flat, the same one he used when describing the actors' abilities. 'We thought you were exotic, but you're just plain old English, aren't you?'

'Sorry.'

Greg returned to the cooking and to the previous conversation. 'The faculty keep to themselves too. I ask them to come see a show and they claim they're working day and night. My roommate is in Gender Studies and they seem more sociable. They hang out here and have long, profound conversations deep into the night. I'd rather discuss art, of course, but I'll take what I can get.'

'You go home to New York at the weekends, right?' I asked.

'Yes. You girls should come to the city. I spend a lot of time with my children watching very bad and very good movies and reading books and eating at brilliant little restaurants. That's my pleasure. And, in the summer, I go to my house in the country and hang out with friends.'

Greg was now bringing plates piled with twisting pasta in a steaming purple sauce to the table.

'Violà, pasta alle melanzane!'

* * *

170

An hour or two later, Jess and I glanced at the empty plates before us, knowing we needed to offer to wash up before we left, but disinclined to hurry that moment. The conversation had moved from theatre to art, then to Rosella gossip and sexuality in general. Greg finished his glass and turned his attention to Jess.

'So, Ms Hunt. What's your story? You're a senior, right? Why haven't we worked together before?'

Jess's cheeks were flushed and she was leaning comfortably upon the table.

'I took a year off to chill out. Basically, I went crazy after dating a professor.'

My eyes widened involuntarily, but Greg sat up casually and laughed.

'Y'all are so funny!' Jess swilled the half-mouthful left in her glass.

'Please expand,' Greg said eagerly. 'What did you do? I hope it was something really terrible.'

'It's not like that.' Jess finished her wine, then sighed. 'Uh, I took an intensive elementary German class and started hanging out with my professor. It was fine and only mildly flirty until the summer. We AIMed all the time and eventually we kind of tried dating, but it was weird.'

'Go on,' Greg murmured.

'I'm kind of messed up about sex. When things started to head that way, my body flipped out and I started throwing up all the time. Eventually I saw a therapist who sent me home when I told her I wanted to die.' Jess added with a forced laugh, 'Good times!'

'That's terrible.' Greg was looking angry. 'This guy should be fired. Is he still here?'

Jess nodded.

'A professor has way too much power to be messing around with students. I may raise eyebrows by having students over to my house, but I'd never do something like that. How old was this creep?'

'Thirty-six.' Jess was not embarrassed. Later, I would ask her about that and she'd say she had spent a year dealing with it and was now going through an 'honesty phase'.

'God, that's really disgusting.' Greg paused. 'So you saw a therapist? Did they put you on Prozac?'

'Yes, actually,' Jess replied and for the first time Greg looked uncomfortable.

'Sorry, I won't make any more jokes about therapy. You could tell us about your therapist. Is that allowed? Male? Female? Mysterious? Helpful? Insane?'

We all laughed and any awkwardness subsided. Jess and I stacked the plates and took them to the sink. Greg disappeared while we washed up to locate a book he wanted to lend me, then walked out with us so he could smoke a menthol cigarette. He thrust the rest of the packet at us and told us he'd given up. Just past the art museum, he uttered, 'Enough, I'm going to bed,' and stalked back into the night.

Greg, Jess and I had dinner two or three times a week for the rest of the rehearsal period. Greg and I learnt more about Jess's scandalous past and I gave carefully censored descriptions of my own relationship history. Greg described growing up abroad, travelling the world, and acting for directors whose names I pretended to recognise, then looked up later. He told me to read his mentors and littered his theatre stories with intense descriptions of following a beautiful girl for thirty blocks only to lose his nerve and turn home, or debauched tales of women climbing through his apartment window so his girlfriend wouldn't find out.

'I've never cheated on my wife,' he said more than once. 'Marriage and children change everything.'

Jess and I would curl under her duvet and discuss what Greg had said. Jess wasn't so sure she believed his protestations of fidelity and the rumours circling the theatre department vehemently contradicted his statements, but I trusted him.

Over the coming weeks, I also used our impromptu sleepovers to pry further details about Jess's past. Her professor had insisted throughout that he'd never done anything like this before and that he was falling in love with her. But one evening, after they'd made out for an hour on his bed and he'd removed her bra, whispering about how they could move to Berlin once she'd graduated and start afresh where no one knew them, Jess had excused herself to the bathroom and burst into tears. When she re-emerged and calmed down enough to be coherent, Atlas had kindly offered to help her with her German homework instead.

Jess was the first person I'd known on anti-depressants and her honesty thrilled me. In return, she'd fish for information from me as I let details slip one by one over many too-tipsy evenings. I was careful to avoid specifics and made her promise not to tell Greg that I may or may not have my own older man waiting for me in England.

17

'Girls, I want to talk to you.'

Greg had been quiet in rehearsals. The tech was tomorrow and things were busy, but everything seemed pretty much on schedule and, in my humble opinion, the play looked fantastic.

'I'm not sure I should have you over any more.'

Jess and I sat opposite each other at his dining-room table and now mirrored one another in the confused and somewhat fearful gazes we directed across the room.

'I do like you and I like being with you in the theatre and having people to chat to afterwards – you both have guts and tenacity and that's refreshing here – but sometimes it scares me.'

Jess and I sat motionless. I was more shocked than embarrassed and an uncomfortable feeling began to creep from my toes. Greg's kitchen was one of the few places I felt truly relaxed in this strange country, but now my calves were tense and an acidity on my tongue told me I might be about to lose this safe place.

'You are such good pals, I am so fond of you, and at times, I admit, I just like being with people so passionate and young. Forgive me if this embarrasses you.'

Stop! Cut! Hold! Freeze! I wanted to shout. I couldn't form it in words but I knew the area of my mind he was about to force me to acknowledge and I knew I didn't want to have this conversation. I was certain Jess didn't either. Sure, we'd had a heavy tipsy chat late one night a while back, wrapped up in comforters in my dorm room, about how we were confused by simultaneously wanting Greg to be our dad and wanting him to find us attractive. And we had contemplated renting from the library the ancient arthouse film the cast kept playing in the green room in which a younger Greg gets naked. But we hadn't rented the film and we hadn't beaten up our psyches over possibly inappropriate desires because there were two of us who felt the same, because we trusted Greg never to hurt us and because we loved the friendship as it was.

'Now, I don't give a damn what the department heads say about me inviting students round,' Greg continued, turning to the counter as if he was about to start preparing us a meal. 'I'd never do anything, you know that.'

There was a pause and Jess shifted her head to her elbow. She seemed calm, perhaps even amused. I held my breath.

'But I find myself hanging out with the two of you, talking about theatre and bodies and Jess's creepy older man. And it's fascinating. But then, when you leave, I feel so alone in this weird place.'

Greg stopped. He fixed his slouch and turned to face us. When he began again, his voice was cold, as if he was suddenly bored by the conversation. I worried he was about to ask us to leave. 'I'm not sure how appropriate it is, that's all. It seems like a kind of creepy Nabokovian thing and I can't excuse myself for it. So I think maybe it's best, especially if you're taking my class next semester, that we try to be a little more appropriate.'

I chewed a fingernail and realised with embarrassment that I would not be able to respond without my voice cracking.

Jess broke the silence. 'Um, not so much.' She sat up straight so her mint T-shirt unfolded and I could read the 'Howdy', which I knew was accompanied by a 'Dammit' on the back. She looked

175

brazenly at Greg. 'Seriously, we appreciate the sentiment, but you don't creep us out and obviously we like your company, so it would be totally lame for us to stop hanging out.'

Greg seemed taken aback for a moment, but eventually the lines on his face smoothed and he began to reassume his characteristically cocky posture. 'Oh really, Ms Hunt? You think you can demand my company?'

'You just need to chill out.'

I looked at Jess in amazement.

'You don't think I'm a creepy older professor, luring you into my trap, like all the other girls seem to fear I am?'

'Whatevs.' Jess didn't appear to have experienced any of the things I had in the last ten minutes.

'And what about you, Ms Lucas? Is this how you feel?'

I looked from Jess to Greg and wondered what to say. I couldn't play Jess's game, even if it might have been the best method of dealing with Greg's little crisis. But I also couldn't even begin to tell Greg how desperately I wanted to keep coming to his house, keep listening to his and Jess's tales, keep feeling like I belonged somewhere.

'Uh, yeah, I think so. I mean, I don't think you're creepy. And, I kind of really like that we can talk about sex and everything, but that I can also trust you and feel safe here. It's only awkward now you've said it.'

'Yes, I see that,' Greg reached for a saucepan. 'I don't really understand you two very well, but as long as you don't mind me perving into your lives a little, I guess I can accept my role as the old goat.'

The conversation that followed was somewhat stilted, but by the end of dinner we were laughing like normal. Jess moaned that she'd never find a boyfriend at Rosella, I told them I was too scared of the militant lesbians to hit on anyone, and Greg told us he thought we were both stupid because Dylan, a boy from the co-ed with a role in *'Twas*, was 'eminently fuckable'.

Shortly after that comment, Jess finished drying the dishes and Greg looked at us pointedly: 'Enough. Now I sleep.'

Jess and I said our goodbyes and stumbled into the chilly darkness.

The following day, I sat at my desk and carefully typed an email:

> **From: Natalie Lucas <sexy_chocolate69@sweetmail.com>**
> **To: Matthew Wright <theoutsider@worldopen.co.uk>**
> **Sent: 12 October 2003, 08:36:21**
> **Subject: Us**
>
> Dear Matthew,
>
> This is hard to write. I don't want to cause you pain.
>
> Please know that I never want to regret anything, but I'm in this new place and I want to try living a new life. I'm sorry I have to hurt you in doing this, but please understand I need my space.
>
> You have made me who I am and I owe you everything, but now I need to learn for myself. I hope we can find a way to be friends.
>
> I will always love you.
>
> Nat x

My nineteen-year-old brain told me this was the friendliest way I could end things with the man I had given my soul to. I did not blame him for anything and I truly wanted to stay friends, but I wanted to be close to him like I was to Greg – without the passion, arguments and lies that had dictated our lives for the past three years.

Matthew's sixty-three-year-old brain, however, told him (and he in turn told me) that I was being an ungrateful, spoiled brat and I was ruining both our lives. My inbox exploded with expletives, curses, begs, threats and flattery.

I stuck to my resolution, though. On a bus back from a party, holding a broken umbrella and tasting sour beer on my breath, I told Jess most of the details, omitting only Matthew's age. The day 'Twas the Night Before . . . opened, she and I donated eleven inches of hair to Locks of Love. Two weeks later, I cropped my remaining bob into boyish spikes and marched into the closest tattoo parlour to have my nipple pierced.

Over the coming months, I worked to construct the normal life I'd desired. I shrugged off Jess's persistent questions about Matthew's age in the same way that each morning, after I closed my bedroom door behind me and reminded myself of the protective Atlantic Ocean, I could ignore the fact I'd just sobbed for an hour before ten violent and accusatory emails. In overheated classrooms, noisy dining halls and on the snowy walkways of the Rosella campus, I was learning to be my new self: a slightly dorky, very shy but sometimes funny little lesbian without a past, without pain and without a head full of poetry beneath her blunt bangs.

18

That first semester, disinclined to return to Atlas's German classes, Jess had taken up Spanish. When one day towards the end of term she asked me to come over and help her pick out an outfit for their final conversation group, I wondered who my straight friend was trying to impress on this campus of women. After some prying, she gushed about a flirtation with Angelo, her Mexican-born professor who always dawdled out of the building with her and observed she was a fast learner.

'It's okay, he's married,' she insisted with her tongue poking out the corner of her mouth as she flecked her eyelashes with mascara. 'Nothing's going to happen; it's just fun to flirt.'

I laughed at Jess, but when Greg found out, he called her an 'asshole' and Angelo a 'creep'.

Angelo was married to a Literature professor from Ireland. A few weeks after *'Twas*, while they were having an innocent coffee, Angelo told Jess that he and his wife were separating. He'd found out she'd had a year-long affair with a female PhD student, herself in a civil partnership with one of the librarians.

Within a month, Jess was spending most of her nights at Angelo's new apartment and Greg was ranting regularly to me about how unethical and idiotic this man must be. Jess began to wear her summer camp 'Love A Teacher' T-shirt and complained that every time she spoke to Greg he made her cry. I had to lie to our mutual friends about Jess's disappearances and began to grow annoyed with the frequency with which I ate in the dining halls alone.

Though I felt happy to see my friend smiling and gushing about how she and Angelo would move in together after she graduated and no longer have to keep their relationship a secret, I also felt betrayed. Each morning and evening I sat in front of Matthew's latest eight-page email with less and less conviction. I wondered what was real, whether I had made a mistake, whether perhaps he was right (perhaps I *was* a child with no brain and no thought of anyone but herself). I tried moving around the furniture in my room, playing Alanis Morissette at full volume, walking aimlessly through the snow and watching *House* on the communal television downstairs, but Matthew's vile and violent words leapt from my laptop screen into my head, followed me around and crawled beneath my skin. How could I have imagined I could be normal? It had seemed possible with Jess and Greg and a play to work on, but when it was just me and my library books in a strange country with the only person in the world I hadn't lied to wanting me dead, the whole notion seemed absurd.

Without Jess to demand food and wine, I also spent less time at Greg's. I think it struck us both as less acceptable if it were just the two of us, and I feared the conversation wouldn't run as easily without our brazen Texan mediator.

Still, after a few weeks of sad 'goodnights' at the end of Tuesday evening classes, I was whining loudly about having no kitchen and being bored with campus food, and Greg finally invited me over alone.

'Thanks, I've missed this,' I murmured as he handed me the things to lay the table.

'I only miss you when I think about you.'

I hiccupped an unsure laugh.

'I have been very nice to Jess and answer all her emails promptly, but she's a fool. Doesn't she know he could lose his job? Doesn't *he* know it? And all this business with the wife.'

I responded appropriately, venting my anger at my friend but trying not to fuel Greg's rage. Jess did know he could lose his job and she also knew how much dating her last language professor had screwed her up, but I understood her desire for drama and the thrill of something so illicit.

Greg's criticism turned to the independent study Jess was supposed to be writing with him and the meetings she kept cancelling. He raved about the department and the miserable students who didn't turn up to his classes and I realised, in the weeks I hadn't spoken to him, Greg had become more misanthropic and lonely than usual.

'You and I, my dear, we know that theatre is not just egomaniacal clowns singing musicals, but also Robert Wilson and Beckett. And that "acting" – or "smacting" as Richard Maxwell describes it – is something that is constantly being renegotiated and examined.'

He paused to drain his glass.

'What do you want to do with your life, Lucas?'

I sighed automatically, 'I dunno.'

'Do you want to direct? I've put so much effort into you, don't let it be a waste.'

'I like it, but I'm not sure I'm so good at it. Academia seems safer.'

Greg looked at me. 'I am, of course, very biased, but I think you should be an artist and take chances and work with your imagination and heart.' He broke his gaze as I blushed and began to clear the plates. 'What are you doing in the summer? You should come to my house in the country and swim in the beautiful river and meet my friends and family who would enjoy you as much as I do. My friends like to get drunk and float down the river and

181

eat. They are all very nice and smart but being older means you are not so worried about being intelligent. You would find them dumb and friendly.'

I helped him wash up and walked back to my dorm alone. I curled onto my bed under the eaves with my laptop and stared at the number 6 beside the word Inbox. In a neat column of blue I read each repeated 'Matthew Wright – RE: Your decision.' I knew I should leave them until the morning or ignore them altogether, but Greg's kind words had left me feeling warm and I suddenly felt a masochistic urge to destroy that feeling by reimmersing myself in my own illicit world. Clicking at random, I read:

From: Matthew Wright <theoutsider@worldopen.co.uk>
To: Natalie Lucas <sexy_chocolate69@sweetmail.com>
Sent: 15 November 2003, 11:14:52
Subject: I'm not throwing you a lifejacket

You're even more foolish than I thought if you think you can reinvent yourself.

I never tried to stop you growing and I always knew you would grow away from me. I knew my situation was a doomed one. But I asked for one thing: respect. And you haven't been able to give me that.

I'm old and I've read and seen a lot, but I know nothing. Nothing except love. That's all that matters. And that is the only thing I tried to teach you. You will learn it one day. But it will be too late for me.

Most men will not swim before they are able to. Ring any bells? It's Hesse.

182

If you carry on this pig-headed search for a new, super, independent you, who doesn't need Uncles and turns left when a friendly stranger suggests right . . .

. . . well then, Natalie, you will not swim:

you will drown.

19

Rosella was to give us three days off for Thanksgiving. To me this didn't seem like very long, but others considered it an adequate length of time to fly to Oakland, Houston, Chicago or Orlando, eat some of Mom's pumpkin pie and fly back again in time for classes on Monday. As the holiday drew near, I realised I was going to be stuck on campus all by myself and, unless I wanted to learn how to knit with the other international students, I needed to make plans.

'Why don't you go to the city?' Greg asked. 'You've been here for almost three months and you haven't visited New York. You're crazy, Lucas. You could stay at my place if you liked, feed my cats while we're in the country.'

'Really?' I gaped at him, wondering a) if he was serious and b) if there was something 'weird' (as defined by this new world of appropriate nineteen-year-old behaviour I was trying to adapt to) about this offer.

'Sure. I mean, you should find someone to go with you, might be a bit strange on your own and I wouldn't want our nice little Brit getting lost in the big ol' city, but you'd be doing us a favour.'

My heart sank. Who would go with me? Everyone at Rosella was returning home.

After an hour or two of moping in my dorm room and

wondering why my exciting year abroad was proving so unexciting, I wandered down to the room shared by three freshers I sometimes hung out with. They were each sprawled on their beds with their laptops open, various Target comforters, 'husband' pillows and posters defining their three separate areas of the room.

'Hey, what's up?' the girl with a chic blown-up black-and-white photograph of a Parisian street above her head asked.

'Not much,' I replied. 'I'm still wondering what to do for Thanksgiving.'

'Oh, poor you,' cooed the brunette surrounded by images of Justin Timberlake. 'I wish I could invite you to mine, but we've already got fourteen for dinner and my mom would freak.'

'Oh, I didn't mean it like that,' I blurted, embarrassed. 'Someone's offered me their apartment in New York and I really want to see the city, but I don't have anyone to go with.'

'Oh wow, you should definitely do that,' piped up the skinny blonde with kittens on her comforter. 'I love New York.'

'Hey,' JT-girl bounced into an excited sitting position. 'You could put a thing on Rosella Social.'

'Is that the weird internet thing you were telling me about before?' I replied, dubious.

'It's not weird,' cut in kitten-girl. 'It's really cool. It's this new thing where you can talk to people on campus and arrange events and things. Like MySpace, but just for us.'

'I never really got into MySpace,' I mumbled.

'Whatever,' dismissed JT-girl. 'Anyway, you can use these event organiser things. Like, you can set up a whole party and invite everyone. Or you can just post messages or questions to all your friends. We could totally set up a note or something to see if any of your friends want to go to the city.'

I took a little more persuading, but eventually I was lured onto the French-photo-girl's bed and quizzed about my favourite films, books and hobbies so they could set me up a profile. I didn't correct them when they automatically listed 'Men' under the category of 'Interested in' and, unsure how it might connect but nevertheless worried about Matthew and his emails, I insisted they set my security settings to the highest available level and that I'd add a photo myself some other time. Twenty minutes later, I had a rather generic sounding profile next to a picture of a cat, my supposed representation of myself. Reminded of Harriet Moore's Gaydar quest, I swallowed a heavy lump in my throat.

'Add me as a friend.' Kitten-girl grabbed the laptop and punched something in until her own, much more detailed profile came up.

'Yeah, and me,' said Frenchy. 'Then we'll search for all your theatre friends and anyone else you know from classes and stuff.'

It felt weird to list the names of someone I'd only said a few hellos to in Dr Broderick's Lit 307 class, the girl in the room directly beneath me who'd lent me her hair-straighteners and the lighting designer for *'Twas the Night Before . . .* , whose name I only remembered because she had the same surname as a girl I'd known at primary school. But with each search, a photo and list of interests appeared and I couldn't help but be intrigued. After finding Rachael Rose, Martha Haas and Jackie Handsford's profiles, it was easy to flick through their friends and add the rest of my classmates, dorm neighbours and those involved with *'Twas*. Within an hour, I had thirty-six friends pending.

'Now for the note,' said JT, dragging the mouse over to a sidebar. 'Here you go, write something about wanting to go to New York, and all your friends will be able to see it.'

'Uh, okay.' My fingers hovered over the keys for a while until I eventually typed a clumsy:

Hey,

So this little international student has no turkey to eat and the use of an apartment in Manhattan – anyone want to ditch the Brit bashing and head to the city with me?

'That's really cool,' giggled Frenchy. 'Now we just click send, and hopefully you'll get some replies.'

I left the girls to their homework and took a shower before dinner.

It was two days before I remembered about Rosella Social again and, thinking I had nothing to lose, I keyed in my password and logged on.

All thirty-six of my friends had been confirmed and, to my surprise, I had three more requests. Nobody had replied to my message, however, and I logged off feeling excruciatingly lonely. The next day, though, I had an email from Dylan, the co-ed student Greg had described as 'eminently fuckable' even as he danced around the stage in an elf costume.

Hey little Brit

I was hanging out with Jackie and she showed me your
message on the social thing. I'm not sure about ditching the
Brit bashing completely, but my family only lives in Kingston,
so, if you like, you could come to mine for Thanksgiving,
then we could drive down to New York on the Friday.
Where's this apartment you have available? Is it central?

Let me know. It'd be rad to hang out with you.

Dylan
x

Dylan. I hadn't imagined going to Manhattan with a boy. After all, I'd only met three since landing in this country. But Dylan seemed nice. We'd danced at the after-show party and I remembered him asking what part of England I was from while we both topped up our drinks. Rumour had it he'd gone home with Katy that night, but there was also some gossip that he wouldn't kiss a

187

girl he wasn't in love with. Of course, I wasn't looking for anything, but Dylan *was* undeniably sexy and it might be fun to get to know him better. Yes, Dylan could be a suitable companion. And if he was offering to drive, that was even better. As the girls down the hall might say: awesome. I had plans.

Dylan's mom made a fuss of me and his brothers shot cheeky smiles that made me wonder what he had told them about us spending the holiday together. After an evening of 'Oooh, I love your accent' and 'Have you really never tasted pumpkin pie before?' Dylan drove us back to his dad's place and I snuggled into the warm wooden-framed bed, imagining what it would be like to have three brothers, a dog and a grandma who cooked secret-recipe stuffing and poured you warm apple cider as you walked in the door.

I woke on Thanksgiving morning to find six inches of snow. The first proper falling since I'd arrived. Tiptoeing excitedly to Dylan's door, I listened to see if he was awake and knocked as soon as I heard a stir. With scarves and coats over our pyjamas, I dragged him through the kitchen and out into the white blanket. The sun had sprinkled gold dust onto the cotton-wool ground and I kicked my boots through the powder as I made my way out into the surrounding fields. Dylan followed and scooped up a handful of snow, deliberately missing me but laughing as I squealed and spun around. We chased each other clumsily, our shoes squidging into the soft ground, compacting the snow and leaving asymmetric patterns in the neat blanket.

'You've done it now,' I growled as one of Dylan's snowballs hit my cheek.

'You'll never get me!' Dylan took off to an untouched corner of the field and I tried to follow, slipping and thrusting out my arms to break my fall.

'Eat it,' he giggled, gently pushing my face into the ground after having doubled back on himself.

'Enough!' I rolled over and gasped for breath between giggles. Dylan sat down in the snow beside me and we both lay back to make snow angels.

'I can't believe it snowed for you on Thanksgiving,' Dylan spoke after a while.

'Yeah, it's pretty amazing,' I said, still out of breath.

'New York's going to be so pretty like this. I have to take you to Central Park.'

'Definitely.' My feet were sweating in their boots and in comparison I was enjoying icy trickles against the back of my neck and the gaps of wrist between my gloves and coat. 'Hey, do you mind if I check my email when we get inside? I think Greg was going to send me some instructions about the cats.'

'Sure. Whatever you like. My dad's cooking dinner for about three.' Dylan rolled over to face me and added with a wink, 'So we can do what we like until then.'

'As if!' I punched him lightly and began to scramble to my feet.

Back in the house, Dylan showed me to an ancient PC in the den and I waited while it booted up and Dylan keyed in the password for the dial-up internet.

'I won't be long,' I promised as I directed the browser to the Sweetmail page.

'Take your time, I'll make some coffee.'

'Thanks.' I typed my username as Dylan shut the door behind him.

My inbox loaded with an accusatory '26' at the top of the page. I had braced myself for this. I was looking for an email from Greg and I was just going to ignore Matthew until I got back to campus. This was my holiday and I wasn't going to let him ruin it.

But as I scanned the list of senders, my eyes accidentally brushed the subject column and saw in neat repetition that every message but one was labelled: 'PLEASE READ: Our friend Rose.'

It was probably a trick. Just another way to shout abuse at me. He was probably telling me how awful I was and how disappointed

189

Rose was in me. Again. But twenty-five times? I shouldn't click, I knew that. I should open Greg's email (impotently sandwiched halfway down the column of Matthew's), then go and drink coffee with Dylan and enjoy my Thanksgiving. But I clicked on one.

From: Matthew Wright <theoutsider@worldopen.co.uk>
To: Natalie Lucas <sexy_chocolate69@sweetmail.com>
Sent: 24 November 2003, 06:37:29
Subject: PLEASE READ: Our friend Rose

Natalie

Rose died last night. In her sleep. She suffered no pain.

I thought you should know.

Despite my ever more desperate quest for queer love, I found myself enjoying Dylan's company that weekend. With his kind smiles and gentlemanly gestures, he reminded me of Tim and, for a fleeting moment, I wondered what I was missing in Durham this year. For three days we ate nothing but bagels. From Greg's third floor apartment, we wandered all around Greenwich Village, checking out market stalls and lingering in bookshops. We took the subway up to an Egon Schiele exhibition Greg had recommended, giggled in the bustle at Times Square, took pictures of each other beneath signs for Actors' Square, hopped over to Long Island to visit PS1 and watched two Pinter plays off off Broadway. Though I occasionally imagined I saw a figure cloaked in red in the shadows beneath fire escapes and in the windows of passing cabs, and I wondered absurdly as I fell asleep in Greg's daughter's bed whether the dead could hear my thoughts, I enjoyed the weekend. By the time we left on Sunday, I'd decided to be in love with New York.

20

I tumbled towards my check-in desk at 8.15, resigned to the fact and half wishing that I was too late and would not be able to fly. It was 23rd December. I'd spent the night on Greg's couch and left plenty of time to get to JFK, but this was the day the metro staff had chosen to strike. My carefully planned trip from Manhattan to Brooklyn and on to Howard Beach had been interrupted by mandatory train and line changes, and here I was with just forty-five minutes until my flight took off.

Matthew and I had managed to be civil via email for the past week and we'd decided to stick to the plan of surprising my mother. A couple of days in the same country might even give us a chance to clear the air, I thought, to begin the friendship I still hoped we'd have. He'd requested I spend time with him in London before driving back to Sussex, as per the original plan. I'd refused his offer of a night in a hotel with some woman he was 'lining up' and endured a brief series of abusive emails as punishment, but we finally settled on a plan to meet at Heathrow, have lunch on the South Bank, see a matinee and drive back together. Nobody else in England knew I was coming home: I was going to hide in a box on my mother's doorstep and, when Matthew rang the bell, pop out as a living Christmas present.

It occurred to me now that it might not be entirely safe that the only person who knew my travel plans was the man who for the past two months had been schizophrenically declaring his passionate love for and vile hatred of me. I was also aware that a day in London with him, especially after a seven-hour flight and a five-hour time shift, was unlikely to go well. Perhaps missing my flight would be a blessing. Perhaps Greg would take pity on me and let me stay for Christmas; I could hole up in his cosy place in the country, sipping whisky and reading books by a log fire, far from England, far from Matthew.

But no, I was fast-tracked through security and made it to my aisle seat with time to spare. The flight was running behind schedule, which would cause Matthew to wait an extra hour at the other end, cause me to feel too guilty to check my matted hair and apply eyeliner in the bathroom before meeting him, and add to the general misery of the day-that-should-have-been-night before me.

'You look like a boy.' Matthew eyed my haircut with disdain.

'Thanks.' I fought my jet lag and apprehension and tried to muster a smile.

'Don't apologise for being late or anything.' He grabbed my bag.

'Um, sorry. It wasn't exactly my fault,' I snapped.

'Never mind. Sorry, that was the wrong foot. Hello Baba.' I winced involuntarily at the familiar nickname. 'How was your flight?'

'Long, but okay,' I shrugged.

'Right, well our play is at two, so I thought we'd go to that restaurant under the train-tracks. Nobody should see us there if that's what you're worried about.'

'Okay.' I swallowed, annoyed that that *was* what I was worried about, even though we were no longer doing anything wrong.

'My car's in C, wherever that is.' Matthew looked confusedly at the blue and yellow signs before us.

I remember only two things about the lunch that followed. The first is diving into the bathroom as soon as we arrived and wincing at my greasy hair and shadowy eyes. My short, blunt, side-parted bob had matted itself to my scalp and, had some cruel person felt the need to attack me with a marker pen as I slept, I would have made an uncanny Hitler. My stomach churned and I sat on the porcelain wishing I could go home and shower and face Matthew another day, in clean clothes and with good hair.

The second thing I remember is the way the waiter treated me as I emerged from the bathroom. Matthew had already found a table and ordered wine and the menus, but my mouth was dry so I approached the bar and asked in my nicest, politest RP if I could please have a glass of water.

'Certainly, um, Mrs Sumac,' the waistcoat replied with a vague curling of his lips.

The play was less mortifying, but perhaps only because I dozed through the second half. Matthew and I discussed the set and how the lead was developing the complexities of Willy Loman's character, but still my cells screamed to be taken home.

Finally I was. I doubt we spoke much as Matthew drove us along the A21 and we arrived at his house. I exchanged stilted pleasantries with Annabelle over a cup of tea and she excitedly presented me with a washing-machine box that she wanted me to jump out of. Though Matthew and I had discussed this plan via email, I now felt sleepy and unimpressed, and asked if maybe we could just ring the bell and have me step from around the corner. While Annabelle was in the loo, Matthew shouted that they'd gone to a lot of effort for me. In the end I folded myself into the cardboard and waited as they rang my mum's doorbell to say a parcel had arrived at their house by mistake.

'Surprise!' I shouted as I burst through the flaps and my mother looked on in astonishment. 'Merry Christmas!'

* * *

As per the tradition I only had my former self to blame for insti-
gating, the neighbours were to descend on my mum's house for
an evening roast on Christmas Day. The morning would be spent
unwrapping presents and drinking tea with my mother and James.
After a late breakfast, my brother and I would cross town to fill
up on chocolate, coffee and clipped small talk with my dad, who
would no doubt be in the middle of an elaborate DIY project
involving a hole in the ceiling and to which he would be keen to
get back. Then we'd return to Mum's, discussing whether or not
we should feel guilty that our father was alone on this of all days,
probably concluding that he'd brought it on himself and moving
on to the more pressing topic of whose present he'd scrimped on
most. The meandering afternoon would be spent half-heartedly
reading books I'd been given, helping my mum in the kitchen
and being beaten by my brother at various PlayStation games.
Around six, I'd rummage through my carry-on-only luggage for
something to change into, despair that nothing looked good,
before wondering whom I was trying to impress now anyway.
Fighting back bile in my throat, I'd choose a red dress and black
tights and try parting my hair on the right instead of the left.
Finishing with a touch more eyeliner, I'd hurry down the stairs
to answer the doorbell, aware that my mum was busy humming
along to Annie Lennox and steaming the veg in the kitchen and
James always figured someone else would answer the door. And
there, before me, would stand the old man I'd loved and fucked
for the past three years, next to his wife and several of our other
neighbours.

'Merry Christmas,' offered Annabelle with a weak smile once I'd
fully opened the door. I wondered how much she knew about my
October email and events since.

'Merry Christmas,' I echoed numbly, before the persona
kicked in and I chirped appropriately: 'Come in! Come in! It's
freezing out there. Can I take your coats? Mum's in the kitchen,

she'll be up in a second. There are drinks laid out in the living room.'

Barbara, Richard, Beatrice, Valerie, Lydia, Hannah, Graham, Lucy, Matthew and Annabelle were ushered into the warm house. 'Oh, I love your scarf, was it a present? America's great, thank you. No, it was all a surprise. Mum nearly fainted. Yes, it's nice to be back. It would have been a long year without a single trip home. Thanks, it's pretty short isn't it? I donated a wig to children with cancer. Oh, yes, I think we might even have some Tanqueray, I'll just check. Make yourselves at home.'

I avoided Matthew's eyes. He was mumbling the same nothings as the rest of them, joining in with the festive chit-chat and laughing loudly in the right places, but I knew his tone betrayed scorn. I knew this would be one of those evenings that we used to dissect together afterwards, laughing at the plebeian sheep who wouldn't know what real living was if it slapped them in the faces. Only, tonight, he would be laughing at me too.

As I asked my mum if there was gin in the cupboard, I began to imagine the email I would no doubt receive tomorrow. Perhaps even later tonight. I shivered involuntarily as I thought of the man upstairs spending the evening scrutinising my clothes and body language, making judgements about how my hair made me less pretty and that my conversation had been flattened by those dumb Americans. I plodded back to our guests, determined not to cry, and handed Valerie her G&T. Annabelle was pulling colourfully wrapped gifts from a carrier bag and my mum appeared behind me, gushing, 'Oooh, is it present time? Hold on a minute, let me get my camera.'

Annabelle gave me a necklace with six garnets set in a swirling silver pattern. It was lovely and I told her so, whilst asking James to help me with the clasp, and blushing as everyone waited to see how it would look against my throat. After a bit, Hannah began tearing into a DVD and the focus shifted, but Matthew's eyes lingered a moment longer. James received a book about cars, my mum was given a cribbage board, Lydia tried on a new pair of chenille gloves and Valerie gushed over an ancient hardback dictionary. My last present was a small rectangular box. I knew the scrawled handwriting and hesitated before tentatively peeling at the corners of the Sellotape. Inside was a black Moleskine pad, the size of an iPod. I fanned my fingers through the pages and found each one printed with a square and half a dozen blank lines.

'For your directorial notes,' Matthew offered, looking me in the eye.

'Um, thank you,' I swallowed, noticing a scribbled message at the front and turning subtly to it, trying to shield the words from those either side of me.

We are but players in her play, ready to laugh and cry at her whim and never expecting more.

You always get what you want Baba, and I'm sure this will be no different.

Your gentle, once-perfect Knight

'Right, I think the pork should be ready. Shall we eat?' sang my mother and everyone began to rise, searching around for their glasses and piling presents neatly beside chair-legs and under tables.

'You're welcome,' whispered Matthew as we descended the stairs.

The rest of the evening was much of the same. I ate and drank and drank and ate, contributing now and again to the conversations around me and trying to ignore the churn in my stomach every time Matthew caught my eye or winked at me while Beatrice related another story about the good old days. After dinner, Matthew wanted to show everyone some W. C. Fields clips, so we piled back into the living room and I gulped my wine before falling asleep propped against an arm of the couch. When I awoke, everyone was saying goodbye and I stumbled blearily from one 'Merry Christmas' hug to the next as people found their coats and thanked my mum for a delicious meal. Matthew's were the final lips to touch my cheek and I found myself half-yawning a 'Sure' as he invited me for tea the next day. Annoyed and drunk, I fell into my childhood bed, still wearing my tights, and dreamt about monsters and lovers and creatures that were both yet neither.

The following day, I trudged reluctantly along the pavement to Matthew's house and pushed the metal gate with a familiar, yet disturbing surge of guilt and secrecy. Matthew opened the door, shielding both of us from the rest of the house with the thick curtain. He was already wearing shoes.

'Annabelle's in. We'll go for a walk.' He held the door ajar with his foot and turned to take his coat from a hook behind him. With one arm in a sleeve, he slammed the door and brushed by me to open the gate.

We walked in silence to Love Lane, which dead-ended in a cul-de-sac but continued in the form of a narrow path leading over a stile and to the top of a hill overlooking the town.

I don't remember exactly what was said once we reached leaves, fields and trees. In the crisp Boxing Day air, we imagined ourselves safe from the others, all of the others, even those quilt-coated souls walking their dogs and hurrying home to hot cocoa or mulled wine. Matthew spoke to me, asked me what I thought I was doing, called me a selfish child no doubt. I suppose I could try to make up the words, follow my writing teacher's advice to 'show, not tell', but my mind was beginning to unravel already and it was not so much the technical details of this scene that lodged it in my memory, as the symbolic nature of our last almost-civil conversation occurring on frost-bitten grass, with moisture in both our eyes. Matthew cried round, plopping tears and hissed accusations through clenched teeth. I think he enjoyed displaying the emotion as much as he hated showing me weakness. I cried in desperation, thin flowing streams of salt-water, stinging in the breeze along with his insults. I wanted him to understand. He wanted me to hurt. At times, we raised our voices, at others we reached for each other's palms. There was no resolution. A spiteful word or two was spat as I left him at my mum's gate and dozens of emails followed, dissecting my delusional attitude and my cruel, uncaring nature. All I got from the conversation was a cold and a bitter regret at having flown home at all. Sniffing my runny nose unselfconsciously, I folded my clothes and packed my Christmas presents into my 33" x 24" suitcase and felt pure relief that I would be back in America this time tomorrow.

Waiting on platform 9 of Philadelphia's 30th Street Station, I wondered why I'd come. I began to question if Becky would still be the girl she'd been in London, and if I was still the person who'd been invited. There'd been no emails or letters, only a brief phone conversation with Becky's mom in which I'd told her what time my train would be arriving. I felt sure the past months had changed me: bruised me a little but also made me more grown up and capable. On this narrow stretch of busy concrete, though, I felt like the lost little girl missing the night bus once more.

As I chided myself for being so pathetic, nervous and desperate, bony arms wrapped around me from behind, halting my breath and squashing the flowers I clutched.

'Nat!' Becky nuzzled my ear before gleefully grabbing my case and marching me happily towards another platform.

On 30th December, after three nights in separate beds, awkwardly not-quite-flirting with one another and neither of us mentioning our last conversation in London, Becky and I found ourselves alone and tipsy in her living room. Her house was a sprawling wooden affair with a piano in the hall, a well-used Aga in the kitchen and plush suede sofas in the living room beckoning you to recline after selecting a book from the shelves and deciding to stay for ever.

Becky and I danced to Billie Holiday and reminisced about the Blue Box. When our spoken chronology reached the final performance, we both fell silent. Becky took my hand. We swayed together and I moved close to tentatively cup her hip. Becky tilted her head to smile at me. After a hideous pause in which my mind whirled with questions and doubts, I reached on tiptoes to kiss her.

'About time!' Becky laughed.

I mocked offence and pushed her to the couch. I kissed her fully now and Becky pulled me close.

We slept in each other's tangled limbs for three nights, playfully stifling one another's moans so Becky's conservatively liberal parents wouldn't hear. We held hands as she showed me the old part of Philly and chased me around the Liberty Bell. Becky's friend Darren brought his one-year-old daughter over and I watched Becky cradle the little girl, a daydream beginning to boil. Becky seemed so maternal, so beautifully at ease, and I thought at that moment I understood the appeal of fatherhood; thought I wanted a child with another woman.

But Becky was cool and self-assured. People fell in love with her every day. At a New Year's Eve party, her male friends jealously told me how lucky I was, but I couldn't help notice with insecurity the boys who winked and the girls who smiled at my date.

In a booth at an all-night diner, Becky told me I complicated things for her. I made her feel, made her care. She didn't seem happy about this. She told me that when she was fourteen she began cutting herself. She had last cut herself badly at the Blue Box, with a Stanley knife while they built the set, right before I'd arrived. She looked up from her syrup-drenched pancakes and focused a hard stare on me.

'If we lived in the same state, I might have to make you date me.'

On New Year's Day, I watched Becky sleep. My January term, in which I'd opted to assistant direct another play, was about to begin. Tomorrow, my friend Bee, one of the actors from 'Twas, would pull up to Becky's house and pop her trunk for my bag, then kindly drive me up Interstate 87, back to my chilly dorm room on the still-snowy campus.

Last summer, I thought, I'd been fascinated by a woman who oozed confidence and sexuality, who looked beautiful in the oddest situation and didn't care what anyone thought of her. Lying in Becky's sheets now, I felt drawn to the very opposite of what had first interested me. Becky seemed weak. She was a normal girl: shy to be touched, embarrassed by her body, worried. My admiration and jealousy had softened to tenderness and desire, and, in this rare moment of confidence, I recognised it as mutual.

Hours later, Becky gripped me in her driveway and whispered so that Bee couldn't hear, 'Would you understand if I said, "I love you for now"?'

I didn't respond. I looked at Becky's hair, still tousled from getting up late. I wanted to take care of her. I wanted to settle down and date her. I wanted to return her words.

Instead I muttered, 'I'll come back in June.'

Becky's face spread into a grin, and with a brief hug and a wave to her parents, I folded myself into Bee's passenger seat.

'CDs are in the glove compartment – you're in charge.'

21

Matthew's daily emails resumed, but I buried myself once more in the theatre department. Carol, the director, had prepared a strict schedule for cast and crew alike. In the building by 8am, we were to spend an hour doing a rigorous warm-up, followed by practical workshops of set-building or costume and lighting design; after lunch, we would rehearse, then give and receive notes before a short dinner break, after which we'd run what we'd changed. Every day, for the whole of January. I was beginning to understand why Jess had opted out of January term, the non-compulsory mini-semester Rosella offered for students to gain extra credit, and escaped back to the snow-free joys of Texas.

On the days things went to plan, we were dismissed from the theatre at 8pm and free to raid the costume closet for impromptu dance parties in the dorm common rooms. Busy every day and surrounded by artists and actors, I felt content. I missed Becky and it worried me slightly that she never emailed, but knowing how she felt about me buoyed my confidence and I even found myself flirting with some of the actors.

I went on a couple of dates with Alexandra, a super-skinny Jewish coxswain I'd kissed briefly after one of the senior pub nights the previous semester. Date is perhaps the wrong word as we were limited to campus and, while I never emerged from the theatre before 8pm, Alex had a strict call to be at the boats by 5am. Instead of going to the cinema or holding hands on long walks, making snowmen together or huddling in cafés with chai tea lattes as I imagined doing with imaginary girlfriends on imaginary dates most hours of most days, Alex and I met each night in Bobst café after rehearsal. I wolfed down curly fries while she scraped the cheese from a Caesar salad and we fast-tracked the 'getting-to-know-you' stage:

'How were rehearsals?'

'Great. How was rowing?'

'Fine.'

'Do you like theatre?'

'I should because I'm an English major, but I'd rather be doing sports.'

'I'm the total opposite. I'm not sure I even know where the sports centre is.'

'That's like cursing in my presence! Hey, are you finished? Want to come to my dorm?'

'Sure.'

I followed Alex out into the snow, my gloved palm sadly empty. She used her identity card to swipe us into her building and took me up to her single room on the third floor. Gesturing for me to sit on the bed, she crossed the room to put on a CD, then walked back to me with a smile.

'Are you going to kiss me then?'

And thus Alex and I made out for the month of January. It can't have been quite as impersonal as that, because I do remember learning about her strict Connecticut parents who still rang her up to say they'd met a nice rich lawyer they'd like her to meet after she'd got over this lesbian 'stage'. She told me about her ex-girlfriend, a rugby player who had broken her heart, and her fears that she wouldn't pass the LSATs and wouldn't get into a decent law school. I babbled about British things because they made her laugh, talked about how absurd the liberalness here seemed in comparison to Durham and made jokes about my failed attempts at being a lesbian since I was sixteen.

But what I remember most is rolling on my or her bed with my lips pressed against hers. I remember sliding my hand up her top and getting it caught in the complicated built-in bra. I remember worrying that my nipples didn't seem as sensitive as hers and thinking she must think I was a freak. I remember the firmness of her stomach, the lack of any fat on her tiny frame and how disconcerting it was to cuddle someone who was all muscle and bone, even if they did cut a truly masturbatory image when they undressed in your doorway. I remember feeling large for the first time in my life and not believing her when she said she liked my curves.

I remember wanting to blow my nose because I'd been lying on my back all evening and I couldn't breathe through my mouth while she was kissing me. I remember trying to move my lips down her belly to where my fingers had explored and being told she only did that in a relationship. I remember her buying me a bottle of moisturiser and laughing at my lack of basic female abilities. I remember kisses dissolving into laughter as we tickled each other.

Finally, I remember Alex arriving at my door as arranged and walking in with only a perfunctory kiss, followed by the clichéd: 'We need to talk.'

I remember saying, 'Okay.'

Then I remember Alex perching prudishly on the edge of my bed and speaking softly, 'I really like you and we're having fun, but I'm not sure we have a connection. I mean, I enjoy it when we hang out, but I don't miss it when we don't. And my ex called me last night and wants to give it another go. I'm sorry, I do really like you and I don't want to hurt you.'

And I remember agreeing with everything she said. I didn't miss her either. I felt awkward when we made out. I thought she was fun, but would usually rather be talking to someone from the theatre. Did I just want a girlfriend so much that I'd convinced myself this was a relationship? Was I that desperate?

So I remember replying, 'I've been thinking the same thing. But, hey, you're really cool and I wish you well with your girlfriend.'

And I remember my pride stinging only a little bit, my tears only slightly moistening my pillow.

With snow still on the ground, January ended, Jess returned from Texas, reading lists were handed out and the play entered 'tech-week'. I signed up for five classes, waved to people in the dining queue and snuck myself into one of the only two bars in the area on the first Friday; this semester would be perfect, I knew it.

Then I met Lizzie Stein.

I fell for Lizzie because she listened to Aimee Mann, drove an SUV, had handcuffs hanging on her wall and introduced me to *But I'm a Cheerleader*. After opening night, I sat in her passenger seat howling to Tori Amos as she reached sixty along 45th Street with the windows open and her hand upon my thigh.

Lizzie was too short and too soft to be butch, but she refused to wear make-up and swore she didn't own a dress. She didn't care. Her daddy was rich and she owned one-of-a-kind Louis Vuitton black sneakers that she coupled with men's slacks and scuffed up backstage at the Ruff.

She was majoring in Theatre Arts, but didn't much like acting. Her minor was in English, but she didn't much like books. We shared a class called Queer American Poetry, in which she never raised her hand, but later agreed with me that the flamboyant 6'5" professor who explained the difference between kitsch and camp with reference to his own outfit was 'dreamy'. She would go on to law school, she supposed.

Studying was a chore to Lizzie and, born in Florida, she hated being stuck in the North-East. But some things made her enthusiastic: watching *Veronica Mars* in bed; fast-forwarding *Tipping the Velvet* to the sex scenes; laughing at my shocked face as she introduced me to www.suicidegirls.com; taking photos with her new camera; IMing me at two in the morning to see if I wanted to hang out in her room; ditching the dining halls to drive ten miles for sushi; telling me I could touch her breasts, but only with the lights off; describing in detail the expensive leather whip beneath her bed; and reading Harry Potter for the fifth time in the back of a lecture about Max Stafford Clark's contribution to directing.

I learnt too late that Lizzie Stein was in love with Lauren Bradbury. After only a week of entertaining the idea that this boyish red-head with a round freckled face might call herself my girlfriend, I accepted my role as second best and willingly began to skip through the snow at midnight to hang out with Lizzie on the days Lauren snubbed her. I wrote terrible poetry about the 'cruel cat who wrapped herself in leather and wound me on her claws', and gleefully titled my final paper for our class, 'The Hermeneutics of Flirtation in (Gertrude) Stein's *Tender Buttons*'.

When Lauren liked Lizzie, I comforted myself with Reena. Reena knitted while watching *Lost* and had a dental dam taped to her door. I slept in her bed three nights in a row, but never managed to kiss her, not even a peck on the cheek. Frustrated, confused and egged on by Jess, I ruined the whole thing by sending a text that expressed something about enjoying spending nights with her but wishing we could do a little more than sleep.

She didn't reply and I stopped staying over.

I recommenced making out with Lizzie on the occasions Lauren rejected her and became agonisingly aware that everyone on the campus except me was having hot, loving, lesbian sex. I developed consecutive crushes on Amy, Rihanna, Jasmine and Jenny. Though I acted painfully self-conscious around them all, I asked none of them out. Amy was too popular, Rihanna was straight, Jasmine already liked someone else and Jenny knew I liked her because Mia had told her so, so if she was interested why didn't she ask me out herself?

There was always a reason to do nothing.

Every time that I cringed while unlocking my mailbox or swallowed hard when someone mentioned Leonard Cohen, I became more and more convinced this would never work. I didn't belong here. Matthew was right: I'd never be normal. Having a girlfriend to walk to class with and sit beside in the library while I did my homework didn't fit with having lost your virginity to a sixty-year-old and not even being able to tell your best friend your darkest secret. My life was tainted and sordid, and however many times I descended the stairs at 8pm for Rosella's complimentary milk and cookies, I would never belong here.

In April, I wore my newly purchased vintage velvet jacket to a dorm party and danced with Andi, who'd bussed in from the co-ed. She got my attention by flashing a pancake breast. Horrified yet impressed, I developed an immediate infatuation with this mohawked Twiglet. Shutting ourselves in the closet, I showed her my nipple bar and we giggled into our cups. Drunk and giddy, I agreed to walk to my dorm with Christine Butler to pick up more alcohol. I failed to make it back to the party and instead slept with Christine, who wore sweatpants to class, played Apples to Apples and didn't seem to trim her fingernails.

Too lethargic and hungover to shower the next morning, I stalked Andi via Rosella Social. Disgusted with myself, yet tickled by the potential flirtation, I left a wall post asking if she'd like to 'get coffee sometime'. I then checked back neurotically, deciding I was a completely unattractive slutty whore who deserved nothing more than the Christine Butlers in life.

Until Andi replied: 'Sure.'

We had two not terribly awkward coffee-shop dates, but neither ended in a kiss or anything more than a friendly, 'see you soon'. Two weeks later, I convinced some friends to attend the Drag Ball at Andi's college as the T Birds from *Grease*. With my hair slicked back and a sock in my drainpipe trousers, I danced shyly with Andi. At midnight, she and a bunch of other students removed their shirts and other items of clothing. Grinding self-consciously with this semi-naked undulating boygirl, I wondered how to initiate a kiss.

After an excruciatingly long time of dancing like that and feeling decidedly overdressed, I told Andi I needed air. Outside, I noticed my last bus was about to leave. I hurried with Andi to the stop, where she sighed that I was sweet but this was not what she was looking for.

Back in my dorm, I IMed with Lizzie Stein until 4am and read more of Matthew's emails. I couldn't date girls who wore pink tank-tops and joined the rowing team, I couldn't hold conversations with friendly actors who needed help with their English accents and now I couldn't even kiss a woman who shaved part of her head and brushed her bare breasts against me while dancing. I wanted to be normal, but how could I be normal with an ankh tattooed on my hip and sixteen new emails in my inbox?

I directed a short play Jess had written in the spring. It was a cocky absurdist student piece in which we could all pat ourselves on the back for our cleverness. I cast only girls I had crushes on, ensuring their company every evening for rehearsals and enjoying their excitement as opening night arrived. I bit my nail as the audience filed in and Rihanna dithered nervously next to me, asking if the set she'd designed was right and should she move this or that object? I noticed Greg's seat was empty. It was a Friday and he must have gone to New York, but I still felt annoyed. I hadn't been invited to dinner for three weeks.

The play went well. Afterwards we snuck into the costume cupboard and dug out bizarre outfits to spend the rest of the night in. Wine and Mike's Hard Lemonade led to Amy and I running across the amphitheatre topless and Jasmine cartwheeling on the college president's lawn. We found a dorm party and stumbled inside. I followed Rihanna back out so she could smoke and we sat shivering on the porch.

'I've never kissed a girl, you know?' she slurred after sucking on the white paper between her fingers.

'Okay.' I mentally kicked myself for being awkward even while drunk.

'I mean, I like boys I think. I've been here three years and never felt like kissing a girl, even just as a joke, but . . .' She trailed off, then looked at me through thick eyelashes.

'But what?' I almost sang, congratulating myself on my coolness.

'But maybe I want to now.' She kept looking at me.

'Oh,' and back to hating myself.

'We could . . .' She wouldn't stop looking at me.

'Okay.' I managed to lean in, still a little nervous of rejection despite the invitation, and tasted her cigarette breath and strawberry ChapStick.

'Whoa, are we interrupting something?' Amy roared with glee as she and Kristin emerged from the building.

I sat back, my cheeks flushed.

'They're out of alcohol inside,' moaned Kristin. 'Where can we get some at this time of night?'

'I have a bottle of wine in my room,' Rihanna said, smiling at me. 'We could all go there.'

'Okay, what are we waiting for?' Amy grabbed Kristin's hand and they began skipping towards North Winthrop Hall.

'Shall we?' Rihanna offered me her arm and I took it.

On the way to her room we picked up a couple of other stray revellers and the promised bottle of wine multiplied into three. We sat in a circle on Rihanna's floor swigging from the bottles before passing them along.

'I have an idea,' whispered Amy before guzzling the last dregs of the second bottle. 'Why don't we play spin-the-bottle?'

She placed the green glass in the middle of the circle and twisted it until it landed on Kristin and Rachel. They each leant over the bottle and touched lips briefly, then sat back flushed.

'You prudes,' moaned Amy, setting up to spin again.

Rihanna and Amy.

Rachel and me.

Kristin and Fran.

Rihanna and Fran.

Then Kristin and Amy and the game paused while they closed their eyes and ran fingers through hair with mouths working passionately and the rest of us making jealous whooping sounds.

'That's how it's done,' smiled Amy, coming up for air.

Rihanna and me.

'Okay,' breathed Rihanna nervously. I touched the back of her head and pulled her into a soft but firm kiss, blotting out the giggles of those around and concentrating on her warm tongue.

'It never lands on me,' moaned Rachel once we'd finished. 'Why do we have to use a bottle, can't we just kiss?'

The question hung for a moment as each of our drenched brains processed it.

'Okay,' Amy broke the silence. She grabbed Rachel from across the circle and pulled her into a half-lying, half-sitting kiss.

Kristin turned to me and hiccuped before doing the same. On my left, I felt Rihanna shuffle towards Fran.

Beneath the fluorescent dorm light, three couples made out on the floor, draped over each other, feet tangling with other couples and giggles and moans blending from one pair to the next. After a few moments, someone, perhaps me, sat up and shouted, 'All change', and without question, each girl found a new partner.

This may have lasted ten minutes or two hours. Natural couples formed and I remember feeling hurt by Kristin and Amy's clear attraction to one another, but flattered by Rihanna's curious-straight-girl attentions.

Stumbling back to our dorm, Kristin and I babbled about how that was exactly like the stuff we'd been talking about in our Performance Studies class. What was the word? Communitas? Mass euphoria? Was that a liminal space? Had we created a sense of abandon? Kristin mused whether she could get away with writing about it for her paper due next week, and we said goodnight on the stairs.

As far as I know, Kristin chickened out of writing about that night for her Performance Studies 301 final, but the story afforded me a meal at Greg's and he congratulated me on finally having a 'real women's college experience'. We laughed together over chicken and rice and he asked why I hadn't seen Rihanna since. I explained she'd been a bit cold, but that it didn't matter, that it was all a one-night thing and he had to promise he wouldn't tell the others that he knew.

He promised and walked me back to my dorm, smoking a menthol before offering me the rest of the packet. I went to bed thinking Rihanna's coolness did matter really.

At Graduation Ball I watched the women I'd spent the year fantasising about arrive in neat pairs. In an attempt to snub Lizzie, I danced on a table with Lauren Bradbury until one of the bar staff told us to get down. I kissed six or seven women, most of them straight, and spilt wine on my dress, then slept in Jess's bed while she went home to Angelo.

Three days later, my bags were packed and my room was as bare as when I'd arrived. I'd stuffed essential items into a travel backpack I'd ordered online and neatly folded the rest of my thrift-store acquisitions into three large suitcases, ready to be deposited in Jess and Angelo's basement until I returned at the end of the summer. I was going to travel, see as much of the States as I possibly could, then meet my mum in Manhattan, drive up to Rosella and fly back using her baggage limit as well as my own.

I'd been babbling about my travel plans for weeks and feeling grown up about exploring places alone, flying from state to state and meeting friends in their different time zones. But now I was leaving this leafy campus with its dining halls and twenty-four-hour porters, its emergency numbers and security men on Segways, I began to grow nervous. Who was I but a little girl, foolishly thinking she could take on the big bad world?

Before I hugged Jess on her doorstep and told her I loved her; before I climbed in a taxi and asked for the station; before I boarded Amtrak and began my summer of adventure, I needed to clear the air with Matthew. Once again, I composed what I thought was an olive branch:

From: Natalie Lucas <sexy_chocolate69@sweetmail.com>
To: Matthew Wright <theoutsider@worldopen.co.uk>
Sent: 11 May 2004, 23:08:07
Subject: Hi

Hello
Thanks for your last couple of letters. Good news about your film.

I'm leaving campus in a couple of weeks, so no point sending much else. Thanks for respecting my space. I'm putting myself together bit by bit, but still struggling to deal with some things. I'd be lying if I said I wasn't dreading coming back a little bit. America has been my liminal space to work out some things. But I still have a few weeks I guess. I'm going travelling – visiting friends all over for a while, then taking this hippy bus that was recommended from one side of the US to another.

I'm sorry for all the pain I caused at the beginning of the
year and am glad to hear things are going well for you.
I'm not ready to analyse the past or read your poems
in great detail, but it's not because everything was an
act or untrue. You and I both know that it was all true
at the time. But I think it was also ill-advised and
immature.

I hope that when I get back we can be friends and talk of
books and theatre without any undertones. I'm really not
strong enough to deal with fights and questions and
attempts to work out what went wrong. I realise this
request is incredibly immature, but I hope you will grant it
because it's the only way I can look forward to returning
home.

I really hope you are doing well and I apologise for my
inability to handle our situation.

I look forward to seeing an old friend in July.

Nat

Once again, however, Matthew read my words rather differently.
In the twelve hours between sending this email and leaving for
Manhattan, I received twenty-four emails, comprising 4,452 words
of vitriol. 'I wash my hands of you, Natalie,' he began, but that
proved an empty promise. Seizing upon my phrase 'ill-advised
and immature', he ping-ponged between incredulous anger and
academic analysis. 'Who is mature in your eyes?' he asked. 'A
handful of writers, perhaps? Our dead poets?' He told me I was
digging myself into a 'cesspool of atrocity' and quoted Ted Hughes
and Leonard Cohen at me. He attacked my mum and my brother,
told me Greg probably wanted to rape me and that I'd never, ever

be anything other than a lonely, stunted child. 'Have you orgasmed, yet?' he asked in parentheses. 'Was I right that, once you were free from true feeling and the power of a real lover, your up-tight mind would allow you that?'

I clenched my fist and bit back the urge to scream. I'd promised myself I wouldn't reply; I wouldn't engage him. I'd let Matthew's anger run its course, allow him to blow off steam and hope with all my might it wouldn't be like this when I returned. I shouldn't have continued reading them. I should have headed out for a final walk around the campus; I should have lain in the grass somewhere and read a book. But instead I sat in my packed-up room and clicked each email open the moment it arrived. It was strange to know Matthew was sitting at his desk this very moment, composing these sentences, feeling this much against me. His next emails listed all the things he'd done for me, told me without him I'd be some stuffy analyst with no concept of beauty. He told me about hooking up his new girlfriend with Rose's manager, Damien, who'd got her a gig at Ealing Studios. Was I meant to be impressed, I wondered. 'Remember Rose?' he asked and I felt a stab of guilt. 'Meg's my breath of fresh air amid your cloud of volcanic ash,' he continued. 'So mature for eighteen! She's applying to Durham. To study a Diploma in Nursing. I told her books are better than bedpans, but she just laughs. I'll let her live in the house I buy there. Perhaps we'll see you on campus.'

I breathed deeply and tried to remain calm. A few minutes later another arrived and this one spoke of love, of the two of us as 'Uncles exiled to different corners of the earth'. It ended with 'By the way, I'm a criminal now. No, not the silly offshore accounts and fake credit cards as I told you before. Worse. Much worse. So stay away. Seriously.'

These emails made me tremble. They blocked out the May sun tickling my window and thrust me into a pit of darkness. I was drowning in a vat of Matthew's love and hatred, bumping into the corpses of dead poets and porn stars. But these were nothing compared to the final email. The final email silenced all metaphors and turned me cold.

From: Matthew Wright <theoutsider@worldopen.co.uk>
To: Natalie Lucas <sexy_chocolate69@sweetmail.com>
Sent: 13 May 2004, 06:20:01
Subject: I'll wait for you

You need to explore, Natalie. I understand. And at the end of your exploring, you will arrive at where you started and know it for the first time. Or so the poem goes. I'll tell you how I'll know it for the first time – I've thought a lot about it, and this really is the only way I'll be able to forgive you and welcome you back:

You can lay yourself down for me. That used to be your speciality, remember?

This is the one, non-negotiable condition of the 'friendship' you are asking me for.

You can walk through my unknown remembered door, go directly to my study and bend over the desk. Straightaway. I don't want to hear you speak. I'll have Annabelle let you in.

Get yourself across my desk like the slut you are. You'd better pull down your panties and hike up your skirt or I'll do it for you and I won't be gentle.

Grip your thighs on the wood and lift your arse for me.

You'll have a choice between my belt and my cane (I refuse to spank you with my palm, you are no longer

214

worthy of that). I'll give you 57 strokes (one for each year of our relationship X 19, your age). If you require cold cream, you'll have to ask Meg to apply it. I won't touch you.

I refuse to fuck you, even if you beg (you're still diseased from that mucky slag Nadiyya), but if you so desire, I'll allow you to bring your own dildo and I'll watch from a distance as Meg slams it into your wretched cunt.

Oh, and if by some miracle you return with a girlfriend, I'd suggest leaving her outside.

She can join the children in the apple-tree and watch through the window if that's how you like it. But she best be not known and not looked for, not even half-heard in the stillness because I can't be held responsible for what I might do.

While she's waiting in the cold, you'll receive even strikes. I'll count aloud.

Whether this pleases you or not is not my concern. It will please me. And, once we are done, I will be able to conduct a perfectly good friendship with you. Of course, we may need to increase the dosage if I am forced to see you often and you start bitching in your usual way.

If you think this is a joke or an empty promise, try me.

Come knocking at my door and you'll see the cane ready and waiting. My belt will slip easily from its loops and

215

wrap around my knuckles. Would you like to be roped to keep you in position? How about a leg-spreader? That's probably a good idea for a nice tight arse.

I won't speak.

Then or now.

This is the last you will hear from me until you grant me this request.

22

Manhattan

This is my summer. Just me and a backpack. I ate lunch with Greg earlier and I'm now sat in a park near the Village. He said he would work with me again in a second and that I have a good eye and work hard . . . that people will see that.

Yesterday Amy and I went to this old speakeasy, Chumley's, for brunch, then to some galleries in Chelsea. One artist had these huge canvases with layer upon layer of smaller images making a larger one. Another had an exhibition of letters and photos and junk from his life. Things that are not art except in context. Both pieces made me think about Matthew, about the layer he occupies in the jumble of my life, about where I'd be and what I'd be doing if I'd walked away from him when I was fifteen, about what my world would look like and how people would react if I stuck it, Matthew and all, to a gallery wall. Amy pulled me out of my thoughts pointing out a disclaimer questioning the authenticity of the letters and photos. Perhaps it was all a story anyway. Perhaps I can write my own, just the way I want it. Perhaps the world is just art and lies. No doubt Matthew would encourage these thoughts.

Even without such sickening echoes, I'm a little scared of the weeks ahead. I'm travelling alone, but mostly I'm nervous about visiting Becky. I hope she still wants to see me.

Philly

I arrived in Philly once again via Amtrak. I rang and told Becky the time of my train, but added, out of politeness, that it was fine if she couldn't make it because I remembered the way. Still, I waited on the platform. She might have been running late. I looked up and down for the messy dark hair and smudged eyeliner I hadn't seen since Christmas. I imagined her running up behind me and twirling me into a kiss. I imagined us holding hands all the way to her house and giggling uncontrollably as her mother explained I could have the blue room once more, then racing up the stairs to lock the door of Becky's own bedroom.

It's her graduation party, though. She has loads to do. I figured maybe she just didn't have time to meet me. Whatever. I bought a ticket and located the right train. I still felt excited. I'm that pathetic. I reapplied my mascara in the carriage and bought flowers at the end of the line.

Then I heaved my bag onto my back and trudged up the hill towards Becky's house. I thumbed the doorbell of 205 and stood straight, ready to smile.

'Hi,' a boy answered.

'Hi.' I couldn't help but grin. 'I'm Becky's friend.'

Squealing, Becky emerged from a doorway inside.

'Nat!' She lifted me in a hug, a safety-pinned bandage on her arm catching on my jumper. 'It's so good to see you!' There was a pause after I untangled myself, then Becky gushed: 'Oh, sorry! This is Tom. You remember I told you about my ex? We got back together.'

Of course I remembered Tom, the infamous Texan from summertime stories over Corona.

I feel surrounded by insincerity and crave the company of the good people. Amy and Jess and Greg. I need Becky in my life as much as I need Matthew. A good realisation I suppose, but what am I supposed to do with it for the next three days?

At the party last night, I sat on the porch with the boys and girls I'd met at New Year's. Inside, Becky danced with Tom. I could hear her through the windowpanes and I saw a circle of guests listening to her jokes about British commercials. Later, I saw her take Tom's palm and lead him to the staircase.

Pretending not to have noticed, the motley crew on the porch took swigs from brown beer bottles and welcomed me graciously into their group. I grabbed a Bud Light from the cooler and realised it was me who had last banished them to this porch. I kissed a girl called Kate. She was pretty and brunette but I was drunk and depressed. Tegan – the ex who tried to pull my hair at New Year's – and I became sort of friends. What else is there to do while Becky takes a guy to her bedroom than make friends with the other rejects?

Becky got more likeable after Tom left yesterday. She told me she's started cutting herself again. Over the past twenty-four hours I've glimpsed a little of the intensity that captivated me at Christmas and found myself, after a few beers, wishing she would creep into my bed during the night. At first I was disappointed with myself, but I guess it doesn't especially matter: it's hardly my biggest shame.

I've been sleeping a lot. My dreams are violent and mostly about Matthew. During a mutual three-hour nap this afternoon Becky said she dreamt about being a devil and me cuddling her on the sofa while we tried to keep it a secret. What am I supposed to do with that information?

Finally, after wanting to scream for days, I'm sat on a plane headed for Portland, Oregon. Too busy applying for a job at a children's

219

theatre, Becky just gave me vague instructions on how to get to the airport by bus. She kissed me on the cheek, then waved as I stumbled down the hill. Had I expected it to be like New Year? Cramped into this window seat, I feel stupid and confused. I should have stayed in New York. Or gone to DC on my own. I feel stronger on my own. I could have kept that bittersweet desire burning and skipped this humiliation.

Fuck it! This is the beginning of my summer. I can't let Becky ruin it. In three hours there will be eight states between us. And her boyfriend's an idiot. He asked if England was in London. Did I really believe her all those months ago when she told me she loved me and suggested that, whatever happens, we could meet up for illicit holidays for the rest of our lives? I feel like a fool for thinking Becky might have understood me, might have swallowed my fucked-up life and said, hey, I've done some dumb things too, who cares? She cuts herself and sleeps with anyone who smiles at her, dances around rooms with no clue whose toes she's treading on, but she's the normal girl: the one with a dozen infatuated friends waiting on the porch, a gleeful extended family congratulating her on her achievements and a stable boyfriend probably about to propose. That's never going to be me. And someone like that will never accept me. My graduation party will consist of friends and family whose relationships to me are tainted by the impossible secrets spun between us. Matthew will always be the cloud darkening my sunny days. He'll always be the wall between me and the world.

Portland, Oregon

State number eight and a huge sense of relief when my plane landed. Becky's house made me feel so socially inept that I was genuinely surprised to be able to hold a conversation and be a normal friend with Rihanna. All awkwardness between us seems to have passed, thank God! And my miseries about Matthew seem less and less pressing after gossiping and shopping my way around

Portland and Oregon City. Rihanna and her friends took me to this huge mountain waterfall and showed me Hood River and its breathtaking scenery. They treated me like a normal nineteen-year-old and maybe I've started believing I am one.

I'm on the train heading to Oakland and I'm overwhelmed by the picturesque views from my upstairs seat. There have been farms that the sun made glow and shadows of mountains on the skyline with the odd snowy one standing out like a lost polar bear. Now it's twilight and we're hurtling through mountains, surrounded by enormous pine trees, cavernous drops and the odd stream trickling down into the lost below. I don't think I've ever seen such enormous geography. I'm taken back to geography classes when I sat fascinated by grainy videos of Mt St Helen erupting. If I press my face to the window, my heart races and my tummy smiles giddily at the terrifying plummet. I feel tiny and insignificant. Vague desires to find my camera are lost to the moment and the joy of sharing my first twenty-four-hour train ride through a foreign land with Evelyn Waugh.

California

. . . is flatter. Miles and miles of what are apparently rice paddies with a few mountains on the skyline. The night was long. About midnight we stopped in somewhere called Dunsmuir. A woman got on and was directed to the seat beside me. She waved over me at a lady waiting on the lamplit platform, then settled down to sleep. Ten minutes along the track, though, she burst into tears, explaining that her sister had cancer and that might have been the last time she'll see her. I comforted her a bit, then tried to read. Apparently cheered up, she interrupted me six times during my first page to tell me she was a people person and had a deck of cards. Sleep was impossible. The woman spilt over onto my seat and snored loudly. Whenever she woke up, her elbow found its way into my ribs and I'd lie there for another half-hour, feeling

221

cruel but staring longingly at those who had double-seats to themselves.

We just passed over a beautiful river, though, and I'm sat in the lounge car now, where I can see miles and miles and somehow the awful night was worth it. We're only an hour from Oakland and my body is tense with excitement. I like being free and alone. I can't wait to see Kristin, take photos of enormous San Francisco hills and be in another city. And my cross-country trip in just a few days. Who knows what that will be like? Greg thinks I'm crazy to be getting on some hippy bus, but I'm excited.

Part of me wonders if it's really me doing these things – the little child with itchy feet who detested growing up in a tiny country town and begged to be taken on family holidays. Now I'm glad to do it all alone, to ride this train with just my thoughts. For the first time, I'm realising I'm okay. All by myself, I'm okay.

Oakland, CA

When I arrived, I was suddenly excited to see the classic things: the Golden Gate and the steep steep hills. Kristin's dad drove us around San Francisco, pointing out interesting buildings and explaining how sixteen years ago a road cut off the city from the water but an earthquake destroyed it and now there's a wonderful street along the waterfront. We went to a couple of viewing points, one just under the Golden Gate, one way up high with the most fantastic views. It's beautiful with the blue bay surrounded by towering mountains and the mist cutting off the horizon.

My second night, we drove to the top of some hills so we could see the lights from the whole Bay area. During the days, Kristin took me to Berkeley and for a picnic lunch at a man-made lake with a beach. Her family's been really sweet too, saying I can come back any time, even if Kristin's not there. They made me a parcel for my trip containing a torch, little pots of dried fruit and John Steinbeck's Travels with Charley. I don't know what to do with so much kindness.

Ruby Mountains, Nevada

I'm sat on a snowy mountain in a pair of shorts and sandals! We're supposedly on our way to Lake Lamoille but we lost the path pretty early. Now, under the guidance of various adventurous males, the group finds itself eating lunch on rocks that required a vertical climb up a mountain face. No one is quite sure where to go next but it's ridiculously pretty.

We met in San Francisco where our strange, awkward introductions barely masked both excitement and nerves. There are more British people on the bus than Americans, which disappointed me somewhat. No more attention for my cute accent. The youngest person just finished her A-levels; the oldest is about to turn sixty.

The hike today was thrilling. My toes were so numb I thought they might fall off, but we kept going and eventually found Lake Lamoille. A couple of people even jumped in a hole in the ice. Coming back was easier once we found the correct path. Sitting on the bus again, it seems unbelievable that we were at the top of that mountain. Ironically my toes got a tan in their hypothermia.

Every night we have to transform the seats of the bus into beds. Our drivers Rob and Eddy did it the first night but I did it with Gill and Charlie tonight. There are eight bunks where bags are kept during the day. Then there are four sets of couples sleeping, two slightly below with no light at all and two above next to the windows. Plus, at the front and back of the bus, there are large padded rectangles for the rest to sleep sardine style. The first night I was a sardine and didn't get a whole lot of sleep because the woman next to me snored. Last night I tried one of the bunks, which, after the initial difficulty of getting in, gave me a pretty good night's sleep.

Idaho

We just arrived at the Salmon River where we'll pull out four long plastic tables and set up the breakfast things while others have a 'bag party' to get at the things we have below. You're only allowed a daypack on the bus and even that you must give up at night.

I went white water rafting along the Salmon River with force four rapids. To begin with it was pleasant but not much of an adrenalin rush. We went swimming in the quiet part and were given a tour of an old gold mine and factory. The boys named our boat The Scallywag Hunter. On the biggest rapid the wave went right over our heads and Charlie fell into me and I fell out. But before I knew it, I was being pulled back into the boat and I hadn't even lost my sunglasses.

We stopped at a campsite and I slept in Mark's tent. I awoke covered in bites that I can't help scratching like a child in need of mittens. I helped cook last night and again this morning because I was one of the first up. We had Jambalaya for tea, which was delicious, and some sort of omelette with tacos for breakfast. When we cook, we stand in a long line chopping and there are systems for washing and packing up that work well. Everyone chips in and it's helped us get to know one another.

Rob, our driver, thought I was American or maybe Italian. Seeing the look of horror on my face as I contemplated going home with an American accent, he's decided to call me an American Princess from now on.

We just hiked two miles up and down mountains to get to delicious hot springs with a view of rolling mountains and waterfalls. For some daft reason we started this hike at 2pm and, with hardly a tree in sight, I didn't think I'd make it. But it feels worth it now. Having sat in the icy waterfall for half an hour, I'm ready for the bathwater springs. I still have to pinch myself to know I'm really here.

We spent four or five hours at the hot springs, then made our way down the mountain. After the first mile, it began pouring and a

224

thunderstorm drenched us. The others, already dry on the bus,
were waiting with clean towels and cheers.

Yellowstone, Wyoming

We stopped in Montana to transform the bus and woke up in
Yellowstone National Park. We made an oatmeal breakfast by
Mammoth Hot Springs, next to elks. We walked along the path
seeing the clouds of steam that spurt from holes in the rock and
the orangey pools of water hot enough to burn your skin off. Now
we're driving towards the Little Grand Canyon, watching out for
bears and seeing only buffalo and elk. The scenery is fascinating
because of the '88 fire. These long thin trunks of pine trees stick
up into the sky, stripped of all branches, but towering over the
smaller new trees. If you look out across the hills, you can see more
burnt trees that have fallen like scattered matchsticks. Apparently
the pine seeds are designed so that they explode when they get hot
and shower seeds everywhere, meaning there are as many new
trees as there are old dead ones.

Grand Tetons, Wyoming

I dreamt of Matthew last night. I woke in a bunk, the bus hurrying
along an empty road with Rob at the wheel and light snores punc-
tuating the regular rumble of the engine. Closing my eyes I saw his
wrinkled grin, imagined his scorn. 'What are you doing, Baba? Do
you think you can fool these people just because you wear hiking
boots and pretend to be a backpacking hippy? Do you think you're
one of them?' I opened my eyes and he flew away. Traipsing through
national parks and swimming in natural lakes feels real and invig-
orating during the day, but at night I lose the people sleeping to my
left and right and feel locked inside my own head, as if Matthew's
been right all this time: as if as hard as I try to cloak myself in
different identities – student, traveller, lesbian, director – I'll never
be anything more than the shy teenager sat on his chaise.

* * *

225

I write this by torchlight in my sleeping bag outdoors at the Grand Teton National Park. We're braving bear country to sleep under the stars. Today we woke at Biscuit Basin in Yellowstone, a collection of pools so hot they boil great bubbles. From there, we walked a couple of miles to Old Faithful. On the way, we passed other magnificent pools as well as whitish rock formations with steam blowing from them. Everyone has to walk on boardwalks because the earth below, though it looks harmless, is often sinking mud. The colours are absurdly vivid and contrast amazingly with the fairly bland landscape of pine trees and dry earth. I checked and it's a constructive plate boundary. I can't explain the excitement I felt when I saw the signs and understood them. I wish I could talk to my old geography teachers who injected such mysticism into these exotic plate boundaries that I now stand (and sleep) upon. I waited for forty minutes at Old Faithful before it blew. It was spectacular, though the touristy atmosphere and attempt to capture both still and video footage meant the sheer impressiveness of water shooting 100 feet in the air because of convection currents below my flip-flopped feet did not sink in until later.

We drove for some hours to our current campsite, stopping only because Virginia decided she needed the loo and didn't tell anyone until she was at a number nine (there's a ten-point system: one=comfortable, ten=oops!). At the campsite, we walked to Jackson Lake, a great spread of still, clear water just below the Tetons. We swam in the late afternoon sun, then dried off by the shore. We tried going back again for the sunset but arrived too late so are planning to seek the sunrise tomorrow morning.

I survived the night with only a few shivers and no bad dreams thanks to the excellent cuddling skills of Charlie with his sub-zero sleeping bag. I had maybe four hours of sleep before we got up to watch the sunrise over the mountains. Actually, it rose behind us, but after an hour and a half of freezing in my pyjamas, the mountains turned pink. Afterwards, us early-birds warmed up by making French toast and now we've chucked everything off the bus for the promised clearout.

We hiked halfway around Lake Jenny, then up to 'Hidden Falls' and 'Inspiration Point'. We ate lunch on rocks by a waterfall – so close that our sandwiches were covered in spray. At the beginning of the trail, we encountered a group of hesitant tourists with one stupid man edging forwards. The ranger hidden in the bushes informed us there was a bear with her cub and tutted through gritted teeth that the man was going for a photo. We saw her walk across the path and the man was extremely close for his snap. We also saw a beaver on the way and some pretty birds too. The Grand Tetons are my favourite scenery so far, which is funny because I just crossed paths with John Steinbeck travelling many decades ago and he said Wyoming was his favourite state. We left at 4.30 and drove to Jackson Hole – a touristy cowboy town. Most people went to bars, but, given my lack of legality, I went to see Superman Returns, *which was a fabulous slice of normalcy.*

Devils Tower, South Dakota
We breakfasted at a picnic site at the bottom of Devils Tower, then circled the tower and read the myths about how it was formed. It's an enormous structure with ridges all around and a flat top the size of a football pitch. They think it might be essentially the centre of a volcano with the outer rock eroded, but there are other ideas too. The Native Americans said a giant bear was chasing a tribe when the earth saved them by rising up and the lines are where the bear clawed at the rock.

Back on the bus people talked about tattoos. I showed mine, but evaded a question about what it means. Should I come up with a lie? I'm going to have to live with it for the rest of my life.

Badlands, South Dakota

We drove for the afternoon, playing cards and reading books. The land became flat as we reached the Badlands, then suddenly these enormous craters opened up in the landscape. We drove along an endless dirt track, all needing the loo but not a tree in sight. Finally we reached a Cowboy Café run by Native Americans. We had Indian tacos and I spoke to Nellie, the matriarch, about her ranch and the history of her tribe. Her life sounded appealing. Imagine living so remotely and having such a strong sense of identity. We camped on her land, somewhere out in the middle of nowhere. Someone lit a fire in a crater and lots of people fell in the cacti during the night. I drank and spoke to driver Rob for most of the evening. He noticed my rainbow bracelet and asked if I was hiding it. I said no, but I'm not flaunting it. (Someone made a gay joke on the first day and everyone laughed, so I'm keeping quiet.) Still, it was kind of nice to be pegged and I like Rob a lot for his subtlety . . . might be nice if he was ten years younger. Funny for me to say that, I suppose.

I was fairly tipsy by the time Rob retired to his sleeper berth and I went to sleep under the stars, again snuggled up with Charlie. We looked at the stars and I kissed him. It was nice, not urgent. He's nineteen, half-Italian, from Vegas and joining the army after this trip.

We made breakfast and drove to White River where half the group is taking a mud bath and the rest sitting in trees, writing and reading. I told Rob last night that I'd go in with him, but this morning I don't feel much like playing around in the mud. Rob is disappointed I think. He just chased me, threatening to give me a bear hug with his mud-caked body.

Wisconsin

Pulling up at a beach by Lake Superior, I jumped off the bus and was the first into the water, full of energy. We spent a few hours there, sunbathing and eating ice-cream. I must have played four or five hours of cards during the on-the-road time. Finally we arrived at our campsite in Copper Falls State Park. I went for a walk with Charlie, but we were eaten by mosquitoes and I felt on edge whenever he tried to touch me.

After showering and eating we huddled around a fire. I sat on the cool box next to driver Rob and we talked for ages about films, music and, eventually, my sexuality. On maybe the fifth beer I decided I had to talk to Charlie, so I lay down with him and told him I'm gay and weirded out by our kiss. I don't know how he took it, I felt bad for being a tease – he's a good guy, just a little immature.

I feel worse now, though. I went back to the fire and sat leaning against Rob. He said he liked it but wouldn't put his arm around me when I shivered. In the end I put my arm around him and we spent some time snuggling, looking for shooting stars and jumping away when someone (especially Charlie) came up with a torch.

We went to get some more beer and, on the way back to the fire, he turned me around and kissed me. I know I should feel terrible about Charlie, but it was the sexiest kiss I've ever had. We slowly edged away from the group and set up a couple of pads and sleeping bags in a corner of bushes. We lay under the stars kissing and cuddling, touching and talking.

I woke at 5.30 and, on my way to the loo, glimpsed Charlie sitting glumly. My heart raced and I hid behind the bathrooms for half an hour hoping to avoid confrontation, unsure whether he had seen Rob and me asleep in each other's arms. When I thought the coast was clear and walked towards the bus, he popped out. He said good-morning and dashed off for a run. I took a shower and, when I re-emerged, it was pouring with rain. I ran into Rob and we decided to hide out on the bench out of the rain. We snuggled and dozed while it poured around us for a long time. Two deer came almost right up to us and I melted sleepily into his arms.

* * *

Rob said he might come to New York after the trip. I hope so. How did I fall so recklessly, so fast, and with so little concern as to how cruel I'm being to Charlie? My whole body aches for a stolen moment with Rob. Jess will laugh. Greg will tut. Thirty-eight's not so old, right? Twice my age. But I like him a lot. And I leave the country in two weeks.

Chicago

Fourth of July. I rode to the top of the Sears Tower – overpriced but an amazing view. I like this city; perhaps I'll add it to my shopping list of possible places to live. We walked through the park where 'Taste of Chicago' was going on and took a boat tour. I queued for a Ferris wheel with Ash and Leah before ditching them and meeting Rob at the Art Institute. We snuck a few kisses and held hands a lot. After being thrown out at closing time, we walked around, across the river and through streets of such fantastic architecture that we cricked our necks with looking up. Later in the evening, we watched the Fourth of July fireworks over the pier.

This time next week, Rob will be out of my life. I seem to make a pattern of getting myself into intense situations with no hope. Perhaps they wouldn't be as intense if they did have hope, but I can't help dreading saying goodbye.

He asked if he was the first boy I've ever dated. He's not, but I think he's the first guy I've really fancied – actually wanted as opposed to falling into something with someone because he liked me, or present company was homophobic, or I was confused. I like him a lot. Too much. I don't like guys like this. It's odd. Nice, though, too. I wish we had kissed in the Badlands and didn't have to be secretive now. I wish I could just be a normal girl with normal romances.

Niagara Falls, New York State

At five this morning I woke up to see a beautiful Ohio sunrise and steal a smile from Rob before sleeping again. We had breakfast on a beach, then drove through Pennsylvania to Niagara Falls. We took the Maid of the Mist *boat tour and tickled one another, poked and smiled at the frustration of having all these blue-raincoated people around. He even snuck a quick kiss.*

I met Rob at the trolley stop after the tour and we wandered around for a while looking for internet access. Dreading Matthew's latest rants, I decided not to check my email, but we booked a private hostel room in Chelsea for next week. Then we had a sandwich in Denny's and talked crazily about random topics – language, semiotics, the bus, relationships . . . He said he's scared by how much he wants to get to know me. Too much.

He thinks Charlie may have seen him kiss me on the boat, so I'm vaguely preparing myself for confrontation but don't really know how to deal with it. I hope Rob doesn't think I'm enjoying the secrecy. I guess it comes easily, but I'm not proud of it. Rob's right, I don't owe Charlie anything, but I still don't want to hurt him. I can't wait to have Rob to myself in New York.

New York State

When they changed drivers in the middle of the night, Rob kissed me before going to bed. I'd just woken from a nightmare about Matthew and being back in England and went to sleep again smiling. We had breakfast by the Delaware River. We're now camping in the Catskills and I have less and less patience for secrecy, but I'm having to entertain myself while he does paperwork. I just jumped in the ice-cold creek – Ash says I'm the 'hardcore girl' when it comes to cold water.

Seeking out the sunset, Rob and I took a walk along the river and finally became too impatient to wait, so I snuck into his tent and he followed shortly after. We snuggled up in a postcoital cuddle and talked about relationships and kids and

231

families. He asked me if he could tell me a secret about himself. He's had a vasectomy. I told him vaguely about my one significant relationship and my new selfish desire for and love of life. He said he's not very good at relationships. Me neither. Perhaps we're perfect for a non-relationship relationship. I know I still can't blurt out everything about Matthew and maybe never will be able to, but unlike Becky and Charlie, Rob seems like he knows I have a history and it doesn't matter. All he cares about is right now. I hope we stay in touch and find each other again somewhere, if only fleetingly. I like his body. I like his kisses and his eyes, his legs and his butt, his mouth and his stubble, I like all his hats and I even like his cute shyness about his greying hair.

We slept cuddled up and woke at 6.30. He woke up in more ways than one and I kissed him until he came, realising without much shame that I'm no good in bed.

Then, for some absurd reason, we went and plunged naked into the river. It was so cold that we came straight back out and tangled in each other's towels, but at least I went skinny-dipping once on the trip.

Manhattan
We arrived in New York at two and there were sad goodbyes. For the first time, I didn't want to be in this city.

He kissed me on the street and climbed back on the bus to drive on to Boston. Now I'm with Amy, giving her the gossip and feeling like a pathetic lovesick woman.

Shopping in Soho with Amy today. Last night we saw a dreadful film, then just hung out with some wine. My mind fizzed and the weird robots on the screen did nothing to cure the depression that was forming about my looming return to England.

Today I feel better. We got henna tattoos at an Egyptian market that made me think of Nadiyya, and walked all over Downtown.

Then we saw a play in promenade at Castle Clinton in Battery Park. In the afternoon, we walked to Dino's apartment to hang out and later headed to an Italian bar in the Village. We had pizza at another Italian place on the corner of Bleecker and Carmine, and from there we walked into Little Italy, where there was some kind of festival going on. We never found out what it was about, but people were waving flags and spilling onto the road, climbing cars and chanting excitedly.

After a bit of negotiating with a bouncer about my lack of ID, we went into a bar. Later Amy, Dino and I walked through the chanting crowds to get to the subway and it felt great to blend in. Perhaps I should learn Italian. 'Reinventing yourself again?' Matthew would tut.

I'm with Rob now and it's luxurious to be in this city once more. Yesterday we met at the hostel in Chelsea around 11am. We left at one, freshly showered and 'annoying to anyone but us'. We headed uptown to the Guggenheim where there was an exhibition of Zaha Hadid. It was awesome just to see the Guggenheim, but spiralling down, immersing myself in futuristic architecture with his palm in mine was pure artistic heaven.

We walked through Central Park a bit and took the subway to Brooklyn, wandered under the bridges, indulgently shared expensive chocolates, then walked along the water and through the neighbourhoods. We crossed Brooklyn Bridge, taking our time to kiss every few steps, and walked all the way over to the Village for dinner. We walked back to the hostel and stayed up talking and fucking.

We woke for sex and philosophy, ate bagels and took the subway to Columbus Circle to hire bikes. Over four hours, we cycled from 59th and 8th to 122nd and 5th, then across to Riverside Park, down along the river all the way to Battery Park and across to Pier 17, where we shared a hot dog and smoothie. Back on the bikes, we cycled up the east side and back across to

59th and 8th. Apart from the last 20 blocks of rush-hour traffic (too much even for my inner adrenalin junkie), it felt really good.

We just came back to pick up his phone and distract ourselves for a couple more hours. Now we're off for Thai food.

We found Thai in the East Village. Along the way, we walked right into Rob's friend Saul. We met up with him later to go to a club on 5th and C. It was pretty cool and we drank and danced until the place closed. Once outside, I realised how giddy I was. We laughed all the way back, buying cookies to share in bed before passing out with the key still in the door.

Four hours later ear-splitting trucks pulled up outside our window to work on who knows what. Once awake, we resigned ourselves to hot, sticky morning sex, then went for a bagel and coffee.

I left Rob so I could have tea with Greg and say goodbye. He told me again that I should think about grad school and said some nice things. He also gave me a hard time about Rob's age and asked why I didn't bring him to introduce them. I'm going to miss Greg horribly.

Boston, MA

Rob and I took the Chinatown bus to Boston and arrived in the late afternoon. We found his bus and went to the infamous Regina's Pizza, followed by a little café for tiramisu. When we returned, we made a bed in the back of the bus. I guess it's pretty hot and kind of kinky with Rob, but it feels tender and good too.

This morning we went out for breakfast and have been all lovey-dovey, sexy and sad. Now we're driving in the bus to New York, where I'll meet my mum and he'll head off on the next trip.

*   *   *

Last night I had a nightmare involving Matthew, and when I woke up I was so happy to see Rob. I feel safe with him. I know he's older and I'm a little stupid, but this is mutual and non-manipulative and so much more innocent. He makes me feel good and my own person. He's a goof and a dork and it's not serious, but, Hell, it's fun and I've finally started to come! And he rides bikes with me. And he just kissed me.

New York City
I'm sat in the hotel with my mum now. I just had a fifty-minute phone conversation with Rob because he won't leave my head. I woke up in the night expecting to see him and I missed him in all the places we went today.

Kissing him goodbye was dreadful. Luckily Mum was jetlagged so I had some time to shower and feel sorry for myself last night. Today we woke early and were some of the first people up the Empire State Building. I looked down at Manhattan and tracked our cycle path around the city. It wasn't a perfectly clear morning, but it was fun to see this city that I'll miss from on high.

I took Mum for bagels in Starbucks and shopping in Macy's at her request. After that, we rode the Staten Island Ferry to see the Statue of Liberty. We ate lunch in Battery Park and walked to Wall Street and Ground Zero.

I've promised Rob I'll come back to the States next month for another trip. I wish I could tell Mum about him, but I'd forgotten how silent and awkward we are about my love life. It's odd that we can discuss our mutual appreciation of Anaïs Nin, but I can't tell her I'm a little bit crazy over Rob. It's my fault, I suppose, for weaving so many secrets and lies between us. I also spent the past few months working up the courage to tell her I'm gay, but I don't suppose I can do that now either.

* * *

A whirlwind tour of Times Square, followed by Lou Donaldson at the Jazz Standard. They played 'Falling in Love with Love', which of course made me think of Rob. He's haunting me in this city. It used to be mine but now I pass the Papaya King and glimpse the Empire State and he's all my mind can handle.

I fantasise about blurting out to my mum, 'I usually date women but right now I'm a little bit stupid over a guy who lives in California.' I don't seem able to, though.

Still, I feel better about the next few weeks. Perhaps I can even handle the Hell of facing Matthew. Perhaps.

I have to stop myself daydreaming about a future I'll never have with Rob. Silly girl that I am.

How can I have spent eighteen years in Sussex and one in Durham and feel completely groundless, but two weeks on a bus and miss it like it's home?

MoMA today. A picnic lunch in Central Park and goodbye phone calls. I cried a little in the park and vaguely told Mum about Rob. She got all parental and said she hoped I was being careful. I blushed but muttered that she didn't need to worry about that with Rob because of his vasectomy. Mum and I are closer than we've been for years, which makes me happy, but I can't help thinking she'd disown me if she knew the truth.

Delaware County, New York State

It's odd to see the Rosella campus empty. I gave Mum a tour, followed by chess and chai in my favourite café for the last time. I said goodbye to Jess and tried to wash this place out of my system.

I fly tomorrow . . . but I'll be back.

My mum and I landed at Heathrow on 19th July. We crammed my four bulging suitcases into the back of a taxi and both dozed through the two hours back to Sussex. I said hello to my dad and glanced at

236

the pile of envelopes with my name on, but essentially slept and cried for two days. On the third day, my birthday, I booked my flight back to San Francisco for 23rd August, where I'd stay with Rob before going with him on another tour. My mum took me out for lunch, and my dad and I propped up the bar in the pub down the road until closing time. I woke with a hangover and began packing my things into boxes for uni. Explaining that I wanted to go to Durham early to find a job, I persuaded my mum to drive me and my stuff up the M1. Tim had emailed a few months ago asking if I fancied being the fifth person in their house and I'd jumped at the opportunity to not return to college accommodation. The house had been ours since 1st July, but nobody was moving in until term started in early October. Still, an empty house in a pretty city was preferable to a month of holding my breath every time I walked out my door in Sussex. Apart from a brief tea party at Valerie's the day after my birthday, where Matthew and I chatted stiffly about The National's autumn programme, I managed to avoid him.

Once I got to Durham, I didn't look for a job. I reasoned there was no point if I was leaving in a month. I read and wrote and went for long walks. I tried to cook Jambalaya for myself and took long bubble baths. Eventually 23rd August arrived.

In my daze of nervous expectation, the journey went quickly. I was frisked twice and had my ChapStick confiscated by security, which caused me to worry more about developing a coldsore halfway across the Atlantic than the class-orange terror alert announced days before my flight. In the very furthest seat in my row with nobody next to me, I spent London to Chicago curled up in three blankets listening to the flight attendants bitch about the passengers. From Chicago to San Francisco, I had a window and watched as the land changed. As we began our descent, I was treated to the sun setting over the Bay.

Rob walked past where I sat and I saw him anxiously scan the screen for my flight number. Leaving my bags, I ran to him and he turned just as I jumped into his arms. Our awkward embrace made us laugh and we smiled giddily as we walked back to my stuff. Rob drove us home in his beat-up truck, and halfway through the journey I slid along the seat to lean on his shoulder. He talked the whole way back, babbling about the city, giving me a night-time tour. I was high with energy for him and waffled words I've now forgotten, giggling and apologising for my incoherence. We ate cereal after I'd showered and sat shyly together on his bed. Finally, after being awake for twenty-eight hours, I fell asleep in his arms.

The following day I woke smiling and we went out to shop for supplies. After a late lunch, we went back to bed. We woke hours later having missed the party we were supposed to attend. Instead, Rob took me out for fries and a shake followed by a movie. Our first real date.

Before the trip departed, we rented bikes and cycled over the Golden Gate Bridge and around Sausalito. Our mornings were frittered away lying in bed talking of showering and doing active things but instead melting into each other without urgency. When we finally got up, we made coffee and eggs and sat on rusty garden chairs on his patio. He showed me around San Francisco on foot; we found pizza, new glasses and a Giants game for him, and a dress, Vietnamese food and a terrible piece of *In-Yer-Face* theatre for me.

The sex was better than before and I wrote silly things in my journal about my newfound orgasms. Rob told me he was a little scared, that he was trying to keep his feet on the ground, but it wasn't working. I doodled some more about wishing I could erase the past and offer myself to him fresh, about feeling suddenly so normal that it seemed abnormal.

We picked up the passengers and the other driver, Louisa, at the meeting point and I sat up with Rob as he drove out of San Francisco. This trip took us on a daredevil hike to Angel's Landing in Zion National Park; to the neon cheesiness of Las Vegas in atrocious heat; to the Grand Canyon exactly one year after my arrival in the US; to breakfast at a cowboy town called Tombstone; to a 'clothing optional' hot spring in New Mexico; to the snow-like dunes of White Sands National Monument; to the mud bath that marks the Rio Grande in Big Bend National Park; to ride the Dillo and eat tacos in Austin; to a bar serving Bloody Marys at 10am in New Orleans; to see dolphins in St Andrew's State Park, near Panama City; to another sprawling beach in North Carolina; and to a final campsite next to the Delaware River.

By the end of the journey, I'd visited thirty-two different states, had sex in eight national parks and swapped 'I love you's from Florida to Massachusetts. When I thought about going back to Durham, I remembered I was twenty and a kid and a dork. I spoke to Jess on the phone and realised I envied her for being able to accept she was different, that she wanted Angelo and didn't care if she fitted in or not. But, as hard as I tried, I couldn't picture Rob visiting me in Durham. Nor could I picture myself as I was now – the person who had sat on a bus in the Grand Canyon wearing a scruffy pair of shorts, Rob's arm around me as he dozed – back at university in England. I was confused. I had too many personas, too many worlds. The normal student in Durham was still entwined with the bizarre child-woman who had been involved with Matthew. However, this intense, satisfying, fun and innocent relationship with Rob left a trace of a similar kind of sordid embarrassment when I tried to reconcile his age with the real world.

We spent my final week in Boston and New York. We hired bikes to see Cambridge, Queens and Brooklyn, sampled tiramisu in every deli we passed and called in on Jess who was settling in as a grad student at Harvard. In New York, we stayed with one of Rob's friends in Astoria, where we tried to make the most of our final few days.

I cried at JFK, unsure if I could force myself to get on the plane, incapable of imagining a day without Rob. I'd slept badly, waking up to look at him until the alarm went off at 4.30am. He drove me to the airport, but there was no parking, so he had to drop me off. Tears rolled down our cheeks as we clung to each other on the sidewalk.

I cried in the line to check in, pulling my hat low over my face and shaking with self-pity. I rang a friend in England, wanting to ask him to come give me a hug at Heathrow, but realising it would be a ridiculous request. I rang Rob, who was stuck in traffic and shouldn't have answered his cell phone, but did.

'I want to be with you,' I said. 'I don't want to be with anyone else.'

'So don't,' he replied and I heard tears in his voice.

'Okay.' I smiled, in spite of myself. 'I'll call you when I'm in England.'

I thought about the bus I had already booked back to Durham and the empty house I'd be in when I arrived. I wondered if I should have planned to return to Sussex, to curl into my mum's cuddles and eat homemade food. Home. But not really. Durham would be safer.

At Victoria Coach Station, unsure who to turn to, I rang my dad's ex-girlfriend, April. We'd stayed friends and often talked about love. Of anyone, I felt she'd understand. She tried to persuade me to go to hers in Guildford instead of Durham. I thought about how much a train ticket would cost and thanked her but declined. Next I rang my mum and she said it must be sad for me, but perhaps I could see him again. I said goodbye and wished I hadn't called her.

I arrived in Durham at 11pm to a quiet house with no internet, so I paid full international rates to let Rob know I'd arrived. I got his voicemail.

Waking to an empty house – an empty bed – was more than I could handle. After less than twelve hours in Durham, I jumped on a train heading south to spend a few days with April and try to sort out my mixed-up head.

A woman on the train asked me if I had a boyfriend. I stumbled at how to explain that yesterday morning I'd woken in the naked arms of a perfect man in Queens and today I was stuck on a delayed train, travelling 300 miles for a cuddle from someone who cares.

23

Term began and I applied for a job at a coffee shop. I loved my first term's class, which was about feminist literature depicting New York City, and I got on well with the other students Tim and I were sharing the house with. Daniel, whom I'd worked with on *Clouds*, asked if I'd like to produce his production of David Hare's *Skylight*, so I found my way back into the drama society. Rob and I made plans for him to visit me in Durham for a whole month just after Christmas, and I called my mum to arrange to introduce them in London after New Year's.

I missed my friends in the US and tried to email Greg and Jess as much as I could, but logging-in to my email always came with an element of dread. Matthew's messages had dried up over the summer when he realised I wasn't responding, but we had seen each other for the first time since Christmas at a tea party at Valerie's house. The encounter was civil, each of us adopting perfect personas, but it prompted the resumption of his daily email attacks. In my replies, I attempted to reason with him, to be polite and to offer him friendship, but everything I typed became fuel for more viciousness. At present, though, they were just words. Words that cut, got inside my head, and made me cry in my bedroom alone; but, thankfully, also words that could be made to disappear with the touch of my laptop's power button.

Then the first letter arrived. Double enveloped. Forwarded from Matthew. Using my real name on the external address.

Rupert Cochrane
F&R Solicitors
PO Box 101
London
SWxxxx

Harriet Moore
Care of Albert Sumac
PO Box 666
London
SWxxxx

31st October 2004

Dear Ms Harriet Moore

It is my duty to inform you that, as requested in the will of Rose Shaw, we are bound to enquire about the status of your relationship with Albert Sumac as of November 2004. At the reading of the will in December 2003, Mr Sumac requested you not be made aware of the terms of the document in case they influenced any decisions you might make, but now it is imperative I bring certain details to your attention.

As laid out in the will of Rose Shaw, written and signed 8th September 2003, Harriet Moore and Albert Sumac were bequeathed (and I quote):

- a rental legacy of £53,000, specifically to be used for a house or flat in Durham.*
- a theatre and foreign travel legacy of £12,195.*

Shaw)'s death on the sole condition that the beneficiaries are
in a committed relationship. Should this not be the case, all
funds should be donated to the Cats Protection Agency.

Thus, it is my duty to enquire whether or not you are currently in a 'committed relationship' with Albert Sumac. I have already contacted Mr Sumac and he has responded in the negative, but I need written confirmation from both parties before I may proceed with executing Ms Shaw's last wishes.

As such, I would appreciate it if you could respond to my query as soon as possible using the above address.

Yours

Rupert Cochrane
F&R Solicitors

One week later, I received another typed letter:

Natalie

You will be hearing from my solicitor, but I thought it polite to inform you myself first. Under advice and with little choice given your inability to discuss such matters reasonably, I am in the unfavourable position of having to take legal action against you (see enclosed).

As I'm sure it will yours, this breaks my heart. I have tried to reduce the sum as much as possible. All the legacy items have been halved, though, of course, you have already lost your own half, and so your total deficit is nearly doubled. I wish it could have been different.

I have also halved the rental cost of the Kew flat, because in theory we were living there together, though, of course, we both know I left for half the summer because you became unbearable.

Gas and electricity are difficult to calculate for the period, so I have let you off there.

My sadness is in knowing that none of this would have been necessary had you been able to show me some respect and follow through on your offer of friendship. I have tried to settle with you, but your stubbornness has made you unable to recognise a friend when you need one, and this, I'm afraid, will now have to serve as another part of your learning process. A lesson more expensive than any of those at Rosella. Perhaps now you will understand that getting your own way and having everything on your own terms is both expensive and lonely. Perhaps, anyway. No doubt you will find a way to blame this on me.

I am willing to discuss this:

- alone
- with my solicitor present
- with your mother present
- with your bus driver present (yes, your Ma has been blathering about your latest bedfellow)
- or any combination of the above

I am sorry it has come to this. I tried not to believe it for a long, long time, but I fear I was avoiding the truth: you are cold, Natalie. You give me goose-bumps.

Yours sincerely

Matthew Wright

Details of funds to be recovered from Natalie Lucas of 30 D***** Road, Durham, DH** 4**

Rental legacy Durham flat/house @ 50% of £53,000	26,500
Furniture (private purchase)	1,254
Travel to and from Durham	150

(two visits with regard to the rental legacy)	
Decorations/books, etc.	70
Three months' rental of Richmond flat	1,275
@ 50% of £2,550	
Theatre and foreign travel legacy	6,097
@ 50% of £12,195	

GRAND TOTAL	**£35,346**

What's your reaction after reading this? Do you laugh? Is your mind's mouth hanging mid-air in amazement? Are you incredulous? Do you have the number of a good lawyer in your address book?

You, reader, whatever your reaction, would surely have known what to do next. But, just in case my powers of authorship have failed thus far, I must reiterate certain details about the girl who found these letters on the doormat of her third-year student home – about me:

- I was twenty years old;
- I had been lying to my family since I was fifteen;
- The only people, apart from the two of us involved, that knew about my affair with Matthew were Rose, now dead, and possibly Matthew's wife;
- Barring a brief stint of work experience at a solicitor's office when I was thirteen, I had never spoken to a lawyer;
- I was certain that confessing the truth, telling my parents, friends, professors and boyfriend that I had willingly conducted a three-year affair with a man forty-four years older than me was not now, nor ever would be, an option.

Thus, once again, my bedroom door was closed and I was sobbing secret tears of self-pity. Downstairs, my housemates made pots of tea and chatted about choosing dissertation topics; in two hours, I would be due at a seminar on Jessica Hagedorn's *The Gangster of Love*; on my computer screen flashed an email from my mum enquiring what my plans were for the Christmas holidays; and beside my bed lay a snapshot of Rob and me taken at a Mets game the second time we were in New York. All around, life was normal and comforting, but in my hand lay a page that seemed to shred my insides. From gallbladder to gut, tiny paper cuts were appearing, slicing my capillaries and dicing my conscience. In itself, this was nothing new: inside, I'd been screaming for months. All across America, in National Parks and Second Cities, I'd peered over my shoulder expecting to see an army of Uncles out for my blood. What was new was that now, on top of all my internal demons, an external and altogether more frightening one was suing me for £35,346.

What did I do? Exactly what I shouldn't have done, of course. I contacted Matthew. I selected an email at random, hit reply and ranted my own schizophrenic barrage of emails, shouting in capitals that he was a SICK BASTARD WITHOUT A LEG TO STAND ON, then begging in italics that we *resolve this and find a way to proceed as friends*.

When my tears finally dried and the agitation in my fingertips turned to cramp, I lowered my laptop lid and paced into the bathroom to wash my face. I chatted to Tim in the kitchen as I buttered a slice of toast, then grabbed my bag and slammed the door. I strode down to campus, climbed the stairs to my class and contributed to a discussion about Hagedorn's depiction of racial dismorphia. That evening, I attended rehearsals for *Skylight* and spoke excitedly to a guy called David about applying for the new student slot at the local theatre: a week's run in their studio space, directed and produced by us, any play we wanted, applications due Monday. Then I cycled home, cooked a bowl of pasta, watched two episodes of *24*, season three, with Tim, brushed my teeth, and closed my door.

At which point, the thoughts I'd stopped myself from thinking all day finally bullied their way into existence.

24

'You have two new messages and no saved messages. First new
message, received today, 10th November, at 13.42, caller withheld their number: (pause) *Look here, Harriet, or whatever your
name is, you bitch. This is Meg, maybe you've heard of me –
Albert's new girlfriend, as in me new and wanted, you old and
unwanted. I don't know what's going on or why you keep
contacting Albert, but you're really upsetting him and he needs it
about as much as a hole in the head. He doesn't know I'm ringing
you and you better not fucking tell him because I had to hack into
his email, but it's for his own good. So listen here, bitch skank,
I'm telling you nicely: LEAVE HIM ALONE! If you don't believe
that's me telling you nicely, try me! Right next to your phone
number, I've found your address. Durham's real nice, isn't it? I
was going to live there too, until you fucked that up by messing
Albert around and banishing us to skankbag—*

'Second new message, received today, 10th November, at
13.44, caller withheld their number: (pause) *Fucking machine,
I'm not done yet. No siree, I'm certainly not done with you yet,
I'm just getting started. You better understand that if you don't
listen to me and leave me and Albert the fuck alone, I'll find a
reason to visit Durham and maybe I'll bring my brother along.*

He likes sport, you know, especially cricket and golf and other things with bats and clubs. I'm pretty sure he wouldn't mind bringing some along and demonstrating how they can be used on dirty bitch skanks like you. Now FUCK THE HELL OFF!'

From: wcarson@worldopen.com
To: Natalie Lucas <sexy_chocolate69@sweetmail.com>
Sent: 15 November 2004, 15:21:38
Subject: Please get in touch

Dear Ms Lucas

My name is William Carson and I am a freelance private detective, formerly an officer of security with the FBI, first in the Criminal Investigative Division and later in the Cyber Division. I am writing to you about a matter that gives me grave cause for concern. I have pleaded with Mr Albert Sumac to give me your postal address and let me contact you directly, but he maintains that your privacy is paramount, even in circumstances like these.

It has come to my attention that you may be the subject of a vicious character attack. An Hispanic woman living in Boston, MA, whom I may legally only refer to as Miss P., has attempted to produce a slur on your character. Her attempts have been stopped for now, but she claims to have found illicit photographs of you on various online websites. My sources suggest she is not responsible for distributing these photographs, but that she has tried to advertise your 'services', presumably with the intention of accusing you of solicitation at a later date. Miss P. claims her grievance against you is that you have 'stolen' her man (it is unclear if she refers to a husband or boyfriend) and left her child (a three-year-old son) without a father.

It is as Mr Sumac's employee that I have discovered this much and Mr Sumac has forbidden me any further investigations without your approval. As such, I implore you to contact me and divulge any information you may have in regards to the case. I do not wish to alarm you, but the consequences of such a matter if not dealt with delicately can be grave, and I would not like to see you hurt. I've been working in this field for years, absolutely years, and trust me I know what I'm talking about. So please, it is imperative that you speak to me as soon as possible.

You can reach me on 0208 *** ***.

Yours

William Carson
PI

From: Michael Hills <mphills@vmail.com>
To: Natalie Lucas <sexy_chocolate69@sweetmail.com>
Sent: 15 November 2004, 16:08:21
Subject: I'll be in Durham

'Naughty Natalie'

I saw your ad and can't get your picture out of my mind. I don't normally do this, but with you, God, with that picture.. I don't care if you're rubbing half the world against your thigh, you dirty slut. I have a business meeting near Durham next week and thought I could get us a hote . so make a place between your legs, baby. I'm happy to ʝay cash.

Ring me: 0777******

Michael xox

From: Matthew Wright <theoutsider@worldopen.co.uk>
To: Natalie Lucas <sexy_chocolate69@sweetmail.com>
Sent: 15 November 2004, 19:42:21
Subject: Re: What the fuck?!

> *When we two parted*
> *In silence and tears*
> *Half broken-hearted*
> *To sever for years,*
> *Pale grew thy cheek and cold,*
> *Colder thy kiss;*
> *Truly that hour foretold*
> *Sorrow to this . . .*

I don't know why I expected anything different. That is just like you: I try to protect you, put myself out, use my own money, all because I am concerned about you and your life, a life I am allowed no part of. And this is the thanks I get. You accuse me. *You accuse me!*

You don't think it could be your filthy bus driver whom you've known all of five minutes? No, much easier to blame me, then you can carry on your casual sex across the globe. I am trying to protect you, Natalie. I can't do more than that. You won't let me.

I've spoken to William. This woman claims to be your bus driver's partner, claims to have a child with him. She has also had a sex test and come up positive for herpes, so I suggest you get checked out because I assume if he wasn't careful with her, he's not been careful with you. This Miss P. says he claimed to have had a vasectomy, and then denied the child when she fell pregnant. I only hope you haven't been so naive.

Do you realise this is your whole life, your whole career on the line? What do you think your universities will say if they see these pictures? William's shown me some of them, they're quite explicit. I've never seen them before, but they're definitely you. A shudder comes o'er me. I've seen one of you sucking on some saggy bird's cunt. She has a tattoo. Someone else must have been there to take the picture. Nadiyya perhaps? Or maybe you slutted around in good old NY? Sorry, I'm not trying to offend you, but you need to see reality. I am not the enemy. It is not a big deal if I see these, hell, I've seen it all before, but what if your professors find them? What if Rosella is told one of their former pupils is advertising as a prostitute? William can help. But I won't tell him to do anything without your consent.

You need to trust me. I'm on your side.

> *I hear thy name spoken,*
> *And share in its shame.*

But with emails like your last, I wonder why I bother, why I ever held you so dear.

> *. . . In secret we met –*
> *In silence I grieve,*
> *That thy heart could forget,*
> *Thy spirit deceive.*
> *If I should meet thee*
> *After long years,*
> *How should I greet thee?*
> *With silence and tears.*

From: wcarson@worldopen.com
To: Natalie Lucas <sexy_chocolate69@sweetmail.com>
Sent: 16 November 2004, 10:11:31
Subject: More information

Natalie,

You have not yet replied to my earlier email and I have
just got off the phone with Mr Albert Sumac, who tells me
you are mistrustful of the information we have approached
you with.

I cannot stress strongly enough the importance of you
working with us in this matter. I have been researching
similar cases for many years. Serial grooming is in fact
my specialty. The laws in the US are good at protecting
its own citizens, but do little to defend the interests of visitors to the country. As such, there are a number of men
around the country – some in almost every state and
often known to the federal authorities, though they have
little power to prosecute – who make a habit of pursuing
young foreign women travelling alone. They befriend these
women and form 'relationships'. While in the United
States, these men often appear charming and generous,
playing on the tragic aspect of an international love affair
and inciting the women to feel passionately.

The aim, however, is to secure an invitation to visit these
women in their home countries. Once there, the man's
true colours are suddenly revealed – when the woman
has nowhere to run, nowhere to go. At best, the woman
can hope to find a sex pervert who forces her to partake
in whatever brand of deviancy he subscribes to, often by
force, with the intention of returning to the United States

253

before criminal proceedings can be brought forward, or in the hope that the woman will be so ashamed she will feel unable to press charges. Even if she does turn to the police before the predator leaves the country, instances of prosecution are rare because these men are unknown to foreign blood and semen databases.

At worst, though – and here I beseech you to think long and hard about your knowledge of the man you are in a relationship with – the man will have laid a complex sexual and financial trap for the young woman. Reassured by the safety he is granted by being born in the U.S.A. he will most likely have given her a false name and made sure everything she knows about his identity has come solely from him. Then, once in her country, at her house, he will begin to manipulate her and those around her, encouraging or forcing her into situations she would normally avoid. To do so, he will most likely enlist the help of a network of contacts already known in the country, possibly met on a previous visit or even just found through the internet. The crimes they then commit could take the form of identity theft or other financial fraud, but they can also manifest as more disturbing sexual crimes, including gang rape, enforced pornography, and in extreme cases trafficking for prostitution. The most disturbing case I have worked on involved a woman such as yourself disappearing from her home in Surrey days after her Texan 'boyfriend' arrived, only to be found six months later being forced to work in a brothel in Thailand.

It is a strange inhumanity that leads people to treat others this way, but sadly it is a truth that it happens all around this world. These men are so dangerous because they spin a web of sin and lay it as a trap for vulnerable women. They are persuasive, but they cannot be trusted. Their manipulations rely on desire, promises and lust, and once they have a woman's trust they will take away her money, time and dignity if possible. Because of the transient lifestyle suited to these individuals, they often choose work in travel or vehicular transportation, often favouring cross-country routes that give them the widest possible net to seek out victims.

I do not mean to scare you Natalie, but I am concerned for your safety. Mr Sumac contacted me because he fears from past experience that your judgment when it comes to sexual situations is poor. He says you have, in the past, displayed an inability to assess a person's agenda or even bodily hygiene before it is too late and that you have been coerced into unfavourable sexual situations using alcohol. It is not my place to comment on these matters, but from everything Mr Sumac has told me about your situation – even without the business with the wife and child – I would advise you to think carefully about what you know about your bus driver that you haven't learned from him. Have you seen his passport or driver's license? Have you met any immediate family or close friends? Mr Sumac informs me he is 39 years of age. In my experience, it would be strange if a man of that age did not have a wife or ex-wife and a certain amount of baggage to bring to a relationship. If he has not told you about such things, you may need to ask yourself why. The other possibility is that he may be bisexual, which again should raise alarm bells in your mind as male bisexuality is the biggest contributor to the spread of HIV/AIDS in the United States.

As it is, I have taped phone conversations recording your bus driver crudely taunting his wife with your sexual willingness, boasting that you give oral without pressure and will do anything he asks. I am in no way defending the actions of Miss P., but please ask yourself Natalie what kind of man taunts his wife with details about his erotic activities with his mistress? Is there any way, do you think, that he could be involved in the business of the internet photographs and allegations of prostitution against you? Could they relate to a more complex plan he has for his visit in January? Could he be dangerous?

If you find yourself doubting the answer to just one of the questions above, you need my help, Natalie. I have seen too many young women just like yourself be manipulated by these disturbed men to sit back and watch it happen again.

<u>Please</u> get in touch.

William Carson
PI

From: wcarson@worldopen.com
To: Natalie Lucas <sexy_chocolate69@sweetmail.com>
Sent: 16 November 2004, 11:32:55
Subject: Postscript

Apologies if my previous email disturbed you. My intention was not to scare you, only to make you understand the seriousness of the situation. I am not trying to interfere with your life or tell you what to do; I am merely acting on behalf of your concerned neighbour. Though Mr Sumac tells me you would like us to just leave you alone, you seem to have troubles and I'm worried something bad is going to happen to you, perhaps in your own home.

I realise this must all come as a shock to you. If you would like to talk to a counsellor who could advise you on coping with the psychological impacts of sex pests and grooming, I have a female colleague whom I could arrange to talk with you on MSN via this email address.

Please let me know.

William Carson
PI

From: Matthew Wright <theoutsider@worldopen.co.uk>
To: Natalie Lucas <sexy_chocolate69@sweetmail.com>
Sent: 16 November 2004, 14:44:10
Subject: Songs of my experience

Each man is in his **SPECTRE's** power, Natalie! But you, you are drowning in your own lake. You cannot see the wood for the trees, you are so blind. Your bus driver is no good. I can see that, your Ma can see that, your house-mates can probably see that, everyone but you. And meanwhile, he's sitting happily in Boston or Chicago or Salt Lake City, wherever his fuck-bus has arrived now, chuckling to himself about his stupid piece of little British 'ass'. But you, you are stubborn and blind and blame me instead.. Remember, though, mutual fear brings peace, only until the selfish loves increase. I assume you still have the intelligence to work out what that means, but maybe I'm wrong. You are only safe, Natalie, until he comes to collect what he wants. He is a predator. And you are a doe-eyed deer, so stupid you don't know when to run and when to wave your fluffy white butt like the slut you are.

Once, I worried about you in a spiritual sense. I worried your mind would be enclosed in a narrow circle and your heart sunk into an abyss by those who couldn't see your worth. But now I realise I was wrong: you are the one who has chosen the circle and the abyss and I wonder why I bother continuing to worry when you refuse to worry about yourself. You won't listen to me because you are stubborn, but YOU ARE IN DANGER, Natalie. Forget your senses, your perception, your gnosis and the pleasure of stolen joys in a barren but eternal world; forget the 'unreal' plain in which we used to live, the dead poets and the lyricism of life: you are in danger in the gross, mucky, mundane world of everyone else. You have dug yourself a hole of pornography, sexual manipulation and jealousy, and you are so far short of being equipped to deal with it that you cannot even see you are in it.

From: Matthew Wright <theoutsider@worldopen.co.uk>
To: Natalie Lucas <sexy_chocolate69@sweetmail.com>
Sent: 16 November 2004, 21:18:35
Subject: Apology accepted

The man hath penance done, and penance more will do. As ever, I will do as you wish. And when you've got what you want from me, you'll cast me aside once more. William says I'm a fool. I'm no fool. I know you'll whistle thrice and cry, 'The game is done! I've won, I've won!' But

I suppose that's love. I once knew a girl called Natalie whom I thought knew love like me. We basked in her glory and made each other young. But I was wrong, she was but the Nightmare Life-in-Death, who thicks man's blood with cold. So now I shiver and dive for any scraps she cares to throw, knowing it will never be enough for her.

Anyway, I've instructed William to continue his investigations..

He is going to act as a character witness for you so that you do not need to appear in court.

I only hope it's not too late.

From: wcarson@worldopen.com
To: Natalie Lucas <sexy_chocolate69@sweetmail.com>
Sent: 18 November 2004, 10:45:06
Subject: Update

Ms Lucas,

It's your lucky day. Though you still haven't contacted me, Mr Albert Sumac has instructed me to continue my work to protect your reputation. Yesterday I appeared in court to defend you against the allegations of solicitation and protest the move to have you subpoenaed. Miss P. was ordered by Judge Dettori to leave you alone. She was also banned from visiting the websites that were mentioned and forced into fierce exile. Her hard drive has been sent for analysis and a piece of software has been installed on her computer to monitor her internet use and to track her emails. If she contacts you, she will be requested back in court.

As for the images on the web, I have taken down those I can find, but I'm afraid there is no guarantee there are no more out there. I would suggest monthly inspections, which I am happy to carry out for an extra fee if instructed.

I will send you my bill for the burdens of the day, plus expenses, shortly.

Yours

William Carson
PI

From: wcarson@worldopen.com
To: Natalie Lucas <sexy_chocolate69@sweetmail.com>
Sent: 18 November 2004, 16:51:29
Subject: RE: Update

Ms Lucas,

I'm afraid this is an issue you will have to take up with Mr Albert Sumac. Personally, I find your attitude quite extraordinary as Mr Sumac has done nothing but protect you thus far and seems only to have your interests in mind.

It is not in my nature to stamp my foot and demand you pay me my money down, but refusing to pay me will, I'm afraid, end in court, where the details of the case will be made public. Whether you want to pursue it to that point is up to you, but I would advise against it as it would negate all efforts to protect your reputation and privacy thus far.

Again, I am shocked at your response and cannot now imagine why Mr Sumac has gone to such lengths to protect such an ungrateful young woman.

Yours

William Carson
PI

From: Gary Hind <biggary69@sweetmail.com>
To: Natalie Lucas <sexy_chocolate69@sweetmail.com>
Sent: 20 November 2004, 23:21:57
Subject: Gimme, Gimme, Gimme

Woah, you are soooo fine! I want you to cover me in roses and blow my mind. I've never done anal before but am well up for it. Do I have to come to Durham or do you travel?

* * *

Natalie

Please find an amended bill below. My solicitor will be in touch.

Yours sincerely

Matthew Wright

Details of funds to be recovered from Natalie Lucas of 30
D****** Road, Durham, DH** 4**

Rental legacy Durham flat/house	
@ 50% of £53,000	26,500
Furniture (private purchase)	1,254
Travel to and from Durham	
(two visits with regard to the rental legacy)	150
Decorations/books, etc	70
Three months' rental of Kew flat	
@ 50% of £2,550	1,275
Theatre and foreign travel legacy	
@ 50% of £12,195	6,097
Services of William Carson, PI	4,100

GRAND TOTAL	£39,446

From: MandyPerrett@vmail.com
To: Natalie Lucas <sexy_chocolate69@sweetmail.com>
Sent: 28 November 2004, 15:01:43
Subject: Natalie, you take my little boy?

You want my man? You have my baby too.
I fly him over to spend christmas with his daddy and
you. I come too and we can all have happy holidays.
You like that? The mother, the father, the baby and the
whore.

Judge told me to leave you alone, but why should I? I've
lost my job. I've lost respect. I've lost my man. Why
shouldn't I lose baby too?

Maybe you wouldn't understand, you childless woman. But I make you understand. I make your womb rattle till you shriek my name and ask forgiveness.

I spoke to Mr Carson and he says there no more money coming from England. Your friend stop paying his bills cos you not grateful for his help. Well so there BITCH. Maybe you need your friend now more than eever.

Judge told me: Complainant Natalie has her name strike from record. Not even say your last name. Just mine. Your no name fucked with my real name.

Bla bla he say, Natalie a nice girl from luvely England with university career and going to be in plays and don't deserve damaging adverts. Made me apologise. I just clean toilets so it's ok. But inside I scream: SHE NOT NICE – SHE FUCK A BUS DRIVER.

So I come see you. I speak nothing but blood to you and make you taste it.

Fuck Mr Carson and fuck the judge. I don't care if I not suppose contact you. I come see you and bring you my little boy.

I work every day. Saturday and Sunday too. Now I count the days till I come to you in Durham and you can work every day for a little boy with no daddy.

BITCH.

25

There were others too, including more explicit emails requesting my 'services' that made me double-bolt my front door even when my housemates were home. When one man mentioned a visit to Durham in January, I vomited into the wastepaper basket next to my desk. Matthew was constantly in contact, of course. I wondered if all of it was an elaborate plan to get me to need his help. I wondered if he was trying to scare me. He knew about Rob because my mother had turned around at a dinner party and said, 'My daughter's in love'. He told me Rob was too old for me. He told me after the 'Nadiyya incident' I obviously had no ability to judge people and I must be in danger. He told me he wanted closure. He told me he wanted to meet in December.

I wanted closure too. I agreed to meet Matthew to talk. And I agreed when he offered to help with the sex scandal. He said he had found my picture online: my name, my body. He blamed Nadiyya. He said he had 'dealt' with the guys in the emails.

Then he screamed at me for being ungrateful. He said I owed him. Big time. He said I must do something nice for him every day until I reached twenty-one and, for every day I didn't do something nice, he would add another day. He said he would be at my house every morning in January to tell Rob what a slut I was. He kept threatening to sue. He said he would bankrupt and ruin me. He said I must meet him in December in a hotel and give him forty-eight hours. He said he still loved me.

I broke. I finally felt my flesh tear in half, splitting right down the middle, separating lung from lung, left from right; my heart beating furiously for all to see and my limbs shrivelling up and dying. I saw white. That was all. No more red anger, no more black fear or blue tears. I simply could not go on, so this was it. I told Matthew to do his worst. I told him to destroy me. Then the threats would have to stop. That was his ammunition. What was the worst he could do? Bankrupt me? Take away my family? My friends? Rob? My degree? Okay. Do it. Then I would pick up the pieces of my shattered self and find a way to go on. Then at least I would be free of his shadow.

A barrage of emails and letters followed. Threats from solicitors. Psychobabble and warnings from the private investigator. Attempts to worm into my head, to question my every belief. Accusations against Rob, assumptions about me, promises that I was in danger. Not just from Matthew either. From the rest of them. From Rose's manager Damien. From her psychiatrist, whom I'd never heard of until I received an eight-page email assessing my need for psychiatric confinement. From Matthew's friends in the 'industry'. All woven together with the investigator and Meg and Mandy Perrett, whoever she was: a Mafioso family from the porn world; a mob with money and supposed links to Ealing Studios. All of them telling me how incredibly wrong I was. How immature and naive I was being. How pig-headed and self-destructive, cruel and ego-maniacal, stone-cold inconsiderate, thoughtless, senseless, unkind, uncaring, uncharitable, unfeeling, unreasonable, irrational, hurtful, spiteful, vengeful, deceitful, blameful, distrustful, frightfully self-centred, insane, deranged, psychopathic, sociopathic, and just plain old pathetic.

I refused to respond. I determined to see Matthew in court. If he came to my house, I would call the police.

My resolve lasted a day. Within twenty-four hours I was back in contact with Matthew, ping-ponging insults and pleas, wailing mercilessly into my pillow and trying desperately to see a way out of my miserable hole.

'How are the spiders?' I asked Tim, burying my head in my cupboard and pretending to root for tins.

'Not bad, not bad. I think I'm going to write my dissertation on this one species that's only found in certain parts of the world.' I could sense Tim leaning against the counter, waiting for me to emerge and face him.

'Cool. Do you think your department will pay for you to travel to see it?' I said to a packet of spaghetti.

'Doubt it, but worth a try. You want a cup of tea?' I heard him step towards the kettle.

'Uh, sure,' I replied, wondering how to extricate myself from the cupboard and get back to my room without Tim noticing my wet lashes. Buying time, I twisted a tin of tomatoes to make the label face front. I heard water gush into the plastic kettle. I reached for a jar of honey at the back and contemplated it as Tim flicked the switch.

'Do you need to borrow something?' Tim said in my ear as the buzz of the kettle grew louder.

'Uh, no,' I breathed, afraid he would touch me.

'Nat,' Tim began softly, 'what's up?'

'Nothing, I'm fine,' I replied to a box of Nutri-Grain.

There was silence while the water boiled furiously against the sides of its container. I held my breath, willing Tim to move away. Finally, the kettle clicked and the water calmed, but instead of moving away to pour the tea, Tim wrapped his arms around my waist and rested his chin on my shoulder.

'It's okay,' he whispered as I crumpled into him and, losing control of my actions, suddenly entered the period Jess had termed the 'honesty phase'.

* * *

266

'Do you hate me?'

My knees were curled to my chest and I was holding my teacup in front of my face. We had shuffled to the living room, my body buzzing with relief and trepidation as I told Tim what I could manage. Now, though, fear was overtaking and I kept glancing at the door, wondering if any of our housemates were in their bedrooms, if they might come down in search of a TV break and find me half-melted into the sofa.

'Why would I hate you?' Tim replied, refusing to sever eye contact.

'Because I lied to you from the moment we met.' I twisted a tissue between my fingers.

'No you didn't.' He wrapped his arm around my shoulder and spoke into my hair. 'And that wouldn't matter.'

'But I'm not who you thought,' I said, pulling away to look in his face.

'I still know who you are,' Tim said, and poked my arm. 'You're Nat. You're my friend.'

'Aren't you disgusted by me?' I asked.

'No.' He placed his palm on my knee and sighed. 'I'm disgusted by that guy. If he ever comes here, I'll rip his head off.'

I tried to laugh, but it came out as a sob.

'Seriously, Nat, you don't need to deal with this alone.'

'That's not how it feels.' I closed my eyes, feeling drained yet somehow calm. 'I still can't risk my parents finding out, and if all of the internet stuff's true, I could get kicked out of uni.'

'Look,' he wrapped me back up in his arms. 'I'm going to take you to the counselling centre tomorrow.'

'I don't know,' I mumbled into his shirt.

'Well I do. They might not be able to do anything, but it's a good place to start. And it's totally confidential.'

'Do you think I have to tell Rob?' I asked, my head still hidden.

'Um, yes, you probably do. When is he coming?'

'Four weeks.'

'And do you think any of it could be true?' Tim whispered. 'About him I mean.'

'I don't know. I don't know what to think.'

'You need to talk to him.' Tim squeezed me into him more tightly.

'I suppose,' I breathed into his chest as another wave of sobs caught up with me.

I still didn't quite believe Tim when he wrapped his arms around me and said, 'It's okay. I'm here for you.'

Regardless of the law, Tim said, this guy was sick in the head and there are no circumstances where a sixty-year-old man should touch a sixteen-year-old girl. I heard what he said. I cried and thanked him. I loved him even more. For the first time in months, I felt safe and incredibly lucky.

But I still shook in bed that night. I still couldn't believe Tim had forgiven me. Not when I couldn't forgive myself. *He must be judging me*, I told myself repeatedly. And over the coming months I'd find with every retelling I'd judge myself a little more. Sure, Matthew was older and it should never have happened, but the fact remained that it had. That, regardless of anything else, I had lied to everyone in my life for four whole years and that made me – in the simple equations of primary-school morality – a bad person. I'd constructed a false life; I'd risked relationships and other people's happiness in order to conduct an affair with a wholly unsuitable man. I may have been seduced, I may have been manipulated, but I had also lied in cold blood for more than a thousand consecutive days and those lies still wrapped themselves around me. How could anyone reconcile that?

'We have a four-month waiting list. You'll have an assessment interview today, but probably not with the counsellor you'll eventually see. Fill in this form and bring it back when you're ready. There are seats just through there.'

The receptionist gestured towards a room across the hall.

Two other people were waiting in silence, reading posters about anorexia and mental health and avoiding eye contact. I took a seat as far away from both as I could and removed my gloves. With the biro I'd been given I made gentle crosses next to statements like: 'I wake in the middle of the night: Never, Sometimes, A lot, Every night'; 'I feel sad: Never, Sometimes, A lot, All the time'; and 'I think about taking my life: Never, Sometimes, A lot, All the time'.

When I was done, I handed the form back to the receptionist, worrying I'd selected too many middling answers to truly deserve counselling.

'Excellent, Trish will collect you in a moment.'

A few minutes after I'd returned to the silent waiting room, a small, round woman with a floaty black skirt and thick dark hair stood in the doorway and smiled as she said my name. I followed her into an office at the end of the hall. Two armchairs faced each other by the window, a plant and a coffee table within reach of both. A bowl of sand sat on the table next to a cup of colouring pencils. There was no paper.

Trish gestured towards the chair on the right and eased herself into the one on the left.

I perched on the edge of the seat, wondering whether or not to take my coat off. This was just an introductory interview, it probably wouldn't take long. I shouldn't look too comfortable.

'Hi,' Trish said, smiling and bobbing her head to catch my eye.

'Hi,' I replied, noticing she had my form in front of her.

'So, today we're just going to briefly discuss how you're feeling and what we can and can't offer you in terms of counselling.' She smiled again.

'Okay.' I thrust my hands under my thighs.

'I'll start with your form.' She shuffled the papers in her lap. 'You say you have nightmares every night and you feel upset a lot, but that you don't have trouble concentrating on your studies.'

'No. I mean yes. I mean, my classes are fine.' My cheeks burnt.

'Okay.' Trish scribbled something in a notebook. 'And what about social interactions?'

'Uh, I don't know.' I glanced at the synthetic blinds shielding us from the world outside.

'It's okay, there are no right or wrong answers.' She pushed a box of tissues towards me.

'Let's try something else.' Trish leant forward. 'Why don't you just tell me, in your own words, what made you come here today?'

I sniffed and looked at the grey carpet.

'Take your time.'

'When I was sixteen,' I began in a monotone, applying 'the Band-Aid principle' and speaking as fast as I could, 'I had an affair with a much older married neighbour and I didn't tell anyone about it.'

'How much older?' Trish interrupted.

'Uh, a lot older,' I swallowed and, for only the second time ever, admitted aloud: 'Forty-four years older.'

I kept my eyes on the floor, not wanting to see her reaction.

'Anyway,' I continued after a pause, 'it went on for three years, until I studied abroad last year and ended it. But he hasn't left me alone and now he's trying to sue me and claiming my current boyfriend, who lives in California, has a child and a wife who wants to kill me and that there are naked pictures of me on the web and that he's the only one who can help and that Durham will kick me out if they find out.' I took a shallow breath and ploughed on: 'And I rang my boyfriend last night and told him all this and he said he still loved me but he was really hurt and started crying, but he never denied any of it and I don't know what to think or do and my housemate told me to come here.'

I looked up and tried to smile, but choked out more tears instead. 'Ridiculous, huh?' I squeaked.

'Not at all.' Trish was still sat forward in her chair, her forehead now creased with confusion and concern. 'I can see this is painful for you, but I need you to give me some more details.'

'Isn't my time up?' I asked, looking at the clock on the wall.

'It doesn't matter.' Trish didn't break her gaze.

'But there are other people in the waiting room.' I pushed myself to the edge of the seat, ready to dart, hoping never to see this kind-eyed woman again. 'There's nothing special about me. I'm happy to go on the waiting list.'

I emerged from that session with an appointment to see Trish the following week and again the one after that. Bypassing the waiting list made me feel at once relieved and petrified. On the one hand, I wasn't crazy: the situation was important and impossible, and it was okay for me to ask for help. But, on the other hand, someone had told me I was more in need of support than anyone else, that my situation really was that bad.

Through the coming weeks, I continued to question myself and, at times, I'm ashamed to say, I also questioned Rob. Who could I believe? People that I'd never met but who came with references from someone who claimed to care for me – someone I'd known almost my entire life and whom my family trusted? Or the man I felt absolutely in love with – the man who'd proved he'd forgive me everything, but who was twice my age and 5,000 miles away? Was I in danger? Who from?

Despite these confusions, I wrote my essays, directed the play David and I had been chosen to put on at the local theatre, and, thinking of how happy I'd felt over the summer, began applying for Masters programmes in America. Tackling the absurdity that had become my life with remarkable efficiency, I'd wake, read the emails, cry for a while, take a shower and get on with my day. If nothing else, having an affair had left me with an amazing ability to compartmentalise.

After Tim, I told a few others. I tried to live honestly for once. When a girl asked me about the boyfriend I'd had in my first year, I said it was a messy situation and now I was dating a guy from

271

America. She asked if the current boyfriend was older and I told her thirty-nine, then she asked about the first boyfriend and I said older still. In an instant, she flipped: she freaked out with high-pitched shrieks and asked me if I was lying to her. I had no idea what to do and realised with horror that this girl would be the first of many to turn on me if the whole truth was ever known.

My close friends reacted more sensitively. I related bits of my sorry story to the producers of my play because I thought they had a right to know if there was potential for my life to blow up in January, just when we'd have to be seriously rehearsing. They hugged me and told me people do much worse. I emailed Jess, finally telling her Matthew's age, and wrote Greg a soppy letter about how he didn't even know what he'd done to help me.

And, of course, there was Trish. As much as I owe my freedom now to the work of that curly-haired woman who sat in the chair across from me every Wednesday morning for three-quarters of a year, those hour-long sessions held some of the most difficult and traumatic moments of the entire period I spent trying to escape Matthew. Despite the relief of no longer having to deal with everything alone, it was scary to have someone tell me that the things I'd been keeping in my head and losing perspective on, the things I'd previously been able to squash into denial, were actually enormously serious.

26

Last night your mother and I planned a Boxing Day party. Please come.

Whatever has gone before.

Though life with you in the not-too-distant past seemed unbearable, it's become undeniably clear to me recently that life without you is much worse.

I'm trying to find the courage. I want to put the past behind us. I've looked at my life and I see it clearly now: it was never for me, always for you. But something is broken between us, something more than my heart.

'We can't solve problems by using the same kind of thinking we used when we created them.' Albert Einstein

I'd like to accept your mother's invitation; I'd like to be introduced to the new you. I'm not sure how I will cope if you say no, if I'm not allowed in your presence at Christmas and if I'm banned from seeing your play in March, from congratulating you at graduation and celebrating your twenty-first birthday in July. **From being a part of your life.**

So please.

Please.

I will be good. I will try very hard to obey your rules, to avoid 'us'.

I've always tried to be there for you and now I just want to be your friend. I'm living my life: walking the streets and making my plans like I always do, but it's nothing without you.

I paid Carson what he was owed because I want you to be safe. I don't want to know the details of what is going on, but I am here to help you. I hope you know I am not requesting this information for myself, nor am I hoping to buy your friendship. It is worth nothing unless freely given anyway.

So please consider it, in the spirit of Christmas and the love I promise not to mention again. I promise, from this point forth, to live by your law.

Yours humbly

Matthew

From: MandyPerrett@vmail.com
To: Natalie Lucas <sexy_chocolate69@sweetmail.com>
Sent: 5 December 2004, 18:32:16
Subject: See you in January

I got plane tickets now. I have work all night and all day. My boy says me, Mummy, why I never see you? I say I saving for him, to make his daddy pay. And now I saved. I buy plane tickets to come to luvvy England for christmas, see his daddy and his girlfriend. I know you live in Durham. I saw his emails to you. Love love love he talks about. They all say he's beside you right now, don't they? How romantic. But you feel ALONE! Haha. You should hear him talking about you in the bars once he stops his Fuck Bus. His little trick. Easy English girl. Cute ass.

Well I teach your ass a lesson.

You better run back to Mummy miss middle class woman daughter. Maybe she let you suck on her titties and protect you, because you going to need it when I arrive.

Mr Carson tell me not to contact you. Well fuck him, Mr court sympathiser. He can't protect you now.

I'm coming and he can't stop me.

You better make me tea when I arrive at your door. Yes. Say sweet things to me.

English muffins and tea. Crumpets too. La di da. You say sorry. Tell Mandy sorry over and over. Down on your knees like the whore you are. S O R R Y.

You will be. Bitch. I make you sorry.

One month not so long.

Then you pay.. You made me a criminal. Now I make you pay.

You write to judge and say sorry, say Mandy not a criminal, I the bitch whore fuck the bus driver like a slutty slut.

Cos if you don't. I mad enough to do anything. I swear I do anything. Why shouldn't I? I a criminal now anyway. So I do criminal thing.

You fuck my man. I fuck you. That fair. Only you stay FUCKED.

You better be home.. Better open the door and say you
sorry. Else I beat down your door and burn down your
house. I hunt you down and make you pay.

S O R R Y

You will be.

My set texts and the library books I'd kept past their due dates
were scattered around my bedroom in various states of dissection:
marginal pencil notes highlighting devices, questioning assumptions and hoping to justify my place at a top-ten university. In
contrast, Matthew's communications were only ever read once,
scanned in horror then placed hastily in a box beneath my bed
or filed uncritically in a corner of my hard drive. If I'd printed all
the emails, bundled them up with the letters and carried them
into a seminar group; if I'd asked six or seven Literature undergraduates to inspect and analyse them, I may have seen a different
story:

Rupert Cochrane
F&R Solicitors
PO Box 101
London
SWxxxx

Harriet Moore
Care of Albert Sumac
PO Box 666
London
SWxxxx

31st October 2004

Dear Ms Harriet Moore

It is my duty to inform you that, as requested in the will of Rose Shaw, we are bound to enquire about the status of your relationship with Albert Sumac as of November 2004. At the reading of the will in December 2003, Mr Sumac requested you not be made aware of the terms of the document in case they influenced any decisions you might make, but now it is imperative I bring certain details to your attention.

As laid out in the will of Rose Shaw, written and signed 8th September 2003, Harriet Moore and Albert Sumac were bequeathed (and I quote):

- a rental legacy of £53,000, specifically to be used for a house or flat in Durham.*
- a theatre and foreign travel legacy of £12,195.*

* These sums are to be paid one year after the testator (Rose Shaw)'s death on the sole condition that the beneficiaries are in a committed relationship. Should this not be the case, all funds should be donated to the Cats Protection Agency.

Thus, it is my duty to enquire whether or not you are currently in a committed relationship with Albert Sumac. I have already contacted Mr Sumac and he has responded in the negative,

---

Handwritten annotations:

No separate contact details? (If solicitor needs H's personal verification, wouldn't they be suspicious of going through A?)

So that's where solicitors come from!

R. Cochrane could be a reference to Ray Cochrane who's a retired jockey

If this is Natalie's torture chamber in the ministry of love, are those guys her saviours or her rats?

Jockeys? What? That seems fairly random (how do you know that?!!)

Hey my dad buys the racing post — I can't help it if I soak up information

So F&R could be Frankie & Ray?

She doesn't exist — does she?

Neither does he! SUMAC = CAMUS a backwards existentialist.

legal?

Also, Rose knew Matthew's real name, so why would she leave an inheritance in a fake name? Wouldn't they need to show ID at some point?

Should she be tempted by the devil?!

Why the hiatus?

Oddly precise — Beginnings of a numerical code ??!!

Dickensian legal battle or Dan Brown conspiracy?

a little clichéd! Why is it always cats? MEOW!

Seems fairly subjective for the legalese that follows

More official

but I need written confirmation from <u>both parties</u> before I may proceed with executing Ms Shaw's last wishes.

As such, I would appreciate it if you could respond to my query as soon as possible using the above address.

WHY? surely if one isn't the other can't be?

Yours

Rupert Cochrane
F&R Solicitors

Natalie

You will be hearing from my solicitor, but I thought it polite to inform you myself first. Under advice and with little choice given your inability to discuss such matters reasonably, I am in the unfavourable position of having to take legal action against you (see enclosed).

As I'm sure it will yours, this breaks my heart. I have tried to reduce the sum as much as possible. All the legacy items have been halved, though, of course, you have already lost your own half, and so your total deficit is nearly doubled. I wish it could have been different.

I have also halved the rental cost of the Kew flat, because in theory we were living there together, though, of course, we both know I left for half the summer because you became unbearable. Gas and electricity are difficult to calculate for the period, so I have let you off there.

My sadness is in knowing that none of this would have been necessary had you been able to show me some respect and follow through on your offer of friendship. I have tried to settle with you, but your stubbornness has made you unable to recognise a friend when you need one, and this, I'm afraid, will now have to serve as another part of your learning process. A lesson more expensive than any of those at Rosella. Perhaps now you will understand that getting your own way and having everything on your own terms is both expensive and lonely. Perhaps, anyway. No doubt you will find a way to blame this on me.

I am willing to discuss this:
- alone
- with my solicitor present
- with your mother present
- with your bus driver present (yes, your Ma has been blathering about your latest bedfellow)
- or any combination of the above

I am sorry it has come to this. I tried not to believe it for

---

Handwritten annotations:

Given the circumstances of this letter this is clearly nonsense!
↳ Purpose is to establish the illusion of politeness

Natalie didn't write the terms of the will — you can't sue someone for breaking up with you, surely?

Seeks to establish diminished responsibility

EXTRAORDINARY! Can't maintain the facade of civility for very long

Adopts the tone of a disappointed parent — superior.
↳ No rent was discussed — would this ever hold in court?

Already claiming kindness again!! What a martyr!

Can't argue with that!

A lesson more expensive — Always the teacher — even now!

Efforts to seem reasonable imply the unreasonableness of the recipient

Surely a shift?

Dismissive of
- USA?
- Education?
- Women?

Is this all about jealousy?

Seems a dig at perceived class/social status of bus driver → SNOBBISH!

a long, long time, but I fear I was avoiding the truth: you are
cold, Natalie. You give me goose-bumps.

Yours sincerely

Matthew Wright

Details of funds to be recovered from Natalie Lucas of 30
D***** Road, Durham, DH** 4**

Rental legacy Durham flat/house @ 50% of £53,000	26,500
Furniture (private purchase)	1,254
Travel to and from Durham (two visits with regard to the rental legacy)	150
Decorations/books, etc.	70
Three months' rental of Richmond flat @ 50% of £2,550	1,275
Theatre and foreign travel legacy @ 50% of £12,195	6,097
GRAND TOTAL	£35,346

Handwritten annotations:

Can't resist a good metaphor!
↳ Also - incredibly informal way of signing of a 'formal letter'

Meant with sarcasm? or just a staggering lack of self-awareness?

— real name - even though legacy was for Albert?

Exactly! Pretty emotive for a lawsuit!

What furniture?

Gifts!

This money doesn't exist? Why not sue for loss of wedding presents whilst you're at it?!

Uses:
- short sentences
- formal language
- superior tone

↳ Plays on gender/age/experience to strengthen argument
Everything is done and designed to undermine the recipient

Willie Carson is another retired jockey
↳ *Still on the jockeys! (is she going to wake up with a horse's head in her bed?)*

Same email provider as Matthew – is this a popular site? Coincidence?

From: wcarson@worldopen.com
To: Natalie Lucas <sexy_chocolate69@sweetmail.com>
Sent: 15 November 2004, 15:21:38
Subject: Please get in touch

Dear Ms Lucas — *Her real name this time!*

Why did he leave?
- drink problem?
- partner stole his wife
- stole huge drugs score (this is a better story!)

My name is William Carson and I am a freelance private detective, formerly an officer of security with the FBI, first in the Criminal Investigative Division and later in the Cyber Division. I am writing to you about a matter that gives me grave cause for concern. I have pleaded with Mr Albert Sumac to give me your postal address and let me contact you directly, but he maintains that your privacy is paramount, even in circumstances like these. *really knows how to build suspense!*

ROBOCOP!

Wiki says they're real divisions, but how would you check something like that?

It has come to my attention that you may be the subject of a vicious character attack. An Hispanic woman living in Boston, MA, whom I may legally only refer to as Miss P., has attempted to produce a slur on your character. Her attempts have been stopped for now, but she claims to have found illicit photographs of you on various online websites. My sources suggest she is not responsible for distributing these photographs, but that she has tried to advertise your 'services', presumably with the intention of accusing you of solicitation at a later date. Miss P. claims her grievance against you is that you have 'stolen' her man (it is unclear if she refers to a husband or boyfriend) and left her child (a three-year-old son) without a father.

Why relevant? (institutionalised racism)

Guaranteed to provoke a response

More mystery

Very coy!

Confirmed? Provided purely to inform or as emotional manipulation?

Presumably not if she's 'Miss P'

It is as Mr Sumac's employee that I have discovered this much and Mr Sumac has forbidden me any further investigations without your approval. As such, I implore you to contact me and divulge any information you may have in regards to the case. I do not wish to alarm you, but the consequences of such a matter if not dealt with delicately can be grave, and I would not like to see you hurt. I've been working in this field for years, absolutely years, and trust me I know what I'm talking about. So please, it is imperative that you speak to me as soon as possible.

You can reach me on 0208 *** ***.

Yours

William Carson
PI

[Handwritten annotations:]

Why did 'Mr Sumac' hire a PI in the first place?

this seems unlikely!

Too personal for a PI? Isn't it Sumac who doesn't want to see her hurt?

Weird!
yeah! Odd use of repetition

In London?

Are PI and Private Detective interchangeable?

Wait! first Google Cit Cas "I've been mad for fucking years, absolute years." It's a line from a Pink Floyd song.

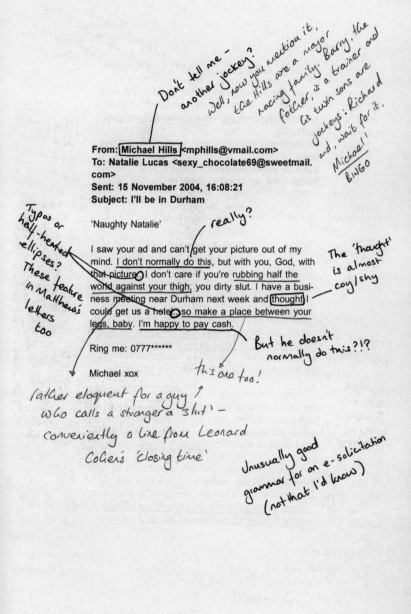

Don't tell me — another jockey?

Well, now you mention it, the Hills are a major racing family. Barry, the father, is a trainer and his twin sons are jockeys: Richard and, wait for it, Michael! BINGO

From: Michael Hills <mphills@vmail.com>
To: Natalie Lucas <sexy_chocolate69@sweetmail.com>
Sent: 15 November 2004, 16:08:21
Subject: I'll be in Durham

Typos or half-hearted ellipses? These feature in Matthew's letters too

'Naughty Natalie'   really?

I saw your ad and can't get your picture out of my mind. I don't normally do this, but with you, God, with that picture, I don't care if you're rubbing half the world against your thigh, you dirty slut. I have a business meeting near Durham next week and thought I could get us a hotel so make a place between your legs, baby. I'm happy to pay cash.

The 'thought' is almost coy/shy

But he doesn't normally do this?!?

this one too!

Ring me: 0777******

Michael xox

rather eloquent for a guy who calls a stranger a 'slut' — conveniently a line from Leonard Cohen's 'closing time'

Unusually good grammar for an e-solicitation (not that I'd know)

From: Matthew Wright <theoutsider@worldopen.co.uk>
To: Natalie Lucas <sexy_chocolate69@sweetmail.com>
Sent: 15 November 2004, 19:42:21
Subject: Re: What the fuck?!

No 'dear'
No 'Natalie'
No nothing,
just VERSE!
Byron at that!

When we two parted
In silence and tears
Half broken-hearted
To sever for years,
Pale grew thy cheek and cold,
Colder thy kiss;
Truly that hour foretold
Sorrow to this . . .

'Not only did you bring this all upon yourself, I am also smart enough to quote poetry to this effect.'

or:
'I spy on you now'

I don't know why I expected anything different. That is just like you: I try to protect you, put myself out, use my own money, all because I am concerned about you and your life, a life I am allowed no part of. And this is the thanks I get. You accuse me. *You accuse me!*

MARTYR!

affected staccato sentences to show outrage

Yep. because nothing validates an argument like repetition and italics.

You don't think it could be your filthy bus driver whom you've known all of five minutes? No, much easier to blame me, then you can carry on your casual sex across the globe. I am trying to protect you, Natalie. I can't do more than that. You won't let me.

I've spoken to William. This woman claims to be your bus driver's partner, claims to have a child with him. She has also had a sex test and come up positive for herpes, so I suggest you get checked out because I assume if he wasn't careful with her, he's not been

Either just doesn't know his name, or still determined to undermine class / status

De-ja-vu of the whole:
'You need to go to the GUM clinic and I'll hold your hand' incident.

Handwritten top left: Did Natalie tell her mum this after she gave her the lecture on being careful? Is it the sort of information one shares with a neighbour? If not this *is* pretty creepy!

Handwritten top right: still claims to have her best interests at heart

careful with you. This Miss P. says he claimed to have had a ~~vasectomy~~ and then denied the child when she fell pregnant. I only hope you haven't been so naive.

Do you realise this is your whole life, your whole career on the line? What do you think your universities will say if they see these pictures? William's shown me some of them, they're quite explicit. I've never seen them before, but they're definitely you. A shudder comes o'er me. I've seen one of you sucking on some saggy bird's cunt. She has a tattoo. Someone else must have been ~~there to take the picture.~~ Nadiyya perhaps? Or maybe you slutted around in good old NY? Sorry, I'm not trying to offend you, but you need to see reality. I am not the enemy. It is not a big deal if I see these, hell, I've seen it all before, but what if your professors find them? What if Rosella is told one of their former pupils is advertising as a prostitute? William can help. But I won't tell him to do anything without your consent.

Handwritten left: He's lying! He saw this one! He knows what happened with Nadiyya and he knows she's ashamed!

Handwritten right: Is this a quote? (or is he just so pretentious that in supposedly furious rages he writes 'o'er'? Yep! Byron again!

You need to trust me. I'm on your side.

Handwritten right: He knows what she cares about

Handwritten left (under "on your side"): Why? If any of this is true?

    I hear thy name spoken,
    And share in its shame.

But with emails like your last, I wonder why I bother, why I ever held you so dear.

Handwritten left: Bitterness present in original letter as subtext is now furiously unleashed!

    . . . *In secret we met –*
    In silence I grieve,
    That thy heart could forget,
    Thy spirit deceive.
    If I should meet thee
    After long years,
    How should I greet thee?
    With silence and tears.

Handwritten right: Everything founded in hiding/ deceit. All unknowable

Handwritten bottom: Also, it's somewhat ironic to sandwich — Smart enough, surely, to see the irony of claiming anything will be me with 'silence' → or is it a threat? — an email with protestations of innocence throughout between the words of a man described by Lady Caroline Lamb as 'Mad, bad, and dangerous to know'!

From: wcarson@worldopen.com
To: Natalie Lucas <sexy_chocolate69@sweetmail.com>
Sent: 16 November 2004, 10:11:31
Subject: More information

Natalie,

You have not yet replied to my earlier email and I have just got off the phone with Mr Albert Sumac, who tells me you are mistrustful of the information we have approached you with.

I cannot stress strongly enough the importance of you working with us in this matter. I have been researching similar cases for many years. Serial grooming is in fact my specialty. The laws in the US are good at protecting its own citizens, but do little to defend the interests of visitors to the country. As such, there are a number of men around the country – some in almost every state and often known to the federal authorities, though they have little power to prosecute – who make a habit of pursuing young foreign women travelling alone. They befriend these women and form 'relationships'. While in the United States, these men often appear charming and generous, playing on the tragic aspect of an international love affair and inciting the women to feel passionately.

The aim, however, is to secure an invitation to visit these women in their home countries. Once there, the man's true colours are suddenly revealed – when the woman has nowhere to run, nowhere to go. At best, the woman can hope to find a sex pervert who forces her to partake in whatever brand of deviancy he subscribes to, often by force, with the intention of returning to the United States before criminal proceedings can be brought forward, or in the hope that the woman will be so ashamed she will feel unable to press charges. Even if she does turn to the police before the predator leaves the country, instances of prosecution are rare because these men are unknown to foreign blood and semen databases.

At worst, though – and here I beseech you to think long and hard about your knowledge of the man you are in a relationship with – the man will have laid a complex sexual and financial trap for the young woman. Reassured by the safety he is granted by being born in the U.S.A. he will most likely have given her a false name and made sure everything she knows about his identity has come solely from him. Then, once in her country, at her house, he will begin to manipulate her and those around her, encouraging or forcing her into situations she would normally avoid. To do so, he will most likely enlist the help of a network of contacts already known in the country, possibly met on a previous visit or even just found through the internet. The crimes they then commit could take the form of identity theft or other financial fraud, but they can also manifest as more disturbing sexual crimes, including gang rape, enforced pornography, and in extreme cases trafficking for prostitution. The most disturbing case I have worked on involved a woman such as yourself disappearing from her home in Surrey days after her Texan 'boyfriend' arrived, only to be found six months later being forced to work in a brothel in Thailand.

It is a strange inhumanity that leads people to treat others this way, but sadly it is a truth that it happens

---

Handwritten annotations:

Unnecessary repetition – Google comes up with a Bruce Springsteen lyric!

Much less coy now!

verily!

– stresses the danger of remaining silent – ie, not getting into contact with him

Plays on perceived notions of imperialism / American dominance.

HA! – Brucey again!

Convenient as neither Matthew nor William have mentioned Rob's name

Surely a far greater risk abroad?

Emotive – The empathetic example

Oddly philosophical phrase? → Yep! – Michael Jackson's 'Dangerous' – "taken by lust's strange inhumanity" all around this world. These men are so <u>dangerous</u> because they spin a web of sin and lay it as a trap for <u>vulnerable women</u>. They are persuasive, but they cannot be trusted. Their manipulations rely on desire, promises and lust, and once they have a woman's trust they will take away her money, time and dignity if possible. Because of the transient lifestyle suited to these individuals, they often choose work in travel or vehicular transportation, often favouring cross-country routes that give them the widest possible net to seek out victims.

I do not mean to scare you Natalie, but I am concerned for your safety. Mr Sumac contacted me because he fears from past experience that your judgment when it comes to <u>sexual situations is poor.</u> He says you have, in the past, displayed an inability to assess a person's agenda or even <u>bodily hygiene</u> before it is too late and that you have been coerced into unfavourable sexual situations using alcohol. It is not my place to comment on these matters, but from <u>everything Mr Sumac has told me about your situation</u> – even without the business with the wife and child – I would advise you to think carefully about what you know about your <u>bus driver</u> that you haven't learned from him. Have you seen his passport or driver's license? Have you met any immediate family or close friends? Mr Sumac informs me he is <u>39 years of age.</u> In my experience, it would be strange if a man of that age did not have a wife or ex-wife and a certain amount of baggage to bring to a relationship. If he has not told you about such things, you may need to ask yourself why. The other possibility is that he may be <u>bisexual</u>, which again should raise alarm bells in your mind as male <u>bisexuality</u> is the biggest contributor to the spread of HIV/AIDS in the United States.

As it is, <u>I have taped phone</u> conversations recording your bus driver crudely taunting his wife with your

Handwritten annotations:

MJ title

Really enjoying his metaphors now!

Natalie's mum could have told Matthew about the bus trips
↙ seems too tailored

Poor? – as in picking Matthew?

No details of which have been mentioned

still no name!

Now he's using US spelling

Presumably he knows the age of 'Mr Sumac'? – What does he know about their relationship?

V. personal attack – designed to shame?
↳ I guess he means the threesome with Nadiyya, but it could just as easily be levelled at Matthew himself

?!?
... where does this come from? → it

, surely illegal?

So definitely his wife now?

Unless it's an elaborate double bluff

'bisexual' is designed as a slur, clearly the writer doesn't know his audience.

sexual willingness, boasting that you give oral without pressure and will do anything he asks. I am in no way defending the actions of Miss P., but please ask yourself Natalie what kind of man taunts his wife with details about his erotic activities with his mistress? Is there any way, do you think, that he could be involved in the business of the internet photographs and allegations of prostitution against you? Could they relate to a more complex plan he has for his visit in January? Could he be dangerous?

If you find yourself doubting the answer to just one of the questions above, you need my help, Natalie. I have seen too many young women just like yourself be manipulated by these disturbed men to sit back and watch it happen again.

Please get in touch.

William Carson
PI

[handwritten margin notes:]

In no way relevant other than to provoke an emotional response

Is there any possibility of her answering objectively now?

leading questions

Always! she's just a little girl who needs saving from the big bad wolf

By mentioning manipulation so explicitly, is this misdirection or an attempted double-bluff to put aside thoughts of manipulation from Matthew/Sumac?

From: Matthew Wright <theoutsider@worldopen.co.uk>
To: Natalie Lucas <sexy_chocolate69@sweetmail.com>
Sent: 16 November 2004, 14:44:10
Subject: Songs of my experience

Each man is in his **SPECTRE's** power, Natalie! But you, you are drowning in your own lake. You cannot see the wood for the trees, you are so blind. Your bus driver is no good. I can see that, your Ma can see that, your housemates can probably see that, everyone but you. And meanwhile, he's sitting happily in Boston or Chicago or Salt Lake City, wherever his fuck-bus has arrived now, chuckling to himself about his stupid piece of little British 'ass'. But you, you are stubborn and blind and blame me instead.. Remember, though, mutual fear brings peace, only until the selfish loves increase. I assume you still have the intelligence to work out what that means, but maybe I'm wrong. You are only safe, Natalie, until he comes to collect what he wants. He is a predator. And you are a doe-eyed deer, so stupid you don't know when to run and when to wave your fluffy white butt like the slut you are.

Once, I worried about you in a spiritual sense. I worried your mind would be enclosed in a narrow circle and your heart sunk into an abyss by those who couldn't see your worth. But now I realise I was wrong: you are the one who has chosen the circle and the abyss and I wonder why I bother continuing to worry when you refuse to worry about yourself. You

---

Handwritten annotations:

Blake references, what a Romantic!

↳ I though SPECTRE was a James Bond ref. (seems to make his suggestion look more ridiculous by referencing an international fiction conspiracy

No nothing!

Token Americanism to convince her these are the driver's thoughts, not his

repetition for emphasis

} 'The Human Abstract' - Blake

whereas he is only the Devil you know

innocence? oh no! of course not!

Never drops his concern (the excuse to stay in touch)

Blake again - 'perception'

won't listen to me because you are stubborn, but <u>YOU ARE IN DANGER</u>, Natalie. <u>Forget your senses, your perception, your gnosis and the pleasure of stolen joys in a barren but eternal world</u>; forget the 'unreal' plain in which we used to live, the dead poets and the <u>lyricism of life:</u> you are in danger in the gross, mucky, mundane world of everyone else. You have dug yourself a hole of pornography, sexual manipulation and jealousy, and you are so far short of being equipped to deal with it that you cannot even see you are in it.

Handwritten annotations:

At least not pretending not to want to frighten her anymore!

The world they hated together

Who in this scenario is jealous? (other than him?)

Telling her to forget this goes against past character - so it must be important!

* no sign of either

More words stolen from Blake - still making his case through <u>dead poets</u>

'The Rime of the Ancient Mariner'

From: Matthew Wright <theoutsider@worldopen.
co.uk>
To: Natalie Lucas <sexy_chocolate69@sweetmail.
com>
Sent: 16 November 2004, 21:18:35
Subject: Apology accepted

Your humble servant...
→ And personal martyr!

The man hath penance done, and penance more will do. As ever, I will do as you wish. And when you've got what you want from me, you'll cast me aside once more. William says I'm a fool. I'm no fool. I know you'll whistle thrice and cry, 'The game is done! I've won, I've won!' But I suppose that's love. I once knew a girl called Natalie whom I thought knew love like me. We basked in her glory and made each other young. But I was wrong, she was but the Nightmare Life-in-Death, who thicks man's blood with cold. So now I shiver and dive for any scraps she cares to throw, knowing it will never be enough for her.

Would you trust a man who writes like this?

I thought she was an angsty teen? No, apparently she's an albatros!

Suddenly casual?

Anyway, I've instructed William to continue his investigations.

He is going to act as a character witness for you so that you do not need to appear in court.

He's never met her!

I only hope it's not too late.

Ominous sign-off (leaves scope for more to come)

From: wcarson@worldopen.com
To: Natalie Lucas <sexy_chocolate69@sweetmail.com>
Sent: 18 November 2004, 10:45:06
Subject: Update

Had to slip Frankie in again Dettori - too neat

Ms Lucas,

It's your lucky day. Though you still haven't contacted me, Mr Albert Sumac has instructed me to continue my work to protect your reputation. Yesterday I appeared in court to defend you against the allegations of solicitation and protest the move to have you subpoenaed. Miss P was ordered by Judge Dettori to leave you alone. She was also banned from visiting the websites that were mentioned and forced into fierce exile. Her hard drive has been sent for analysis and a piece of software has been installed on her computer to monitor her internet use and to track her emails. If she contacts you, she will be requested back in court.

on what grounds?

back to 'Miss'? now?

another oddly poetic phrase

As for the images on the web, I have taken down those I can find, but I'm afraid there is no guarantee there are no more out there. I would suggest monthly inspections, which I am happy to carry out for an extra fee if instructed.

! everything is left open again

comes out of nowhere - reads like a 'just when you thought it was safe to go back into the water' kind of line.

I will send you my bill for the burdens of the day, plus expenses, shortly.

There is no way this is legal!

Yours

William Carson
PI

He's had no contact with or instructions from Natalie. He only knows her through a teenage email address - and she's seen no proof of his work!

From: wcarson@worldopen.com
To: Natalie Lucas <sexy_chocolate69@sweetmail.com>
Sent: 18 November 2004, 16:51:29
Subject: RE: Update

Ms Lucas,

I'm afraid this is an issue you will have to take up with Mr Albert Sumac. Personally, I find your attitude quite extraordinary as Mr Sumac has done nothing but protect you thus far and seems only to have your interests in mind.

It is not in my nature to stamp my foot and demand you pay me my money down, but refusing to pay me will, I'm afraid, end in court, where the details of the case will be made public. Whether you want to pursue it to that point is up to you, but I would advise against it as it would negate all efforts to protect your reputation and privacy thus far.

Again, I am shocked at your response and cannot now imagine why Mr Sumac has gone to such lengths to protect such an ungrateful young woman.

Yours

William Carson
PI

From: MandyPerrett@vmail.com
To: Natalie Lucas <sexy_chocolate69@sweetmail.com>
Sent: 28 November 2004, 15:01:43
Subject: Natalie, you take my little boy?

You want my man? You have my baby too. I fly him over to spend christmas with his daddy and you. I come too and we can all have happy holidays. You like that? The mother, the father, the baby and the whore.

Judge told me to leave you alone, but why should I? I've lost my job. I've lost respect. I've lost my man. Why shouldn't I lose baby too?

Maybe you wouldn't understand, you childless woman. But I make you understand. I make your womb rattle till you shriek my name and ask forgiveness.

I spoke to Mr Carson and he says there no more money coming from England. Your friend stop paying his bills cos you not grateful for his help. Well so there BITCH. Maybe you need your friend now more than eever.

Judge told me: Complainant Natalie has her name strike from record. Not even say your last name. Just mine. Your no name fucked with my real name.

Bla bla he say, Natalie a nice girl from luvely England with university career and going to be in plays and don't deserve damaging adverts. Made me apologise. I just clean toilets so it's ok. But inside I scream: SHE NOT NICE – SHE FUCK A BUS DRIVER.

Handwritten annotations:

Amanda Perrett is a racehorse trainer

is this related?

Occasional lapses in grammar feel affected

↳ This is the title of a Sylvia Plath poem: "The womb rattles in the pods, the moon..."

Why would this conversation take place?

Capitalisation and larger font like in Matthew's emails

She can't construct whole sentences or capitalise 'Christmas' but she can spell complainant?

Judge is Anglophile?

What has this to do with anything?

(implication of class divide? – or just showing she knows about her)

So I come see you. I speak nothing but blood
to you and make you taste it.

Fuck Mr Carson and fuck the judge. I don't
care if I not suppose contact you. I come see
you and bring you my little boy.

I work every day. Saturday and Sunday too.
Now I count the days till I come to you in
Durham and you can work every day for a
little boy with no daddy.

BITCH.

Last night your mother and I planned a Boxing Day party. Please come.
Whatever has gone before.

Though life with you in the not-too-distant past seemed unbearable, it's become undeniably clear to me recently that life without you is much worse.

I'm trying to find the courage. I want to put the past behind us. I've looked at my life and I see it clearly now: it was never for me, always for you. But something is broken between us, something more than my heart.

'We can't solve problems by using the same kind of thinking we used when we created them.' Albert Einstein

I'd like to accept your mother's invitation; I'd like to be introduced to the new you. I'm not sure how I will cope if you say no, if I'm not allowed in your presence at Christmas and if I'm banned from seeing your play in March, from congratulating you at graduation and celebrating your twenty-first birthday in July. **From being a part of your life.**

So please.
Please.

I will be good. I will try very hard to obey your rules, to avoid 'us'.

I've always tried to be there for you and now I just want to be your friend. I'm living my life: walking the streets and making my plans like I always do, but it's nothing without you.

I paid Carson what he was owed because I want you to be safe. I don't want to know the details of what is going on, but I am here to help you. I hope you know I am not requesting this information for myself, nor am I hoping to buy your friendship. It is worth nothing unless freely given anyway.

So please consider it, in the spirit of Christmas and the love I promise not to mention again. I promise, from this point forth, to live by your law.

Yours humbly.
Matthew

Handwritten annotations:

Pure, schizophrenic 180° turnaround. Classic manipulation by confusion: he can't be angry and aggressive all the time because that would make it too easy to blame him. He has to play nice so that he can be offended when she rejects his olive branch.

odd coalition – invasion of home

incomplete sentence

The greater good!

Didn't he use an Einstein quote when he was trying to seduce her?

from Leonard Cohen's 'There for you'

guilt trip!

all the effort is his!

Seemingly defeated?

Doth he protest too much?

Philosophical to the last!

clutching at straws?

a doomed romantic hero, cruelly spurned, etc, etc.

Perhaps this activity might have saved me weeks of insomnia and months of anguish; perhaps it could have pointed all fingers at Matthew and eased my mind into labelling him a miserable, psychotic freak rather than questioning its own sanity and directing the same words inwards. Or perhaps such marginal notes as these are only the manifestations of my psyche as I try to make sense of a seemingly senseless situation; perhaps they only bleed onto these pages as I try so hard to capture Matthew's distinctive tone, cadences and voice without pilfering his exact phrases and opening myself up to a plagiarism prosecution. Either way, they haunt me now, niggling at my nervous system in the same way a phantom whiff of Matthew's aftershave seems to find my nostrils once or twice most weeks, causing me to swivel in the supermarket aisle or turn on the street.

Unfortunately, at the age of twenty, my literary common sense was relegated to the classroom. My reactions in my bedroom, on the hallway floor where the post landed, in the living room where I half expected Matthew's face to emerge from the darkened garden at the window, and in the shower where I soaped and scrubbed my foolish tattoo, were anything but rational.

Finally, three more counselling sessions and another breakdown in front of Tim later, I went to the police. An officer came to my house. She sat at the Argos table in my dining room and listened while I sobbed through an incoherent account of what had happened. I held printouts of the most recent emails. She glanced briefly at the one on top and told me it seemed like one of the men was lying. I should talk to both Matthew and Rob. I should also close the email account and encourage no more communication.

'Ring this number if you have any more problems.'

I glanced up the street as she climbed back into her blue-and-white car, relieved that none of my housemates had returned from lectures.

I then sobbed in the hallway and shrieked at the stairs.

* * *

'Hey you.'

'Hey.'

'Isn't it like 3am for you? What are you doing up?'

'I need to ask you something.'

'Uh oh, that doesn't sound good. Are you okay?'

'Not really.'

'What's up?'

'Uh, quite a lot.'

'More about the old creep? Well, you want to tell me?'

'Do you have a wife?'

'Excuse me?'

'A wife? Do you have a wife and a child?'

'What is this?'

'I'm sorry, but do you? I need to know.'

'You're serious? You think I have a wife I haven't told you about?'

'No . . . I mean, I just have to ask.'

'Wow.'

'Now you're mad.'

'Well, yeah. Why would you ask me that?'

'Because I've been getting more emails and I had to go to the police and they told me to ask you.'

'So, you don't trust me any more?'

'I don't know who to trust. I don't know what's going on.'

'Some old creep has been harassing you for more than a year, but you think it's *me* who's lying to you? Jeez.'

'No, don't be like that. I just needed to ask.'

'I'm hurt that you have.'

'I'm sorry.'

'I mean, you only told me about all this shit a few weeks ago. And I'm on your side, I think it's awful and I want to help, but you gotta know this is a lot for me to take in anyway. And now I'm being dragged into it too and you don't trust me.'

'I do.'

'You obviously don't, or you wouldn't have rung.'

'I'm sorry, I'm not coping very well.'

'I know. I'm sorry too. But I don't know how this makes me feel.'

'Please understand.'

'I do, but I'm still hurt.'

'Sorry.'

'Stop saying that.'

'Sorry.'

'I think I have to go.'

'What?'

'I can't deal with this right now.'

'You can't just hang up.'

'I'll, uh, call you tomorrow.'

'Are we okay?'

'Get some sleep.'

'I love you.'

'Bye.'

Click.

* * *

Natalie, you were once the actor, the actress, the voter, the politician, the emigrant and the exile, the criminal that stood in the box. I was the stammerer, the well-formed person, the wasted and feeble person. And together, for the briefest of moments, we were something beautiful. But now, we stand, simply a man and a woman's body at auction, waiting for the highest bidder in this heartless world. You became she who adorn'd herself and folded her hair expectantly, who cried for more and tossed her withered lover away. As I undulated into the willing and yielding day, you bit into its sweet flesh and spat it out, demanding something sweeter, crying out to be filled with the charge of the soul even as you closed your own soul off to the world.

Don't worry, closing your email account doesn't mean you'll

get a flood of letters from me instead. I've tried not to be involved. I too have cut my email connection to the 'mafia' that is Rose's lawyers and to Carson. I haven't wanted to know any details so that I couldn't be accused of being involved. I've always had your interests at heart, you must know that. I would have done more had you asked. I saw one of the adverts and I was in shock. I jumped in as I'm sure you would have in my place: to help. To save your reputation, and you. **Your safety has always and will always matter to me.**

I'm sorry if I've hurt you and your opinion of me in the process. The world is yours now. I'll avoid your places, our places. I give it all to you. I always have. I won't come to Durham in January, unless you ask me to. **As of this letter, all the money you owe me is written off.** I will stay out of your life unless you ask me back into it, unless I have written instructions in a letter or email. I will avoid your play in March if you want me to stay away.

All I ask is that you come to the Boxing Day event at your mother's. You know how I feel about socialising with them all; my only reason for going is to see you. So please, come for an hour, just one hour. Smile at me doing my droll persona thing, then leave. Let's begin a truce with a smile.

You wanted your 'normal' life and you almost got it. *Almost* because, however many times your mother tries to say it is, there is nothing 'normal' about a relationship with a middle-aged bus driver on another continent. But it is your life and you'll see that soon, I hope. Or perhaps he'll grow bored with your tantrums and your stubborn inability to take advice.

I forgive you, though. And I forgive your mother for making you who you are. For all of your impossibilities, you are still that wonderful woman and girl I met in 2000. We wouldn't struggle with each other so if it wasn't the purest of loves. We knew it back then, even if we sometimes forget it now.

You have left me in the dark, Natalie, but even in my blindness, I pray for you, and I beg of you never to forget that if anything is sacred, the human body is sacred. Look after yours, my truant lover.

Have a nice Christmas. I wish you laughter and happiness and I hope to see you, for just one smile.. that's enough for now.

Matthew

What happened on Boxing Day? Not much: nothing out of the ordinary, nothing devastating or unexpected. But the day haunted and tortured me from the moment I woke from my worried non-sleep to the first polite opportunity I could find to excuse myself to bed. Before the party, my mum snapped at me for not helping her prepare the house and told me I was spoilt when I muttered I wasn't in a sociable mood. I fluffed cushions and arranged cutlery with a sense of impending doom. Two years ago I'd been excited to help set up for our festive meal; I'd spent the day buoyed by the euphoria of my erotic secrets, and I'd probably disappeared to masturbate and text Matthew about it just before our guests arrived. I'd offered people drinks and made idle chatter while stealing glances across the room and whispering more and more dangerous things as I became increasingly tipsy. Even a year ago, brooding for a seven-hour flight and wishing I could have stayed in America, I hadn't dreaded the joint of pork and strawberry trifle with such alarming intensity.

This year I felt haunted by the ghosts of my past selves. Child, lover, liar. Had Matthew known the familiarity would turn my stomach? Had he hoped I would be lured back into my pre-Rosella state? Was I supposed to forget the emails, the private detective and the promised lawsuit because he smiled and handed me a Christmas present? Or was he planning something? Should I be afraid rather than just apprehensive? Might he ruin the evening with a clink of his spoon against a glass and tell everyone everything? Would he get me kicked out of my house on the day after

Christmas in the hope that, with nowhere else to go, I might knock on his door? Could he tear apart my family at a time when it should be most united? Or perhaps he would protect himself and just bring up the emails, the woman in Boston, Rob and the pictures on the internet? Might he call me a whore in front of my mother and her friends?

But Matthew created no scene, he made no pointed comments during general conversation, and I noticed no furtive glances. He was polite and charming to everyone. He persona'd his way around the dinner table and enquired about my studies. He and Annabelle gave me a notebook and a candleholder, and once we were done with dessert, he suggested we take our coffees to the lounge to watch the Charlie Chaplin shorts he'd dug out this morning. He didn't even try to sit next to me. As he'd promised in his letter, he was on his best behaviour. And somehow that was worse. I clutched a teddy bear in my old bed and tried not to close my eyes for fear of drifting into the dream world that so often pricked the backs of my eyelids lately: a monsterless nightmare where Matthew and I didn't hate each other and I still snuck off to see him, still told him I loved him, still touched my lips to his. I woke in sweats from images of us laughing at the others and playing cards in his kitchen, making love and checking into hotels. I lay in the dark trying to bring myself back to now, but reaching out my hand and tormenting myself with disgust, I touched the wall of my childhood bedroom; the wall on which I'd stuck poems and quotes and the bronze ankh Matthew'd given me summers ago. There was no escape here.

27

'Am I speaking to Natalie Lucas?' an officious voice blared from the wall-mounted telephone beside Arrivals.

'Yes,' I replied, feeling as if I'd done something wrong.

I'd arrived at Heathrow an hour early and waited by the Arrivals rail for Rob's delayed flight. I'd then watched all the passengers file out of baggage claim and into the arms of friends and relatives until the corridor was empty and I was standing alone on the fluorescent-lit waxed floor.

'And are you here to meet Robert Evans?'

'Yes.'

Finally, as I was pacing and wondering what to do, watching the next flight's passengers file through the corridor, an announcement was made: 'WOULD ANYONE WAITING TO MEET ROBERT EVANS PLEASE CONTACT THE ARRIVALS INFORMATION DESK.'

'Natalie, I need to ask you a few questions.'

'Okay. I mean, is Rob okay?'

'Robert's fine, Natalie. We're just a little concerned about his motives for visiting the country, so our immigration officers are conducting an interview with him.'

'Oh.'

'Natalie, how old are you?'

'Twenty.'

'And could you confirm how old Mr Evans is for me?'

'Uh, thirty-nine.'

'And can you confirm you are in a relationship with Mr Evans?'

'Yes.'

'And how did you meet?'

'Um, when I was travelling last summer.'

'Where were you travelling?'

'All across America.'

'And was Mr Evans travelling also?'

'No, he was the trip guide and driver.'

'Right. So, how long have you been in a relationship with Mr Evans?'

'About six months.'

'And would you say it's serious?'

'Sorry?'

'Would you consider your relationship with Mr Evans serious?'

'Uh, I don't know, I guess.'

'Are you engaged?'

'No.'

'Do you have any plans to marry while Mr Evans is in the country?'

'*No.*'

'Good, because I have to inform you, Natalie, that it would be against the law for you to become engaged to Mr Evans or to marry without first contacting the embassy.'

'Oh.'

'Yes, it could result in deportation and a fine.'

'Okay, he's just here to visit me, though.'

'How long does Mr Evans intend to stay?'

'One month.'

'And where will he be staying?'

'With me. I mean, we've got a hostel in London tonight and tomorrow, but then we're going back to mine.'

'Okay, thank you, Natalie. I'm going to return to Robert now and ask him a few more questions. Please could you wait near the information desk where you are now?'

'Sure.'

'Thank you for your help.'

Forty-five minutes later Rob trudged through the Arrivals corridor with his giant backpack slung over one shoulder and his hat pulled beneath his eyebrows.

'Hey!' I smiled, relieved and excited.

'Hey,' he replied in a monotone. He accepted my kiss with half a smile, and then looked me up and down with a frown.

'I'm glad you got through. How ridiculous, just for a holiday,' I burbled.

'Yeah, well it wouldn't have been a problem if I'd been able to give them the address of where I was staying, but as you wouldn't tell me the name of our hostel . . .'

'Oh,' I swallowed guiltily. I hadn't wanted to email Rob the details of the booking I'd made as a final insurance against him possibly having a crazy wife who might follow him to England. I'd told him it wasn't about trust, but that the woman had known details about me that she shouldn't have, so I was worried someone might be hacking into our correspondence. 'Couldn't you have given them my Durham address?'

'I didn't know it. I didn't think I'd have to write to you while I was with you,' Rob snapped, and then looked away.

'Sorry.' I took his hand and moved into his eye-line. 'Hey, I'm glad you're here.' I stood on tiptoes and kissed him again.

'Yeah, me too.' He pulled away. 'I'm just tired, I guess.'

It took an hour and a half to get to our hostel, which was dingy and small. I'd paid an extra £20 for a private room that was little more than a double mattress crammed into an oversized closet. Rob dropped his bag onto the one patch of carpet, leaving us only the bed.

'D'you want to get food?' I asked as he flopped onto one of the two flat pillows.

'Yeah, I'm pretty hungry. I need a shower too.'

'Okay.'

I read while he showered, then we found a cheap Italian on the other side of the roundabout to our hostel. I asked Rob about his flight and the movies he'd watched, who was covering for him at work and what his Christmas was like. He answered in monosyllables and eventually we grew quiet.

Jetlagged, Rob didn't sleep well that night or the next. We paced around London, dutifully visiting the tourist spots and taking photos of each other standing by famous buildings. We had moments of laughter, chasing each other along the South Bank and kissing over the table after Rob's first full-English, but most of the weekend was strained. We made polite conversation and avoided talking about Matthew. We trudged exhaustedly through the whole of the V&A and perched in a patisserie with my mum and her new boyfriend, all smiling inanely and pretending to have fun. By the time our train pulled into Durham and Rob and I had sat for three hours reading separate newspapers instead of chatting to or holding the person we'd sent trans-Atlantic 'I love you's to since September, it was clear we needed to talk.

My housemates weren't back from Christmas yet, so we had the whole house to shout in. It wasn't a fair fight, of course: Rob was battling on my turf, aware he needed somewhere to stay for the next three and a half weeks. We yelled a little, then cried a lot. We went back and forth, telling each other we were still in love and still wanted what we had had over the summer, but that something had changed. He said he'd known it since I made that phone call, but he'd decided to come anyway, just to make sure. He held me while I cried.

He stayed for two weeks, before booking himself into hostels in London and Oxford. We slept side-by-side, but did our own thing during the day. I went to seminars while he walked by the river, watched films and photographed the city walls. A few times, I rubbed his back and tried to unbutton his shirt, but was always shrugged off or pushed away by a roll to the other side of the bed.

My housemates were nice enough not to say anything about our whispered fights and my tear-stained cheeks, and Rob cooked a meal to say thank you for their hospitality before he left. I walked him to the bus stop and he hugged me goodbye but didn't wave out of the window. I sat on Millennium Bridge and sobbed for what felt like days. We had been over since he'd arrived, but it was only now that I was alone.

There was a letter waiting for me when I returned to the house.

> Thy beauty shall no more be found,
> Nor, in thy marble vault, shall sound
> My echoing song; then worms shall try
> That long preserv'd virginity,
> And your quaint honour turn to dust,
> And into ashes all my lust.

Andrew Marvel 'To His Coy Mistress'

Little Meg and I spent the weekend looking at houses in Bath. I've convinced her to do her nursing there instead of Durham – 'It's too cold up in the North,' I said. 'More like she's too cold,' she replied. She's not stupid. But she's happier being far from you. Perhaps I will be too.

Did you have a nice time with your bus driver? I hope, for your sake, that you are right about him. I can't help but worry. Even if you don't care. I haven't spoken to Carson, so I don't know what's going on with the wife, but your mother hasn't told me about any scandals, so perhaps all has gone quiet. Or perhaps you're dead and raped in a ditch somewhere and your cold housemates haven't even noticed your absence. I'm sure I'd be the last to know.

Your former Uncle

My play was turning into a disaster. My lead actor had been cast in three of the nine plays scheduled for the term and had started to waltz into rehearsals forty-five minutes late and stop run-throughs to quiz me about his character's motivation or ask whether I really thought this blocking would work. The other actors began to follow suit until I felt like a kitten crawling into a lion-pen each afternoon. These six-foot boys with their gym-worked muscles and their experience of standing before an audience reminded me, with their playground rebellion, that I was just a five-foot girl pretending to know something about directing because a professor a few thousand miles away had told her she was talented.

I was also in the middle of my Post-War Italian Cinema module and trying to grapple with middle-class alienation in Antonioni's 'trilogy of feeling'; final papers would be due in the third term, but essay topics were to be handed to tutors by Friday of the eighth week of this term. Plus, one of my housemates had seen a mouse and was demanding a deep clean of the entire house this coming weekend, the department secretaries were being wholly unsympathetic to my claims that transferring a 3.92 GPA into three grades of 68%, 71% and 73% wasn't entirely fair, and my bank balance was flirting shamelessly with its overdraft limit.

The proverbial straw arrived on a Wednesday morning. I opened it with a mouthful of toast.

Are you content?

I call on Uncles to judge what I have done. Infirm and aged I might stay, but my meditation was always on the supreme theme of **Art and Song**.

Art and Song, do you remember it? When all your other lovers are estranged or dead, Natalie, you might. You sat in my kitchen laughing at me and calling me an old man, but I never saw you as a young girl. You are an old soul and we are both young and old, old and gay, O so old. We were everyone before us, remember? Thousands of years. We loved each other and we were ignorant. We sang in our bridal sleep in Kew, where you told me you loved me and spoke of marriage. Remember?

Well, man runs his course between extremities I suppose. You're devolving, Natalie. You already struggled with your mind, in my study and at my kitchen table, reading Hesse in your mother's house and arguing with me about what was right. But now here you are again: all alone in the frozen North, waging fights against your heart and mind. (And perhaps your body too? You've looked like a boy every time I've seen you with daft haircuts, and no doubt you sit in the bath trying to scrub away my ankh – or have you had it removed already? I hope it hurt.) Well, sorry to be the one to tell you, but you're going to lose. Better men than you have tried and failed. You'll be left with clouds about a fallen sun and no one to help you pick up the pieces.

You'd like it if I said I'd arise and go now, leaving you to enjoy your loneliness. But it's not just about you, Natalie. This is my life too and I can't bear the hypocrisy. I'm sick of hearing your mother blather about you and your silly play and having to make excuses as to why I can't come, because you'll have a conniption if you see me in the auditorium. Annabelle's sick of it too. It's making me ill. It makes her want to move. I can't stand it any more. I'm going to tell Heloise what her ungrateful, selfish, slutty daughter is really like. I'll tell her I tried to give you poetry and love and you threw it back in my face, that as you can't pay me, she owes me for all the rubbish I've been put through. Yes, I know I said I'd call off the lawsuit, but I've been thinking about it and it's just not fair that you should get off scot-free for all the lives you've ruined. We're having your Ma over for dinner on Friday. I plan to tell her everything. I'm cooking shepherd's pie. We'll have trifle for dessert and we can work out a payment plan over coffee.

You're more than welcome to come if you can descend from your icehouse up in Durham.

310

On second thoughts, I'd rather you didn't. I've had enough of you and your whining.

I want this sorted. Now.

I was okay. My blood had turned cold and my hand was screwing up the envelope, but I was okay. I had a counselling session at eleven. I felt a wetness on my cheek, but I was okay. In any case, in two hours and thirteen minutes, I would be okay. I would shower and dress and walk down to campus. I could go early and get a coffee, be around people, not curled up in my room. Trish would make things better. She would help me work out what to do. She would tell me it would be okay.

I pushed back my chair and carried my plate to the sink. I climbed the stairs and placed the letter in the shoebox beneath my bed labelled 'Fuck Off and Die', then locked the bathroom door and removed my pyjamas. I stood in the shower before switching it on and endured a blast of ice before the water turned scorching. I dried myself, then pulled on jeans and my oversized Rosella hoodie. I tied a bow in my Converse and drew a defensive line of kohl beneath each of my eyes. I took a deep breath, opened the front door and directed my feet towards the counselling centre.

Everything would be fine. Trish would help and a coffee in a crowded place would calm me down. Matthew couldn't get to me here. I was safe.

As I queued for a drink, my phone rang. Number withheld.

Deep breath.

'Hello?'

'May I speak to Natalie please?'

'Speaking.'

'Hi Natalie, this is Rebecca from the university counselling service. I'm afraid I'm calling to cancel your appointment this morning. Trish is unwell and unable to come in. Would you like me to reschedule you for next Monday?'

I hung up the phone, put it back in my pocket, and walked out of the café.

One hour and £57 later, I was sat on a train destined for Sussex. I rummaged through the rucksack I hadn't repacked since yesterday's classes and found my Italian cinema notebook and a green biro. I tore a sheet of lined paper from the back and, placing it on the plastic fold-down table before me, began:

Dear Mum and Dad
I had an affair with Matthew.

PART THREE

28

Some things that happened in March 2005:

- Chancellor of the Exchequer Gordon Brown delivered his ninth Budget.
- Approximately 1,300 people were killed by an earthquake measuring 8.7 on the Richter scale off the west coast of Northern Sumatra.
- Sixty-six people went on trial for child sex abuse and prostitution in Angers, France.
- Martha Stewart was released from prison.
- The UK became the first country to officially recognise darts as a sport.
- Changes to the capital punishment system in the United States made sentencing someone to death for a crime committed before they were 18 unconstitutional.
- Paris Hilton appeared on the cover of *Playboy*.
- London police claimed to have foiled a £220 million attempted bank robbery.
- NBC's version of the British comedy *The Office* premiered in the United States.

And I told my parents the worst possible thing I could imagine, thus beginning my third life.

My dad sat beside me on the sofa in his office reading my letter; my mum stood in her kitchen and tore it up unopened, requesting with tears in her eyes that I say whatever it was to her face.

My dad said he'd hoped I wouldn't have to deal with people like that until I was much older; my mum said she wished I'd told her sooner.

My dad said he'd been suspicious of Matthew, but chalked it up to his own warped mind; my mum said she'd had no idea.

My dad said he felt sorry for not preventing it; my mum said she felt betrayed by both Matthew and Annabelle.

My dad said he wanted to go over to Matthew's house right away; my mum said she didn't know how it would affect her friendships, but she was glad she knew.

My dad said he was really angry – but not with me; my mum said the affair was one thing, but it was much worse that Matthew wouldn't leave me alone.

My dad said he'd been to counselling a few times and hadn't found it much use; my mum said at least I'd find it easier to come home now.

My dad said he didn't mind that I liked girls, because he'd had a threesome once; my mum said she'd once had a fling with a married man and it had made her feel horrid.

My dad said I could always come to him; my mum said I was her little girl.

My dad said he'd protect me; my mum said she loved me.

29

On the day Durham ejected me from its student body, shut off my email account and threw me into the world of alumni, I dyed a bottle of wine blue.

The bottle clunked in my tote next to the back-up red as I paced past Sam's door three times.

On the fourth approach, I knocked. I put my jacket on the peg and pulled the blue bottle out of my bag before we walked into the kitchen. It was only then that I saw the pans and the chopping boards, the meat marinating and some fancy starter bubbling on the stove.

It was June and we were almost graduates. In two months I would be moving to Chicago to begin a Masters degree and Sam would be staying in England to write scripts. We were theatre kids and these outings that we'd jokingly labelled 'HOT dates' were no more than play. Sam had already donned a medallion and I spiky heels for a Posh & Becks picnic, and we'd both worn suits and cardboard FBI badges for a Mulder & Scully coffee morning.

With no further word about a lawsuit from Matthew, I'd tentatively begun acting like a normal student. After handing in my final essay, I'd frivolously spent the remainder of my student loan on a trip to Barcelona with a girl in my seminar group. Upon landing in Newcastle on our return, my mum had phoned to tell me Matthew had stopped her in the street to shout red-facedly about how pathetic it was that I couldn't confront him. She thought it was a sign he was panicked and losing control. I'd sat on the train back to Durham scanning the lines of my book, absorbing nothing – *He's shouting in the street now? Does he want everyone to know? Does he think he has nothing to lose? Might he get violent?* – but I'd stepped off at the station and walked straight to Sam's house to smilingly present him with the ('extra hot') chillies I'd brought back from Barcelona, hopefully like any carefree twenty-year-old might gaily give to a friend. Days later, Sam had brought a homemade apple pie to the bar one evening, telling me I was 'sweet enough to eat'.

But these were joke dates: nothing more than a bit of fun to fill the final weeks of university. They meant nothing and, as Emma pointed out with a mouthful of cinnamon crust, 'Sam makes cake for *everyone.*' This boy was sweet, but I was going to marry a rich American who could get me a green card. Or live a fabulous bohemian life as a lesbian artist.

Still, suddenly self-conscious, I tried to hide my blue wine in the fridge. The shelves, however, were bare, and the clean white glowed against the royal glass. Sam was moving the next day and nothing remained in his house except nude bookcases, the landlord's flimsy furniture and the muddle of kitchen utensils he was using to cook for me. The sparse surroundings didn't lend themselves to conversation, and though this was still supposed to be a fake date, I reminded myself how idiotic it would be to begin liking someone at the end of the year.

I'd already sent my things home with my dad and was wearing the only dress I had left. I looked at my toenails, which were painted green inside batik sandals, and wished I were more sophisticated. With relief, I noticed Sam's pink shoes and smiled.

His last-remaining housemate, John, peeked into the kitchen.

'Don't worry, I'm heading out soon. I'll leave you two *love-birds* to it.' He winked with the sickening superiority of a safely coupled friend.

'Look in the fridge!' Sam smiled with delight, but my heart sank as John peered at my absurd offering.

'It's just the bottle!' John insisted until I poured a glass. Glancing in turn from the sapphire liquid to my and then Sam's face, John declared, 'I give up on you both,' and flounced out of the room.

I found out later that John had heard every detail of the Posh & Becks picnic and Mulder & Scully coffee morning. Later still, when Sam snatched his phone away from me as I opened a photo album, I bullied him into admitting that he was hiding self-portraits taken before each of our dates to consult John on shirt selection. For now, though, Sam and John were intimidating aspiring playwrights who the drama society referred to as 'Gilbert and Sullivan'. I'd met them both in the bar after the opening night of my play. They'd said sweet, noncommittal things about what I knew was a far-less-than-impressive production, soothing my embarrassment and massaging my battered ego.

John's departure left us in silence. Looking sheepish, Sam presented one of those tiny bottles of champagne you find on the ends of aisles in the supermarket, a pink ribbon curled around its neck. Thinking of the blue wine, my odd earrings and cucumber toenails, I squirmed at my lack of elegance and tried to make a joke about the champagne being pink like his shoes. He laughed kindly and I wondered if other people were this socially awkward.

We hovered on the kitchen tiles, staring through the one window at the dull garden wall, sipping pink fizz and making inane conversation about waiting for degree results until there was a clatter in the hall.

'Fuck, fuck, fuck!'

We hurried to see what had happened and found John at the bottom of the stairs with an empty cardboard box and two smashed espresso cups on the floor. I made inadequate gestures towards helping him clean up while Sam returned to his cooking. John threw the pieces in the bin and grumpily said he'd had enough of packing. Just before he slammed the door, he instructed me with a wink to 'Have fun!' and the roof of my mouth dried up.

Sam and I were alone.

This is not a real date, I reminded myself, and wondered why, if that was true, my palms were sweating.

What followed was a cringe-worthy ritual of small talk interspersed with brief moments of relaxed conversation. We ate on a fold-out table in the empty living room, then sat on opposite ends of the sofa. Both the TV and stereo had been packed, so every nervous giggle echoed in the silence.

I could not have known then, in those excruciating pauses between stilted conversation, that within three days we would be holding hands in the street and confirming our relationship via Facebook. Equally, I couldn't have known we'd drag a mattress into the closet of his new house and fumble away his virginity in our makeshift den. I couldn't have known Sam would persuade me to follow him to the Edinburgh Fringe Festival and we would spend the month of August sharing strawberry crepes and watching bizarre performance art. I couldn't have known my first night in Chicago would also be my first night without Sam in six weeks and my tears wouldn't cease all the way from airport security desk to Sears Tower. I couldn't have known that, against all my expectations, we'd make a long-distance relationship work and share a nothing-short-of-filmic embrace at Heathrow upon my return. Nor could I have known that in eighteen months' time we'd look to rent our own terraced house in Durham, and on our second anniversary, we'd name a kitten Shakespeare.

On this sultry June evening, neither of us knew anything. But, somehow, after we'd each attempted several hesitant shuffles and the last drops of blue liquid had stained our incisors, we managed to bridge the gap between us and share our first kiss.

* * *

In the following weeks, I engraved an umbrella as a birthday present, only to find its recipient had never seen *Breakfast at Tiffany's*, and Sam painted me in black and white to look like Audrey Hepburn for mine. We discovered our matching distinctions together and endured the teasing from our friends. There were dinners and breakfasts, and I triumphed in converting him to coffee over tea. We woke together in a single bed every day in August and climbed Arthur's Seat in flip-flops and canvas shoes.

When the guy behind the desk at the American Embassy informed me, 'You don't have the right documentation, mam, I can't issue you a visa at this time, mam, please don't get upset, mam,' I wondered whether to drop out of my overpriced Masters course and stay in England. Meanwhile Sam was calculating the cost of coming to Chicago for Christmas and paying for a year's worth of calling cards. Sam came home with me to Sussex to help me pack and I sat in the back with him as we drove to the airport. He kissed me goodbye next to the security entrance and, while I was being herded onto British Airways, he was crying on a tube somewhere on the Piccadilly Line.

At some moment amid all of this, after a bottle of regular-coloured wine and another gourmet meal, he whispered to me in the dark, 'I think I'm falling in love with you.'

And like any normal twenty-year-old with a potentially useless humanities degree and an uncertain future before her would have done, I smiled and mouthed, 'Me too.'

Epilogue

2012

Dearest Sam,

A long time ago you told me you'd never ask questions because you only wanted me to offer what I felt comfortable sharing. That was a couple of years after my convoluted sobs in your darkened bedroom the night before graduation, when you told me the past was past and you were falling for the me of the present. But it was before you understood quite how dreadfully I didn't want to visit my hometown, or to play cards with your family, or stay in a Travelodge on our way to Scotland.

We'd moved in together and I was sobbing to an NHS counsellor once a week and curling into disproportionate foetal rebellion whenever my car broke down or someone said something shitty at work. I was trudging through a thicket of depression. You were kind to me. You didn't always understand me, but you wrapped me in your arms and made much of my world better. But still I thought you'd leave if you knew the truth. Still I imagined you'd pack your bags if I admitted to waking beside you from dreams in which my mouth sought Matthew's, or if you discovered the thoughts I sometimes had about losing my mind. You said you loved me, but I wondered what kind of love could survive my absurd psyche.

On a brave day, though, I wrote you a letter. I tried to tell you everything: all the miserable details, all the sordid, cringe-worthy secrets. I wanted you to know inside my head. I hoped you might arrive with shining armour to tackle my demons, but deep down I expected you to run. That letter was a dozen pages long. I left it on your keyboard and went to work.

Your response was simple. A hand-written note by the kettle. You said you worried I liked drama and you feared I would hurt myself, but you never expressed shock, never called me bad. You folded me back inside our cosy relationship as if I hadn't just told you things that would make your mother stop inviting me for Sunday lunch. You cooked me dinner and we started the next series of *The West Wing*. You didn't care.

You didn't care!

Today I sit in my chilly attic office with a blanket around my shoulders and the cup of tea you've just brought me. The diaries I scrawled so earnestly in a decade ago sit on a bookshelf up here, but the photos I've pinned to the walls, the anthologies stacked up high, the scattered save-the-date stickers and the endless Post-it notes attest to my present eclipsing my past. I don't know how you saw through the frightened and confused girl you met in 2005, how you continued to look beyond the depressed and disturbed girlfriend you found yourself living with from 2007. But somehow you did. Through some sixth sense or superhuman power, you knew the woman I'd become and knew she'd be the one you'd love. Well, finally, I've caught up; I've got to know her too. A month ago, wearing an Alice-in-Wonderland dress and bright red shoes, she stood before you and vowed to be your wife. And, in the simplest possible way, it made her very happy.

Nat

Thanking

The following is a list of people I need to thank not just for making this book possible, but for helping me through its events and, thus, making my present possible. I consider myself a bit of a loner and sometimes worry I don't have many friends, but this list is proof I have some of the kindest, most generous and forgiving friends in the world. So, from the bottom of my battered but healing heart, I'd like to thank those who listened to my early, utterly ineloquent confessions: Trev, Dave, Emma, Nat, Frances, Kristin, Emily, Rob, and in particular Jess and Greg. Thank you also to all three of my counsellors, each of whom helped me in different ways; to my writing tutor Megan and those in my classes for patiently suffering through my first cathartic explosions; to the other teachers and editors, who coped with me with remarkable grace; to my best friend Laura for reading all of my rubbish; to the wonderful, supportive members of the Authonomy community, without whom I would not have a publisher; to my editor, Rachel, for her endless patience and my publicist, Jo, for holding my hand; to my husband, whose perfection I cannot put into words; and, finally, to my brilliant family, especially my mum.*

*whose primary concern upon publication is that the world will think she reads only Barbara Taylor Bradford novels – she doesn't!

About Authonomy

Authonomy is an online community of authors, readers and publishers, conceived and developed by editors at HarperCollins. It was launched to provide unpublished authors with a platform to showcase their work. Authonomy is also dedicated to seeking out and publishing the very best new writing talent. To find other exciting new books or to join our brilliant community, visit www.authonomy.com.